KNITTING TODAY'S CLASSICS

KNITTING TODAY'S CLASSICS

65 BEAUTIFUL SWEATERS from the Studios of CLASSIC ELITE

KRISTIN NICHOLAS

Lark Books
ASHEVILLE, NORTH CAROLINA

DEDICATION

This book is dedicated to all the knitters of the world, who continue to inspire us to create fresh, new designs, yarns, and colors season after season.

EDITOR **Leslie Dierks**

ART DIRECTOR **Chris Bryant**

PHOTOGRAPHY **John Goodman, Philip Newton, Peter Ogilvie**

ILLUSTRATIONS **April Carder**, *pp. 135–137*

EDITORIAL ASSISTANCE **Valerie Anderson**

PRODUCTION ASSISTANCE **Bobby Gold**

Library of Congress Cataloging in Publication Data

Nicholas, Kristin.
Knitting today's classics : 65 beautiful sweaters from the studios of Classic Elite / Kristin Nicholas.
p. cm.
Includes index.
ISBN 1-887374-36-1
1. Knitting—United States—Patterns. 2. Sweaters—United States. 3. Classic Elite Yarns (Firm) I. Classic Elite Yarns (Firm) II. Title
TT819.U6N5323 1997
746.43'20432—dc21 97-13162
CIP

10 9 8 7 6 5 4 3 2 1
First Edition

Published by Lark Books
50 College Street
Asheville, North Carolina 28801
USA

Distributed by Random House,Inc., in the United States, Canada, the United Kingdom, Europe, and Asia

Distributed in Australia by Capricorn Link (Australia) Pty Ltd., P.O. Box 6651,
Baulkham Hills Business Centre, NSW 2153, Australia

Distributed in New Zealand by Tandem Press Ltd., 2 Rugby Rd., Birkenhead, Auckland, New Zealand

You can purchase Classic Elite Yarns throughout the United States at better yarn stores. Classic Elite Yarns are distributed in Canada by: S. R. Kertzer, 105A Winges Road, Woodbridge, Ontario, Canada L4L 6C2. Phone: 905–856–3447. For more information about Classic Elite Yarns, contact the company at 12 Perkins Street, Lowell, MA 01854. Telephone: 508–453–2837. Web site address is http://www.classiceliteyarns.com

Printed in Hong Kong

ISBN 1-887374-36-1

Contents

Introduction

Knitting is a common thread that binds together people of many different ages and personalities. Ask knitters why they knit, and they will give a variety of reasons. Some knit to express their creativity, others do it for therapy, some like to make things, others knit for fashion's sake, and some knit just to pass the hours.

Most knitters are highly intelligent women and men who enjoy creating fabrics with their hands. Many aren't concerned with the product of their knitting; instead, they enjoy the action they repeat with their hands. Some like trying new techniques and experimenting with stitches, and they never repeat a stitch, ever. Other knitters purely enjoy the process of knitting plain fabrics, of passing the time while talking to friends, watching television, or going to the movies, and of creating a simple fabric with integrity.

For many knitters, the tactile quality of the fibers becomes addictive. They enjoy the yarn running through their hands as a row nears completion. Each project moves on and develops a life of its own. Knitters remember where they were in their lives or in the world when they were making certain projects.

Some knitters are just beginning this journey of discovery. They're attracted to the craft, the yarns, the colors, the fashions. In their professional lives they do something very important, so knitting is their escape. Knitting allows them to develop their creativity, and they release urges that have been bottled up inside them since grade school. They begin with a sweater in simple stockinette stitch, then move on to more and more difficult projects. They begin to like the challenge. It's safe to conclude that they will never stop knitting their entire lives.

Knitters make different kinds of knitted objects. Some knit very personal gifts for family members and newborns; other knitters decorate their homes with their projects; some knit for charities, such as Warm Up America, to make others' lives better. Whatever the finished product, a handknitted piece is not one that is tossed away easily. Handknits get passed from child to child, cousin to cousin, generation to generation. They have lives of their own, and more times than not, handknits have well-worn holes in the elbows and ribs falling off before they become relegated to the ragbag. Even then, handknits can be cut and pieced together to form a patchwork quilt of past projects.

All knitters know that any other knitter is a special person, that a knitter sees things differently and gets more out of life than most people do. Those unfortunate souls who don't or can't knit must run to the nearest mall to buy a ready-made sweater in whatever color or style is available. On the other hand, a knitter selects a yarn for its texture and color, then chooses a stitch and needle size. Each piece of the garment is painstakingly knit and seamed together, and the buttons are carefully added.

If you're a new knitter, you have a lot to look forward to! Years of creativity, experimentation, and satisfaction await you. You won't tire of the craft, and it cannot be exhausted. If you've been knitting for a long time, there are still hundreds of techniques to try. Consider knitting a good luck charm that can follow you throughout your life. It will keep you happy, content, and pleasantly occupied.

In this book I've tried to include projects for all types of knitters. I hope you will enjoy working your way through the collection and trying designs for various skill levels. Just like a knitted wardrobe, this book includes ideas, techniques, yarns, and stitches from several different designers. It's a collection of classic styles that you and your family will wear for many years.

HOW A COLLECTION EVOLVES AT CLASSIC ELITE YARNS

Each season the Classic Elite in-house design team scours the pages of current fashion magazines to glean the newest silhouettes, colors, and stitch techniques in knitwear. Ideas from the fashion world are combined with what we think knitters will enjoy making and wearing for years to come. We search libraries for old magazines and books, including knit stitch dictionaries, which offer invaluable inspiration to our designs. Although many of the stitch books are more than 20 years old, the stitches found on their pages still look current. We also work with selected handknit designers to produce sweater designs exclusively for us. Designers such as Deborah Newton, Sally Lee, and Norah Gaughan add their distinctive, imaginative styles to our in-house collection.

Yarns are chosen, and the process begins for creating a swatch for each sweater design. There may be from five to ten separate attempts to get a swatch just right. Once the swatch looks perfect for the collection being developed, rough draft instructions are mapped out and sent with the yarn to one of our talented knitters. While the first sweaters are being knit, many other designs are being developed. It's better than Christmas when the boxes of sweaters begin to arrive back at the studio!

After the sweaters are properly steamed or washed to even out the irregularities of the handmade pieces, a photo session occurs. Instructions are rewritten and carefully proofread before publication. Then the new collection is revealed to the stores, where the yarns and new designs are made available to knitters. If all goes well, many of these designs will look classic enough to be included in a compilation of favorites such as this one.

1

Knits for the Family

Every member of the family loves sweaters! In the office and at home, in the playground and on the golf course, men, women, and children live in modern knitwear. Knitted fabrics move easily from situation to situation, and knitters have the luxury of planning colors and textures for heirloom-quality handknits for the entire family. Family members can watch their garment as it grows on the needles, then enjoy wearing it for years. Handknit sweaters are often passed from child to child and even from generation to generation. Most of the designs in this chapter are unisex sized and styled so that they look equally flattering on men and women. There are choices in texture, color, and silhouette for everyone in your family.

Family Portrait

design: **Linda Pratt**

knitting rating: **Intermediate**

photography: **Philip Newton**

An oversized diamond cable wraps around a simple center cable, making an eye-catching design for intermediate knitters. The remainder of the design is worked in a broken rib stitch. Chunky two-by-two ribbing edges this design, which includes a cardigan and pullover for adults and a pullover for children. It is shown in two different textures of bulky yarn—a loosely twisted blend of wool and llama (all of the pullovers) and a brushed mohair (the woman's cardigan).

SIZES

Adult: Small (Medium, Large, Extra Large)

Child: <2 (4, 6, 8)>

Finished measurements: 40 (44, 48, 52)" (101.5, 112, 122, 132 cm) <27 (29, 30, 32)" (68.5, 73.5, 76, 81.5 cm)>

NOTE: *Cardigan is sized for adults only.*

MATERIALS

PULLOVER: Montera (50% llama, 50% wool; 100 g = approx. 125 yds/114 m): 9 (9, 10, 10) <3 (4, 5, 6)> hanks

Equivalent yarn: 1143 (1143, 1270, 1397) yds (1045, 1045, 1161, 1277 m) <508 (508, 635, 750) yds (465, 465, 581, 686 m)> of bulky wool

CARDIGAN: La Gran (74% mohair, 13% wool, 13% nylon; 1½ oz. = approx. 90 yds/82 m): 14 (15, 15, 16) balls

Equivalent yarn: 1260 (1350, 1350, 1440) yds (1152, 1234, 1234, 1317 m) of bulky brushed mohair

Knitting needles: sizes 8 and 10 U.S. (5 and 6 m), 16" (40.5 cm) circular needle in size 8 U.S. (5 mm), cable needle (cn)

GAUGE

Broken rib stitch on larger needles: 16 sts = 4" (10 cm)

Big and little cable: 24 sts = 5" (12.5 cm) when blocked

Take time to save time--check your gauge.

PATTERN STITCHES

■ **2 x 2 Ribbing** (over multiple of 4 sts plus 2)

Row 1 (RS): *K2, p2*; rep bet *s, end k2.

Row 2: *P2, k2*; rep bet *s, end p2.

■ **3 x 1 Broken Rib** (over multiple of 4 sts plus 3)

Row 1 (RS): *P3, k1*; rep bet *s, end p3.

Row 2: P all sts.

■ **Big and Little Cable** (over 26 sts and 40 rows)

NOTE: For child's version, omit rows 17 through 28.

PRC: Sl next st to cn, hold in back, k3, p1 from cn

PLC: Sl next 3 sts to cn, hold in front, p1, k3 sts from cn

C4R: Sl next 2 sts to cn, hold in back , k2, k2 from cn

C6B: Sl next 3 sts to cn, hold in back, k3, k3 from cn

Row 1 (RS): K1, p9, k6, p9, k1.

Row 2 and all even rows: Work sts as they appear.

Row 3: K1, p9, C6B, p9, k1.

Row 5: K1, p8, PRC, PLC, p8, k1.

Row 7: K1, p7, PRC, k2, PLC, p7, k1.

Row 9: K1, p6, PRC, k4, PLC, p6, k1.

Row 11: K1, p5, PRC, p1, C4R, p1, PLC, p5, k1.

Row 13: K1, p4, PRC, p2, k4, p2, PLC, p4, k1.

Row 15: K1, p3, PRC, p3, C4R, p3, PLC, p3, k1.

Row 17: K1, p2, PRC, p4, k4, p4, PLC, p2, k1.

Row 19: K1, p1, PRC, p5, C4R, p5, PLC, p1, k1.

Row 21: K1, PRC, p6, k4, p6, PLC, k1.

Row 23: K1, PLC, p6, C4R, p6, PRC, k1.

Row 25: K1, p1, PLC, p5, k4, p5, PRC, p1, k1.

Row 27: K1, p2, PLC, p4, C4R, p4, PRC, p2, k1.

Row 29: K1, p3, PLC, p3, k4, p3, PRC, p3, k1.

Row 31: K1, p4, PLC, p2, C4R, p2, PRC, p4, k1.

Row 33: K1, p5, PLC, p1, k4, p1, PRC, p5, k1.

Row 35: K1, p6, PLC, C4R, PRC, p6, k1.

Row 37: K1, p7, PLC, k2, PRC, p7, k1.

Row 39: K1, p8, PLC, PRC, p8, k1.

BACK

With smaller needles, c.o. 74 (82, 86, 94) <42 (46, 50, 50)> sts.

Work 2 x 2 ribbing for 4" (10 cm) <2" (5 cm)>.

On last row of rib (WS), inc 9 <5 (5, 9, 13)> sts evenly to give 83 (91, 95, 103) <47 (51, 59, 63)> sts.

Change to larger needles and work in 3 x 1 broken rib patt until piece meas 16½ (17, 17½, 18)" (42, 43, 44.5, 45.5 cm) <8¾ (8¾, 9¾, 9¾)" (22, 22, 25, 25 cm)> from beg.

Mark for armholes.

Work until piece meas 26½ (28, 29, 29)" (67.5, 71, 73.5, 73.5 cm) <14 (14½, 16, 16½)" (35.5, 37, 40.5, 42 cm)> and b.o. all sts.

PULLOVER FRONT

With smaller needles, c.o. 78 (86, 90, 94) <46 (50, 54, 54)> sts.

Work in 2 x 2 ribbing for 4" (10 cm) <2" (5 cm)>.

On last row (WS), inc 16 (16, 20, 24) <12 (10, 12, 14)> sts evenly to give 94 (102, 110, 118) <58 (60, 66, 68)> sts.

Change to larger needles and set up patt as foll: P2 <0 (1, 0, 1)>, k1 <1>, work 31 (35, 39, 43) <15 (15, 19, 19)> sts in 3 x 1 broken rib, 26 sts in big and little cable, 31 (35, 39, 43) <15 (15, 19, 19)> sts in 3 x 1 broken rib, k1 <1>, p2 <0 (1, 0, 1)>.

Work as for back until piece meas 22½ (23, 24½, 25)" (57, 59.5, 62, 63.5 cm) <9½ (10, 11½, 12)" (24, 25.5, 29, 30.5 cm)> from beg.

NECK SHAPING: Work 30 (33, 37, 40) <15 (15, 17, 17)> sts, sl center 34 (36, 36, 38) <28 (30, 32, 34)> sts to holder, join another ball of yarn, and work rem 30 (33, 37, 40) <15 (15, 17, 17)> sts as est.

Working each side sep, b.o. 1 st at each neck edge every other row 5 <2> times to give 25 (28, 32, 35) <13 (13, 15, 15)> sts at each shoulder.

When piece meas same as back, b.o. all sts.

CARDIGAN LEFT FRONT

With smaller needles, c.o. 38 (42, 46, 50) sts.

Work in 2 x 2 ribbing for 4 " (10 cm), ending on a RSR.

On the next row (WS), inc 7 sts evenly to give 45 (49, 53, 57) sts.

Change to larger needles.

Next row (RS): P2, k1, work 15 (19, 23, 27) sts in 3 x 1 broken rib, 26 sts in cable pattern, ending k1.

Work as for back until piece meas 24½ (26, 27, 27)" (62, 66, 68.5, 68.5 cm) from beg, ending on a RSR.

NECK SHAPING: On next row (WS), b.o. 14 sts at beg of row, work as est to end.

Dec 2 sts at neck edge every other row 5 times.

Work until piece meas 26½ (28, 29, 29)" (67.5, 71, 73.5, 73.5 cm) from beg and b.o. all sts.

CARDIGAN RIGHT FRONT

Work as for left front, reversing shaping.

SLEEVES

With smaller needles, c.o. 42 (42, 46, 46) <26 (30, 34, 38)> sts.

Work in 2 x 2 ribbing for 3" (7.5 cm) <2" (5 cm)>.

Inc 9 (9, 13, 13) <5> sts evenly in last row to give 51 (51, 59, 59) <31 (35, 39, 43)> sts.

Change to larger needles and work in 3 x 1 broken rib, inc 1 st each end every 4th row 15 <6 (6, 7, 8)> times to give 81 (81, 89, 89) <43 (47, 53, 59)> sts.

When piece meas 18½ (18½, 19½, 19½)" (47, 47, 49.5, 49.5 cm) <8 (8½, 8¾, 9)" (20.5, 21.5, 22, 23 cm)> from beg, b.o. all sts.

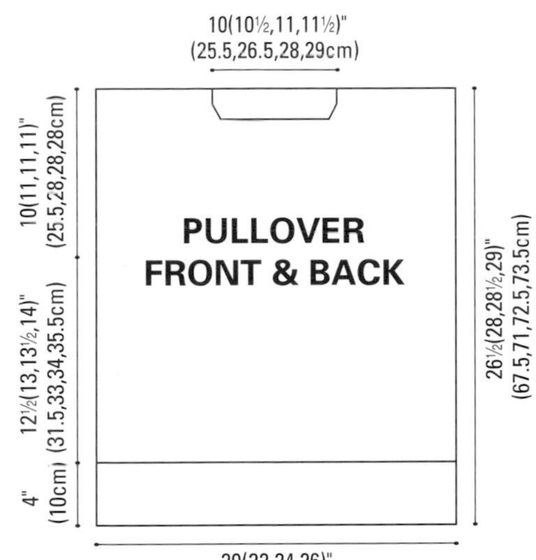

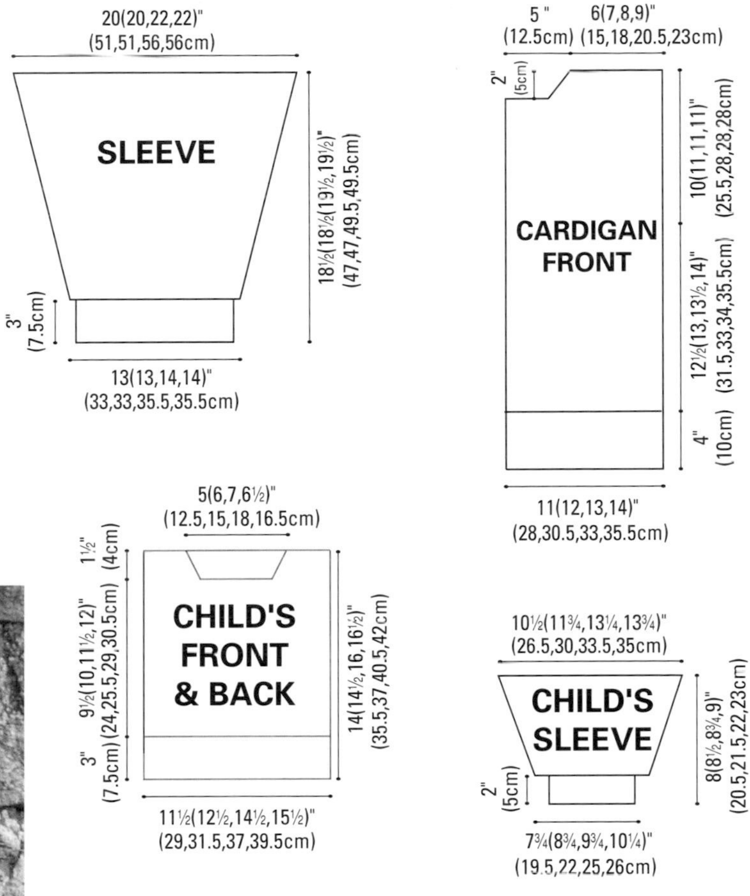

PULLOVER FINISHING

Sew shoulder seams.

With circular needle, p.u. 76 (80, 80, 84) <60 (64, 72, 72)> sts evenly around neckline, including those sts on stitch holder(s). Work in 2 x 2 rib for 2½" (6.5 cm) <1½" (4 cm)>.

B.o. loosely in ribbing.

CARDIGAN FINISHING

*With smaller needles, p.u. 94 (98, 102, 102) sts evenly along right front edge.

Work in 1 x 1 rib for 5 rows,* making 6 buttonholes in row 2 (by yo, k2tog).

Rep bet *s for left front.

P.u. 92 (96, 96, 100) sts around neckline and work in 1 x 1 rib for ¾" (2 cm).

B.o. loosely in ribbing.

Set in sleeves bet markers.

Sew underarm and side seams.

Steam or block gently if desired.

Color Options

design: **Kristin Nicholas**
knitting rating: **Experienced**
photography: **Philip Newton**

Children love bright colors and clashing motifs. This group of cardigans and pullovers, sized for the entire family, uses ethnically inspired motifs in stripes of colorwork that are separated by ridges of brightly colored garter stitch. The possibilities for these sweaters are endless, since motifs and colors can be rearranged to make a new sweater for each member of the family. After gaining confidence with the pattern, you may want to experiment with designing your own colorwork motifs. The edges are worked in many ridges of multicolored garter stitch. Duplicate stitch can be applied to the completed garments, if desired, to add yet more color and texture.

Child's Pullover

SIZES

1 (2, 4, 6, 8, 10)

Finished measurements: 20 (22, 24, 28, 32, 36)" (51, 56, 61, 71, 81.5, 91.5 cm)

MATERIALS

Montera (50% llama, 50% wool; 100 g = approx. 130 yds/119 m): 1 (1, 1, 2, 2, 2) hanks each of colors A (dark color), C (medium color), and D (dark color); 2 hanks of B (light color); 1 hank of E (medium color)

Equivalent yarn: 130 (130, 130, 260, 260, 260) yds (119, 119, 119, 238, 238, 238 m) each of bulky wool in colors A, C, and D; 260 yds (238 m) of color B; 130 yds (119 m) of color E

Knitting needles: sizes 7 and 9 U.S. (4.5 and 5.5 mm)

Tapestry needle for working duplicate stitch

Colored markers to fill in the squares relating to your 5 chosen colors

GAUGE

St st on larger needles: 16 sts and 20 rows = 4" (10 cm)

Take time to save time—check your gauge.

PATTERN STITCHES

■ Garter Ridge

Due to the different numbers of rows in Fair Isle patterns, you may end on a RSR or a WSR. Work garter ridge as follows:

End on RSR: Beg with WSR facing, p 2 rows.

End on WSR: Beg with RSR facing, k 2 rows.

Garter ridges are worked over 2 rows in specified colors or color of your choice. Many of the sequences require multiple garter ridges on top of each other.

■ Duplicate Stitch

Where there are very small areas of a color in a patt, work this color in duplicate st to avoid carrying many colors behind work.

■ Stockinette Stitch

Row 1 (RS): K all sts.

Row 2: P all sts.

NOTE: *This pattern is designed to stretch your horizons and help you begin designing colorwork patterns on your own. If you're following the pattern exactly, you will be determining your own starting points as explained in the directions that follow.*

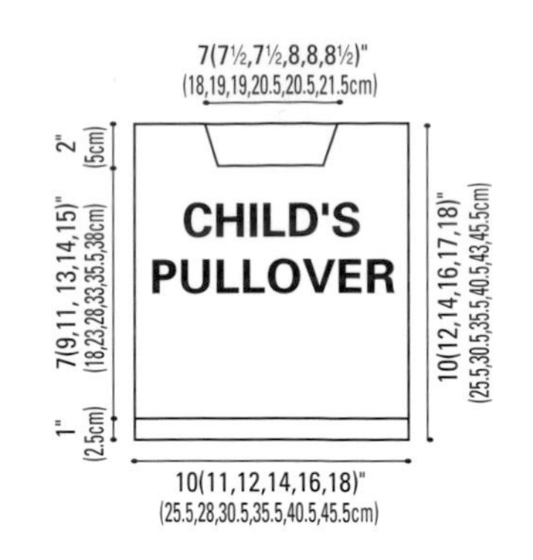

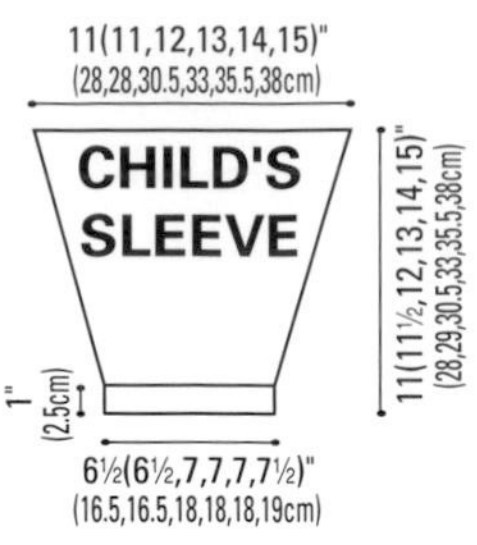

BACK

With smaller needles, c.o. 40 (44, 48, 56, 64, 72) sts.

Work 4 garter ridges as follows: D/B/E/A or in any color sequence you desire.

Change to larger needles and beg working in Patt A.

TO CENTER PATTERN: Determine where to start by doing the following (this example given is for size 4 on patt A):

Take total number of sts for size you are making–size 4 has a total of 48 sts in front or back–and divide this by patt rep (48 divided by 20 = 2 rep with 8 sts rem).

Divide rem sts by 2 to determine the number of sts for which you must compensate in order to center the patt (8 divided by 2 = 4).

Begin patt 4 sts in from end of patt, work 2 complete reps of patt, and end with 4 sts from the beg of patt.

Now you are accomplished at figuring out a rep, and the sky is the limit.

Work patt A over 21 rows.

Work garter ridges (2 rows) in color E, then A.

Work patt B over 9 rows.

Work 1 garter ridge in color D.

Omit patt C for sizes 1 and 2; otherwise, work patt C over 12 rows.

Work garter ridges (2 rows) in color C, then B.

Work 13 (23, 18, 28, 18, 18) rows in patt D.

Work 1 garter ridge in C.

Omit patt E for sizes 1 (2, 4, 6); work patt E over 15 (20) rows for sizes 8 and 10.

B.o. all sts.

FRONT

Work as for back until piece meas 8 (10, 12, 14, 15, 16)" (20.5, 25.5, 30.5, 35.5, 38, 40.5 cm).

Work 10 (11, 13, 16, 20, 23) sts, join a 2nd ball of yarn, b.o. center 20 (22, 22, 24, 24, 26) sts, and work to end.

Working each side sep, b.o. 1 st at each neck edge every other row 4 times to give 6 (7, 9, 12, 16, 19) sts at shoulder.

When piece meas same as back at shoulders, b.o. all sts.

SLEEVES

With smaller needles, c.o. 26 (26, 28, 28, 28, 30) sts.

LEFT SLEEVE: Work garter ridges in following sequence: A/C/B/A.

Change to larger needles and beg working patt F, centering in middle of sleeve.

At the same time, work in St st, inc 1 st each end every 4th row 2 (8, 3, 6, 10, 10) times, then every 6th row 7 (1, 7, 6, 4, 5) times to give 44 (44, 48, 52, 56, 60) sts.

When piece meas 11 (11½, 12, 13, 14, 15)" (28, 29, 30.5, 33, 35.5, 38 cm), b.o. all sts.

RIGHT SLEEVE: Work garter ridges as follows: D/B/A/C.

Work as for left sleeve, using chart F.

FINISHING

Sew one shoulder seam.

With smaller circular needle, p.u. 56 (56, 58, 62, 68, 72) sts evenly around neckline.

Work in garter ridge as follows: B/A/C/A; then b.o. sts loosely.

Weave in all loose ends.

Sew other shoulder and neck seam.

Using cross-stitch embroidery techniques, decorate the different pieces with multicolored embroidery.

If you planned to work some of the colors in duplicate stitch, do this now.

Mark underarm points 5½ (5½, 6, 6½, 7, 7½)" (14, 14, 15, 16.5, 18, 19 cm) down in front and back from shoulder.

Set in sleeves bet points.

Sew underarm and side seams.

Adult's Cardigan

SIZES

Small (Medium, Large)

Finished measurements: 46 (50, 54)" (117, 127, 137 cm)

MATERIALS

Montera (50% llama, 50% wool; 100 g = approx. 130 yds/119 m): 2 hanks each of colors A (dark) and D (dark); 4 hanks each of colors B (light), C (medium), and E (medium)

Equivalent yarn: 260 yds (238 m) each of bulky wool in colors A and D, 520 yds (475 m) each of colors B, C, and E

Knitting needles: sizes 7 and 9 U.S. (4.5 and 5.5 mm), 36" (91.5 cm) circular needles in sizes 7 and 9 U.S. (4.5 and 5.5 mm)

Very long stitch holders (or scraps of yarn)

Tapestry needle for duplicate stitch

Eight 1½" (4 cm) buttons

GAUGE

Same as for child's sweater, above

BODY

NOTE: *Body is knit in one piece to armholes, then split into back and two fronts, which are worked separately.*

With smaller needles, c.o. 180 (196, 212) sts.

Work 7 garter ridges as follows: A/C/D/B/A/E or in any color sequence you desire.

Change to larger needles and beg working in Fair Isle pattern.

(To determine where to start your pattern, see the explanation in the child's version, above.)

Work in the following pattern sequence or take creative license and change the colors to suit yourself.

Work pattern H for 26 rows.

Work one garter ridge in E.

Work one garter ridge in C.

Work in pattern J for 6 rows.

Work one garter ridge in C.

Work one garter ridge in A.

Work pattern C for 12 rows.

Work one garter ridge in A.

Work pattern I for 17 rows.

Work one garter ridge in A.

Work one garter ridge in C.

Work pattern J for 6 rows.

Work one garter ridge in C.

Work one garter ridge in B.

Work pattern K for 20 rows.

Work one garter ridge in B.

Work pattern B for 9 rows.

Work pattern D for rem 3½ (4½, 5½)" (9, 11.5, 14 cm) of sweater.

When piece meas 17½ (18, 18½)" (44.5, 45.5, 47 cm), split work for armholes to give 44 (48, 52) sts for front, 92 (100, 108) sts for back, and 44 (48, 52) sts for rem front.

BACK

Work 92 (100, 108) sts.

Work back straight until piece meas 27 (28, 29)" (68.5, 71, 73.5 cm); then b.o. all sts.

RIGHT FRONT

Work 44 (48, 52) sts at each side of opening until piece meas 24 (25, 26)" (61, 63.5, 66 cm).

SHAPE NECK: B.o. 8 (9, 10) sts at neck edge.

Work 1 row even.

B.o. 1 st at neck edge every other row 4 times to give 32 (35, 38) sts at shoulder.

When piece meas same as back, b.o. all sts.

LEFT FRONT

Work to correspond with right front, reversing neck shaping.

SLEEVES

Make two different sleeves: With smaller needles, c.o. 34 (36, 38) sts and work in garter ridge to correspond with body of sweater.

Inc 4 sts evenly across last row to give 38 (40, 42) sts.

Change to larger needles and work in patterns given below while inc 1 st each end every 4th row 19 (20, 21) times to give 76 (80, 84) sts.

SLEEVE A:

Work in pattern G for 8" (20.5 cm).

Work one garter ridge in color A.

Work in pattern C for 12 rows.

Work one garter ridge in E.

Work in pattern D for rem 5 (5½, 6)" (12.5, 14, 15 cm) of sleeve.

SLEEVE B:

Work in pattern F for 21 rows.

Work one garter ridge in color C.

Work in pattern E for 16 rows.

Work one garter ridge in E.

Work in pattern D for rem 8 (8½, 9)" (20.5, 21.5, 23 cm) of sleeve.

FINISHING

Sew shoulder seams.

Sew sleeve seams.

Sew sleeves into armhole openings.

CARDIGAN BAND: With RS facing, use smaller circular needle and color E to p.u. 110 (115, 120) sts along front edge, pm, p.u. corner st, pm, p.u. 85 (90, 95) sts around neckline, pm, p.u. corner st, pm, p.u. 110 (115, 120) sts down rem front of cardigan edge.

Knit 1 row in color E, completing first garter ridge.

Work rem garter ridges in the following sequence: A/B/D/C/A.

To miter corner sts: Work to marker, inc 1 by backward loop method, work st, inc 1 before next marker.

Work this inc every RSR at top sides of cardigan.

BUTTONHOLES

Using safety pins, mark work 2" (5 cm) in from bottom of cardigan--this number seems large, but the button is 1½" (4 cm) in diameter.

Mark 2 sts in from marked st at top of cardigan.

Then evenly mark 6 more buttons.

To make buttonhole, work to marked st, b.o. next 3 sts, cont working to the next marker, and so forth.

To finish buttonhole on next row: C.o. 3 sts where sts were b.o. on previous row.

Sew on buttons.

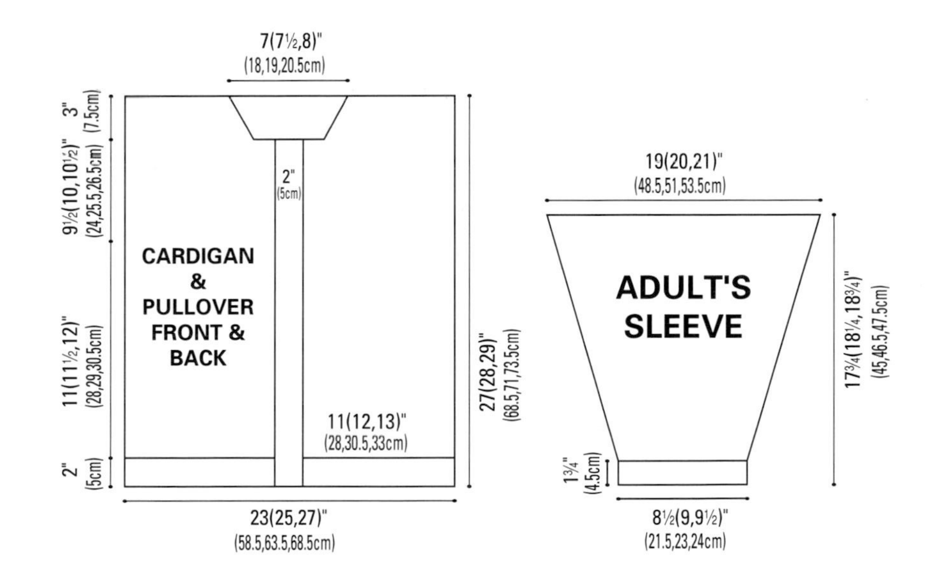

Adult's Pullover

MATERIALS

Same as adult's cardigan

BACK

With smaller needles, c.o. 92 (100, 108) sts.

Work as given for body of cardigan, following same color sequences.

When piece meas 27 (28, 29)" (68.5, 71, 73.5 cm), b.o. all sts.

FRONT

Work same as back.

When piece meas 24 (25, 26)" (61, 63.5, 66 cm), shape neck.

Work 36 (39, 42) sts, join a 2nd ball of yarn, b.o. center 20 (22, 24) sts, and work to end.

Working each side sep, b.o. 1 st at neck edge every other row 4 times.

When piece meas same as back to shoulder, b.o. all sts.

FINISHING

Sew shoulder seams.

Sew sleeve seams.

Sew sleeves into armhole openings.

With smaller needles, p.u. 84 (86, 90) sts evenly around neck.

Work in garter ridges to correspond with bottom of ribbing of sweater.

B.o. loosely.

FINISHING FOR BOTH SWEATERS

Weave in all loose ends.

Using cross-stitch embroidery techniques, decorate selected areas with multicolored embroidery.

If you planned to work some of the colors in duplicate stitch, do this now.

(Duplicate stitch can be used to outline an entire motif with a darker or lighter color to provide greater contrast between patterns.)

COLOR KEY

- ● = Color A (dark)
- ◇ = Color B (light)
- ☰ = Color C (medium)
- ★ = Color D (dark)
- ■ = Color E (light or medium)

GARTER RIDGE ROW

In any color, you will work two rows:

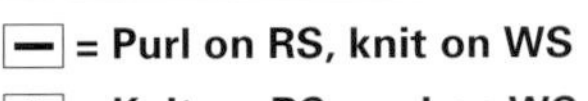

- — = Purl on RS, knit on WS
- I = Knit on RS, purl on WS

NOTE: *To avoid carrying long sections of colors not being used, work extra colors in duplicate stitch when your sweater is completed.*

■ Pattern A (over 20 sts and 19 rows)

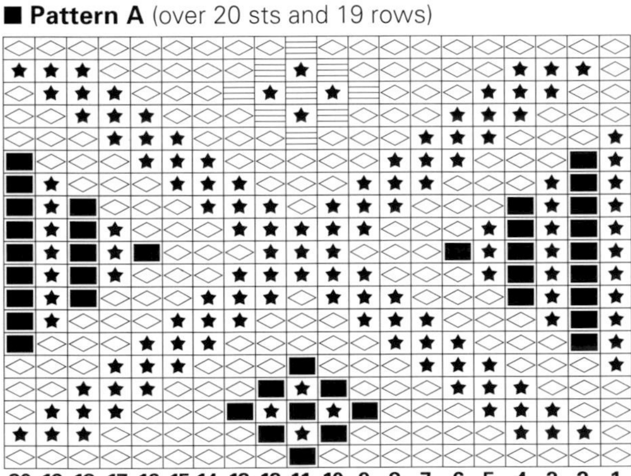

■ Pattern B (over 20 sts and 9 rows)

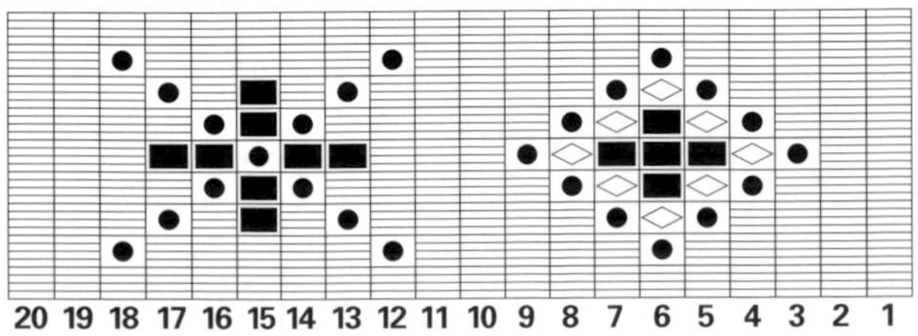

■ Pattern C (over 20 sts and 12 rows)

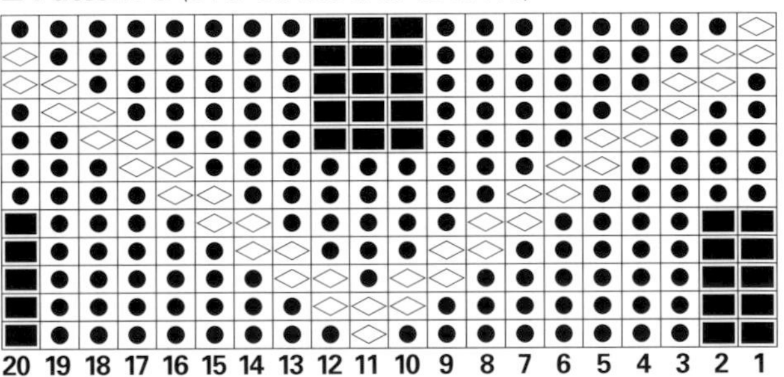

■ Pattern D (over 6 sts and 6 rows)

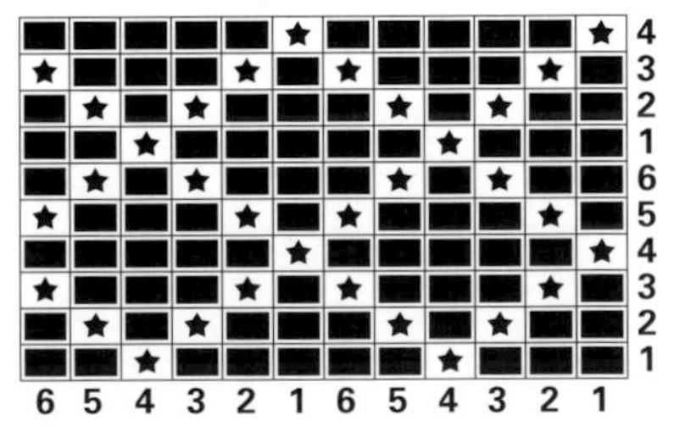

■ Pattern E (over 8 sts and 8 rows)

■ **Pattern F** (over 10 sts and 6 rows)

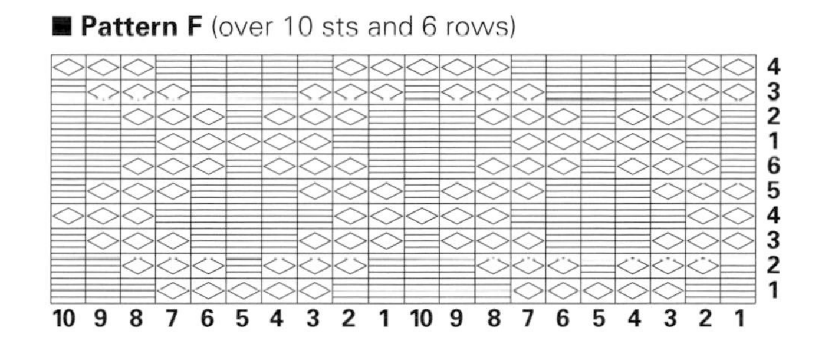

■ **Pattern G** (over 8 sts and 8 rows)

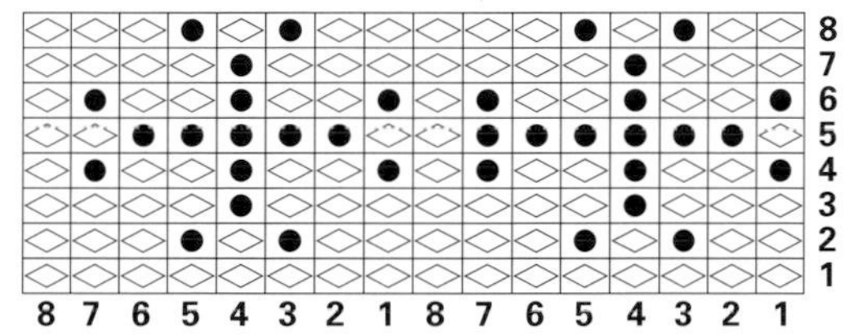

■ **Pattern H** (over 30 sts and 26 rows)

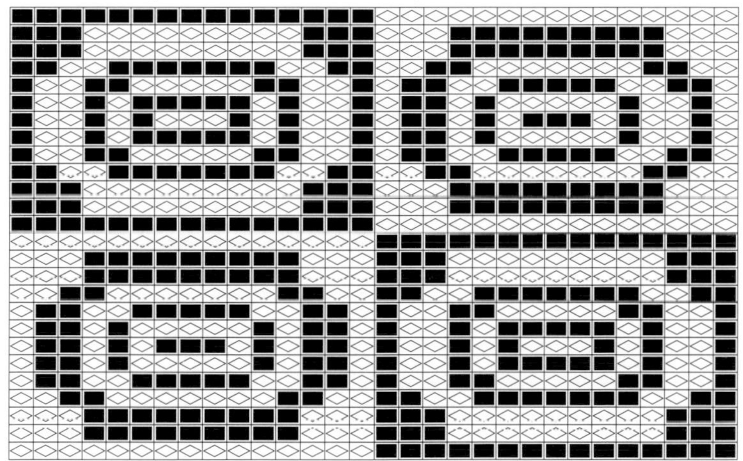

■ **Pattern J** (over 7 sts and 6 rows)

■ **Pattern K** (over 17 sts and 20 rows)

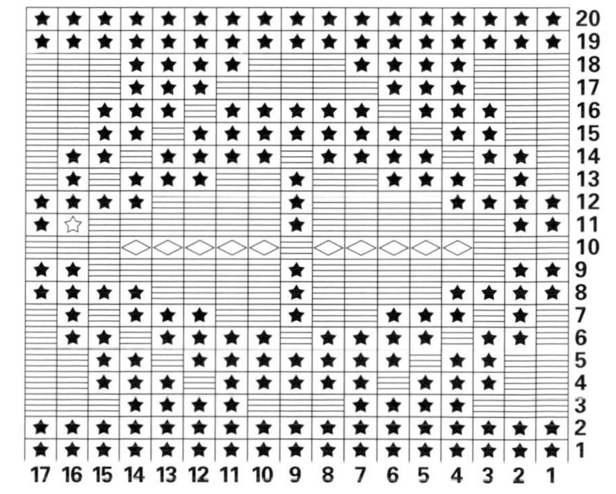

■ **Pattern I** (over 20 sts and 17 rows)

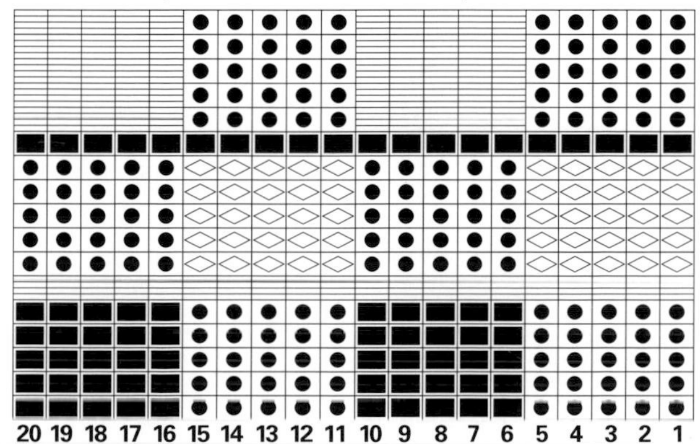

Native American Aran

design: **Kristin Nicholas**

knitting rating: **Experienced**

photography: **Philip Newton**

Two favorite traditional knitting techniques are combined in this group of pullovers for the family. The solid-colored sweaters are knit throughout in the Aran pattern. In the multicolored versions, two-color Fair Isle knitting is worked in bold motifs on the lower sections, and the hem is trimmed with multicolored corrugated ribbing. The yoke is made up of an array of Aran cables separated by small columns of twist stitches. For the experienced knitter, this design offers the challenge of working with two techniques for a project that is exciting and technically inspiring.

Solid Aran Sweaters

SIZES

ADULT: Small (Medium, Large, Extra Large)

CHILD: <6 (8, 10, 12, 14)>

Finished measurements: 42½ (48, 53, 57½)" (108, 122, 134.5, 146 cm) <28 (34½, 38, 40, 42½)" (71, 87.5, 96.5, 101.5, 108 cm)>

MATERIALS

Tapestry (75% wool, 25% mohair; 50 g = approx. 95 yds/87 m): 18 (18, 19, 20) <9 (10, 11, 12, 13)> hanks

Equivalent yarn: 1710 (1710, 1805, 1900) yds (1564, 1564, 1650, 1737 m) <855 (950, 1045, 1140, 1235) (782, 869, 956, 1042, 1129 m)> of worsted-weight wool

Knitting needles: sizes 5 and 8 U.S. (3.75 and 5 mm), circular needle in size 5 U.S. (3.75 mm), cable needle (cn)

GAUGE

Twist stitch cable pattern: 19 sts and 25 rows = 4" (10 cm)

Braid cable = 4½" (11.5 cm)

Open cable = 3¼" (8.5 cm)

Take time to save time—check your gauge.

PATTERN STITCHES

■ **Reverse Stockinette Stitch** (RSS)

Row 1 (WS): K all sts.

Row 2: P all sts.

■ **Twist Stitch** (over 2 sts)

Row 1 (WS): P2.

Row 2: TW2 (skip first st, k 2nd st without removing from needle, k first st and remove both from needle).

■ **Twist Stitch Rib** (over multiple of 5 sts plus 3)

Row 1 (WS): *K3, p2*; rep bet *s, end k3.

Row 2: *P3, TW2*; rep bet *s, end p3.

■ **Twist Stitch Rib in Round** (over multiple of 5 sts)

Row 1 (WS): *P3, k2*; rep bet *s.

Row 2: *P3, TW2*; rep bet *s.

■ **Twist Stitch Body Rib** (over multiple of 6 sts plus 4)

On larger needles:

Row 1 (WS): *K4, p2*; rep bet *s, end k4.

Row 2: *P4, TW2*; rep bet *s, end p4.

■ **Open Cable** (over 21 sts)

BC3/2: Sl 2 sts to cn and hold in back, k3, p2 sts from cn.

FC3/2: Sl 3 sts to cn and hold in front, p2, k3 from cn.

FC3/1: Sl 3 sts to cn and hold in front, p1, k3 from cn.

BC3/1: Sl 1 st to cn and hold in back, k3, p1 from cn.

Row 1 (WS): K6, p6, k9.

Row 2: P9, sl 3 sts to cn and hold in back, k3, k3 from cn, p6.

Row 3 and all WS rows: Work all sts as they appear.

Row 4: P7, BC3/2, BC3/1, p5.

Row 6: P5, BC3/2, p3, FC3/1, p4.

Row 8: P3, BC3/2, p6, FC3/1, p3.

Row 10: P3, k3, p9, k3, p3.

Row 12: P3, FC3/1, p6, BC3/2, p3.

Row 14: P4, FC3/1, p3, BC3/2, p5.

Row 16: P5, FC3/1, BC3/2, p7.

Row 18: P6, sl 3 sts to cn and hold in back, k3, k3 from cn, p9.

Row 20: P5, BC3/1, FC3/2, p7.

Row 22: P4, BC3/1, p3, FC3/2, p5.

Row 24: P3, BC3/1, p6, FC3/2, p3.

Row 26: P3, k3, p9, k3, p3.

Row 28: P3, FC3/2, p6, BC3/1, p3.

Row 30: P5, FC3/2, p3, BC3/1, p4.

Row 32: P7, FC3/2, BC3/1, p5.

■ **Braid Cable** (over 30 sts)

BC: Sl 2 sts to cn and hold in back, k2, k2 from cn.

BC2/1: Sl 1 st to cn and hold in back, k2, p1 from cn.

FC2/2: Sl 2 sts to cn and hold in front, p2, k2 from cn.

BC2/2: Sl 2 sts to cn and hold in back, k2, p2 from cn.

FC2/1: Sl 2 sts to cn and hold in front, p1, k2 from cn.

FC: Sl 2 sts to cn and hold in front, k2, k2 from cn.

Row 1 (WS): K1, *k4, p4*; rep bet *s 3 times, k5.

Row 2: P1, *p4, BC*; rep bet *s 3 times, p5.

Row 3 and all WS rows: Work all sts as they appear.

Row 4: P4, BC2/1, FC2/2, BC2/2, FC2/2, BC2/2, FC2/1, p4.

Row 6: P3, BC2/1, p3, FC, p4, FC, p3, FC2/1, p3.

Row 8: P3, k2, p2, BC2/2, FC2/2, BC2/2, FC2/2, p2, k2, p3.

Row 10: P3, k2, p2, k2, p4, BC, p4, k2, p2, k2, p3.

Row 12: P3, k2, p2, FC2/2, BC2/2, FC2/2, BC2/2, p2, k2, p3.

Row 14: P3, FC2/1, p3, FC, p4, FC, p3, BC2/1, p3.

Row 16: P4, FC2/1, BC2/2, FC2/2, BC2/2, FC2/2, BC2/1, p4.

BACK

With smaller needles, c.o. 103 (113, 123, 133) <63 (73, 83, 83, 93)> sts.

Knit 3 rows.

Work twist stitch rib, beg with a WSR.

When piece meas 2½" (6.5 cm) <1½" (4 cm)> incl garter stitch, inc 31 (33, 35, 37) <27 (31, 29, 35, 31)> sts evenly across in RSR to give 134 (146, 158, 170) <90 (104, 112, 118, 124)> sts.

Change to larger needles.

FOR BOTH SOLID ARAN AND FAIR ISLE ARAN VERSIONS, est cabled patt on WSR as follows:

ADULT: *K4 in RSS, p2 for TW*; rep bet *s 0 (1, 2, 3) more times (over 6 (12, 18, 24) sts), work open cable over 21 sts, p2 for TW, work open cable over 21 sts, p2 for TW, work braid cable over 30 sts, p2 for TW, work open cable over 21 sts, p2 for TW, work open cable for 21 sts, *p2 for TW, k4 in RSS*; rep bet *s 0 (1, 2, 3) more times (over 6 (12, 18, 24) sts).

CHILD: K0 (2, 0, 3, 0) in RSS, *k4, p2 for TW*; rep bet *s 0 (1, 2, 2, 3) more times (over 6 (12, 18, 18, 24) sts), work open cable over 21 sts, p2 for TW, work braid cable over 30 sts, work p2 for TW, work open cable over 21 sts, *p2 for TW, k4 in RSS*; rep bet *s 0 (1, 2, 2, 3) more times (over 6 (12, 18, 18 24) sts), end with k0 (2, 0, 3, 0) sts in RSS.

Work as est in patt, twisting the 2 St sts every RSR and keeping other sts in RSS.

Work straight until piece meas 25 (25, 26, 27)" (63.5, 63.5, 66, 68.5 cm) <13 (14, 16, 18, 19)" (33, 35.5, 40.5, 45.5, 48.5 cm)> for Aran version or 26¾ (27¼, 27¾, 28¼)" (68, 69, 70.5, 71.5 cm) <13 (13¼, 15, 17¼, 18½)" (33, 33.5, 38, 43, 47 cm)> for Fair Isle version.

B.o. all sts.

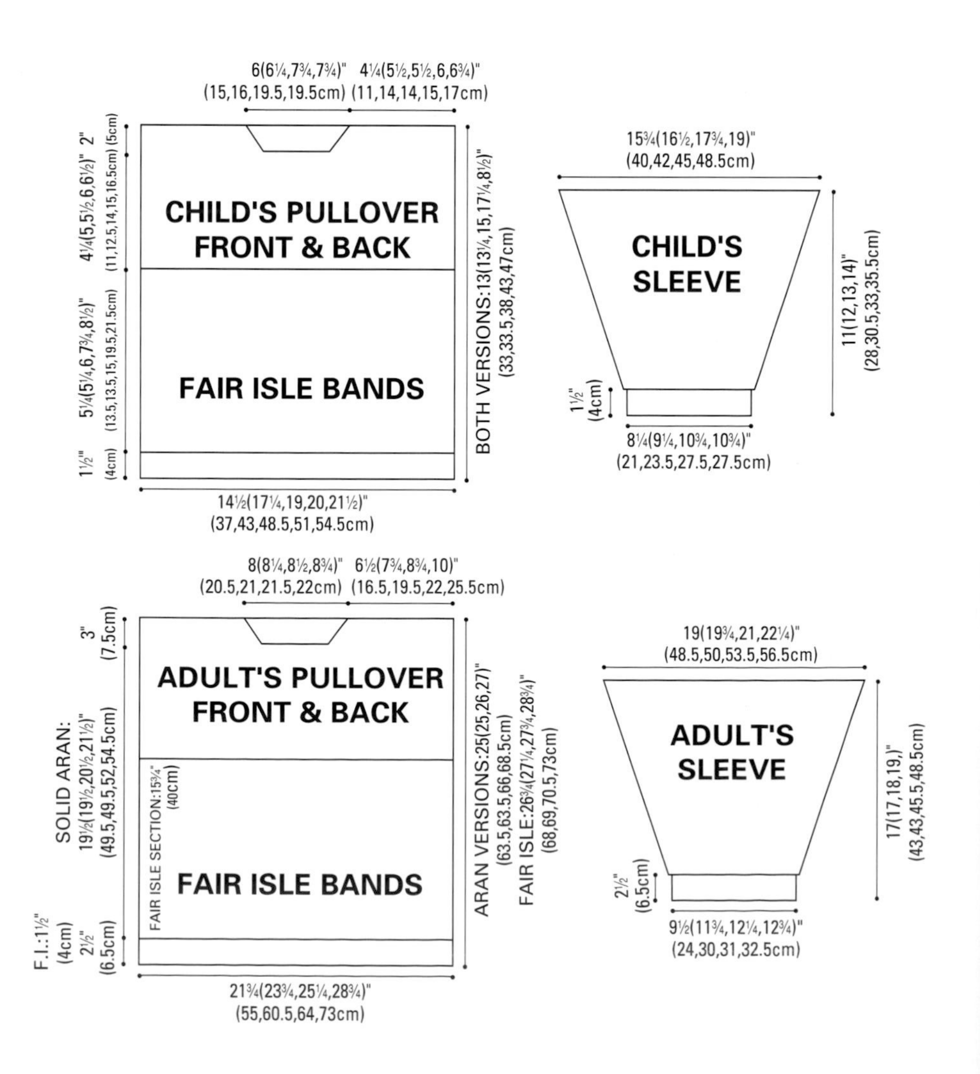

FRONT

Work same as back until piece meas 22 (22, 23, 24)" (56, 56, 58.5, 61 cm) <11 (12, 14, 15½, 17)" (28, 30.5, 35.5, 39.5, 43 cm)>.

SHAPE NECK: Work 49 (54, 59, 64) <30 (37, 41, 44, 47)> sts, join 2nd ball of yarn, b.o. center 36 (38, 40, 42) <30> sts, and work to end.

Working each side sep, b.o. 1 st every other neck edge 9 <5 (5, 6, 7, 7)> times to give 40 (45, 50, 55) <25 (32, 35, 37, 40)> sts at shoulder.

When piece meas same as back, b.o. all sts.

SLEEVES—BOTH VERSIONS

With smaller needles, c.o. 39 (43, 48, 48) <33 (38, 38, 43, 43)> sts.

Knit 3 rows, ending with a RSR.

Work in twist stitch rib for 2" (5 cm) <1½" (4 cm)> incl garter st rows.

When you have finished a RSR, change to larger needles and inc on WS as follows: *K2, inc 1, k1, p2*; rep bet *s, ending with k2, inc 1, k1 to give 46 (52, 58, 58) <39 (45, 45, 51, 51)> sts.

Cont to work in twist stitch rib for sleeve as est in last row by k4 on WSR and p4 on RSR as inc in last row.

At the same time, inc 1 st each end every 5th row 10 (9, 13, 9) <10 (8, 7, 10, 3)> times, then every 4th row 11 (12, 8, 15) <5 (7, 10, 7, 17)> times, incorporating new sts into patt to give 90 (94, 100, 106) <69 (75, 79, 85, 91)> sts.

When piece meas 17 (17, 18, 19)" (43, 43, 45.5, 48.5 cm) <10½ (11, 12, 13, 14)" (26.5, 28, 30.5, 33, 35.5 cm)>, b.o. all sts.

FINISHING

With smaller circular needles, p.u. 105 (110, 115, 120) <70 (75, 80, 85, 90)> sts evenly around neck.

Work in rnd in twist stitch ribbing for 4" (10 cm) <1½" (4 cm)>, ending with a twist rnd.

K 3 rows in garter stitch.

B.o. all sts in purl.

Fair Isle Banded Versions

This sweater is knit in the rnd to the armholes, then split and worked back and forth in Aran stitches.

MATERIALS

ADULT: Tapestry (75% wool, 25% mohair; 50 g = approx. 95 yds/87 m): 5 (6, 7, 8) hanks each of colors A and E; 1 hank each of colors B and F; 9 (10, 12, 13) hanks of color C (main color); 2 hanks of color D

Equivalent yarn: 475 (570, 665, 760) yds (434, 521, 608, 695 m) each of worsted-weight wool in colors A and E; 95 yds (87 m) each of colors B and F; 855 (950, 1045, 1140) yds (782, 869, 956, 1042 m) of color C (main color); 190 yds (174 m) of color D

CHILD: <4 (5, 5, 5, 6) hanks of color A; 1 hank each of colors B, C, and E; 2 hanks of color D>

Equivalent yarn: <380 (475, 475, 475, 570) yds (347, 434, 434, 434, 521 m) of color A; 95 yds (87 m) each of colors B, C, and E; 190 yds (174 m) of color D>

Knitting needles: 24 or 36" (61 or 91.5 cm) <24" (61 cm)> circular knitting needles in sizes 5 and 8 U.S. (3.75 and 5 mm), 16" (40.5 cm) circular knitting needle in size 5 U.S. (3.75 mm)

GAUGE

As above and:

Fair Isle St st on larger circular needle: 20 sts and 24 rows = 4" (10 cm)

CHILD'S BODY

With smaller needles and color A, c.o. 125 (155, 165, 170, 185) sts.

Join in rnd, taking care not to twist.

P 1 rnd; k 1 rnd; p 1 rnd.

Beg working rib in rnd as given in multicolored twisted rib stitch:

■ Twisted Rib In Round

Rnd 1: *P3 in B, k2 in A*.

Rnd 2: *P3 in B, TW2 in A*.

Rnd 3: *P3 in C, k2 in A*.

Rnd 4: *P3 in C, TW2 in A*.

Work for 8 rows, inc 15 (17, 25, 30, 27) sts evenly around to give 140 (172, 190, 200, 212) sts in last rnd.

Change to larger needles and beg Fair Isle patterning.

In order to have pattern repeats work out evenly, it is necessary to dec or inc some sts in the first rnd of some of the patterns; stretching and blocking the fabric will accommodate these minor changes.

■ Pattern A (repeat over 2 sts and 4 rows)

Work even over all sizes.

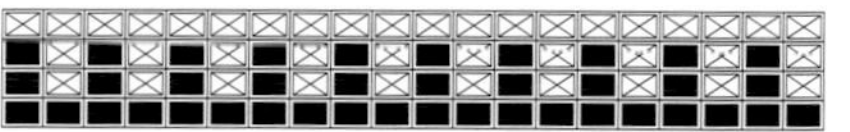

■ Pattern B (repeat over 10 sts and 10 rows)

SIZE 6: Work even on 140 sts.

SIZE 8: Dec 2 sts in first rnd to give 170 sts.

SIZE 10: Work even on 190 sts.

SIZE 12: Work even on 200 sts.

SIZE 14: Dec 2 sts in first rnd to give 210 sts.

Work for 15 (15, 20, 30, 35) rnds.

■ Pattern C (repeat over 16 sts and 7 rows)

SIZE 6: Inc 4 sts in first rnd to give 144 sts.

SIZE 8: Inc 6 sts in first rnd to give 176 sts.

SIZE 10: Inc 2 sts in first rnd to give 192 sts.

SIZE 12: Dec 1 st in first rnd to give 199 sts and beg where indicated on chart. Pattern will not repeat exactly.

SIZE 14: Dec 2 sts in first rnd to give 208 sts.

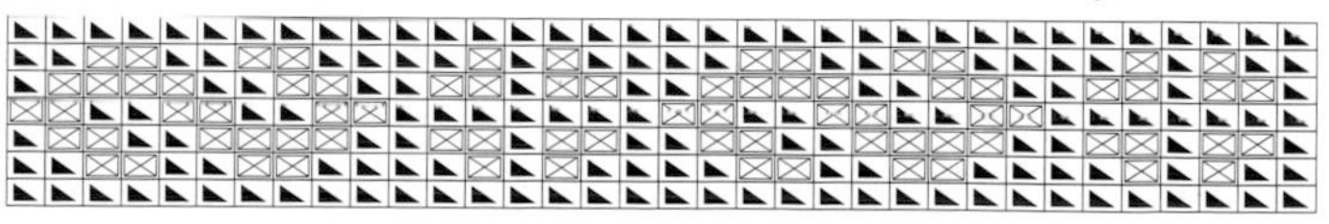

■ **Pattern D** (repeat over 6 sts and 5 rows)

SIZE 6: Work even on 144 sts.

SIZE 8: Dec 2 sts in first rnd to give 174 sts.

SIZE 10: Work even on 192 sts

SIZE 12: Dec 1 st in first rnd to give 198 sts.

SIZE 14: Inc 2 sts in first rnd to give 210 sts.

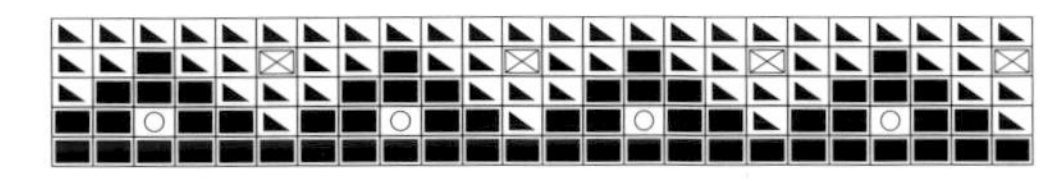

Work patterns A, B, C, and D as given above.

When 31 (31, 36, 46, 51) rows have been completed, change to color A and beg patterning.

Purl 1 rnd, inc 36 (34, 32, 38, 38) sts evenly around.

Split work in half and beg working back and forth for front and back to give 90 (104, 112, 118, 124) sts.

Go to * in instructions for child's back in the solid Aran version and beg working in Aran sts on WS of sweater.

Then work front as back.

Work rest of sweater as given for solid Aran version.

Make sleeves in color A.

ADULT'S BODY

With smaller needles and color C, c.o. 185 (210, 230, 250) sts.

Join, taking care not to twist.

P 1 rnd, k 1 rnd, p 1 rnd.

Work in rnd in multicolored twist stitch ribbing as follows:

■ Twisted Rib In Round

Rnd 1: *P3 in F, k2 in C*.

Rnd 2: *P3 in F, TW2 in C*.

Rnd 3: *P3 in D, k2 in C*.

Rnd 4: *P3 in D, TW2 in C*.

Rep until rib meas 1½" (4 cm), including garter st edge.

In last rnd, inc 27 (30, 34, 38) sts evenly to give 212 (240, 264, 288) sts.

Change to larger needles and beg working Fair Isle patterning.

In order to have pattern repeats work out evenly, it is necessary to dec or inc some sts in the first rnd of some of the patterns; stretching and blocking the fabric will accommodate these minor changes.

■ **Pattern A** (repeat over 4 sts and 4 rnds)

Work even over all sizes.

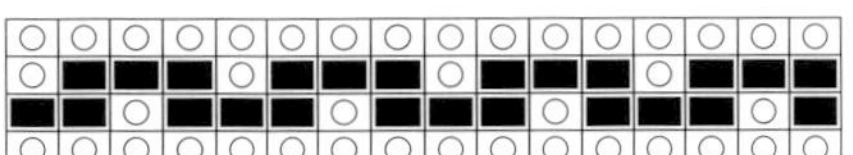

Pattern B (repeat over 2 sts and 4 rnds)

Work even over all sizes.

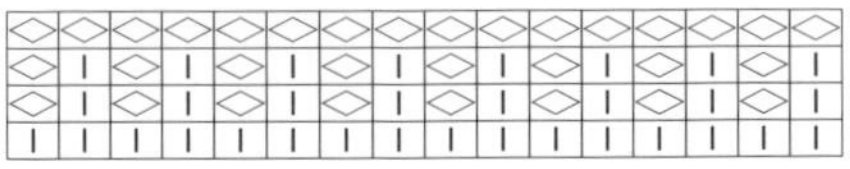

■ **Pattern C** (repeat over 32 sts and 51 rnds)

SMALL: *Work panel C over 9 sts, work 97 sts of Pattern C, beg where indicated; rep from *.

MEDIUM: *Work panel C over 9 sts, work 111 sts of pattern C, beg where indicated; rep from *.

LARGE: *Work panel C over 9 sts, work 123 sts of pattern C, beg where indicated; rep from *.

EXTRA LARGE: Work 9 repeats of pattern C evenly around.

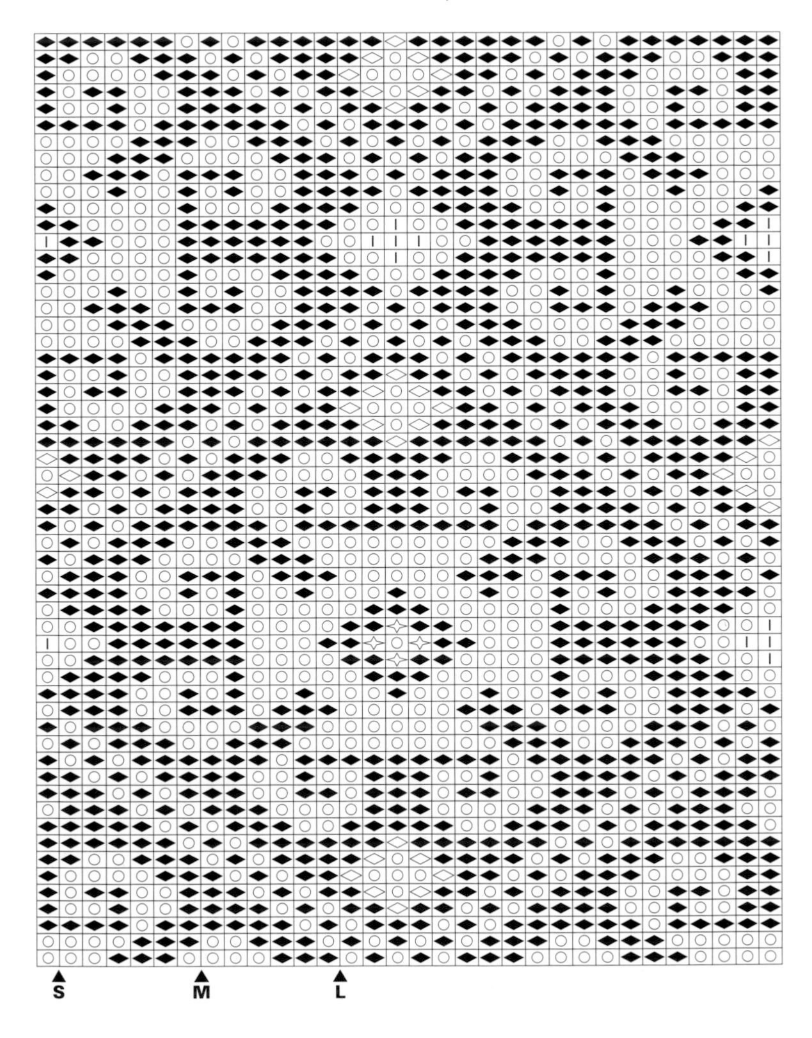

Panel C

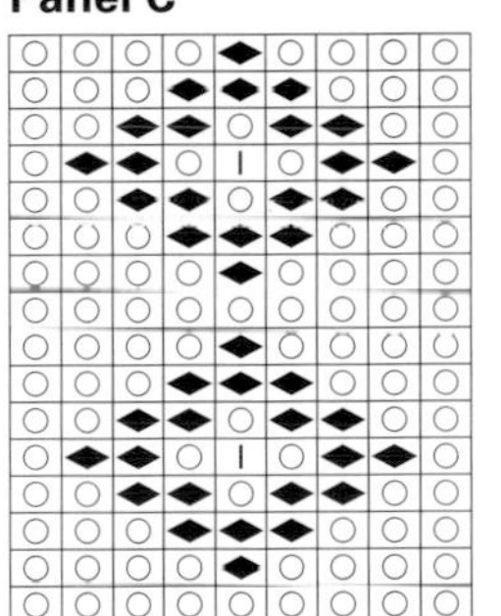

■ Pattern D (repeat over 6 sts and 5 rnds)

SMALL: Dec 2 sts evenly around to give 210 sts.

MEDIUM: Work even on 240 sts.

LARGE: Work even on 264 sts.

EXTRA LARGE: Work even on 288 sts.

■ Pattern E (repeat over 32 sts and 13 rnds)

SMALL: *Work 8 sts of pattern F, work 3 repeats of pattern E; rep from *.

MEDIUM: *Work 10 sts of pattern F, work pattern E starting and ending where indicated; rep from *.

LARGE: *Work 4 sts of pattern F, work pattern E starting and ending where indicated; rep from *.

EXTRA LARGE: Work 9 repeats of pattern E.

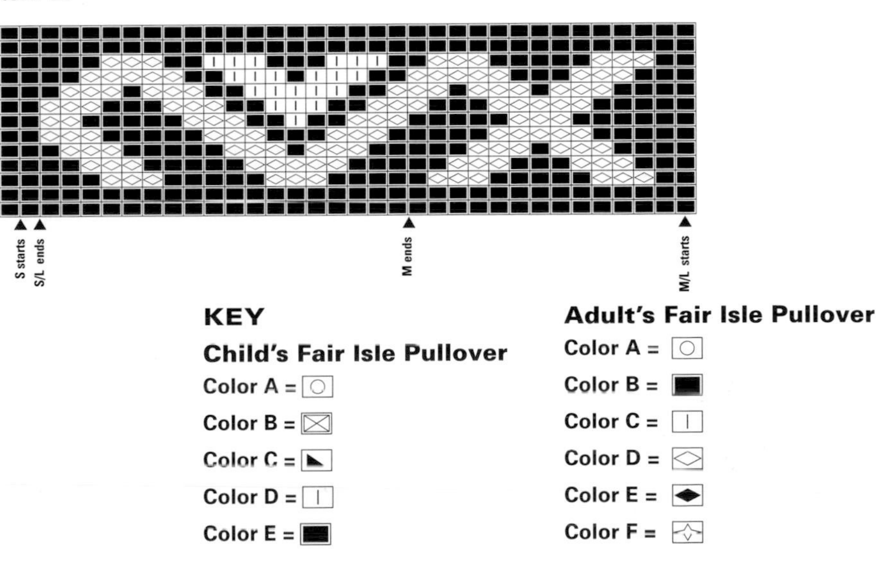

KEY

Child's Fair Isle Pullover

Color A = ○

Color B = ☒

Color C = ◣

Color D = |

Color E = ■

Adult's Fair Isle Pullover

Color A = ○

Color B = ■

Color C = |

Color D = ◇

Color E = ◆

Color F = ✧

■ Pattern F (repeat over 4 sts and 4 rnds)

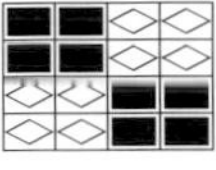

■ Pattern G (repeat over 4 sts and 5 rnds)

SMALL: Inc 2 sts evenly around to give 212 sts.

MEDIUM, LARGE, EXTRA LARGE: Work evenly as est.

■ Pattern H (repeat over 6 sts and 7 rnds)

SMALL: Dec 2 sts evenly around to give 210 sts.

MEDIUM, LARGE, EXTRA LARGE: Work evenly as est.

In the last rnd of pattern H, inc 58 (52, 52, 52) sts to give 268 (292, 316, 340) sts.

Purl 1 rnd in color C (main color).

Split work in half and beg working back and forth in Aran sts as given in the instructions for the adult's back in the solid Aran version.

Clark's Falls

design: **Kristin Nicholas**
knitting rating: **Intermediate**
photography: **Philip Newton**

Guernsey styling from Great Britain has been readily adopted by American knitters, who have added their own slight modifications. For example, traditional Guernseys are knit very tightly with fine yarns, but Americans prefer chunkier gauges. This design includes children's sizes, and it comes in two lengths for adults—a tunic length preferred by women and a shorter version for men. The yoke is worked in a very easy version of basket stitch that has cable crossings in only three of the 18 rows of the pattern. At the edges are horizontal garter ridges.

SIZES

ADULT: Extra Small (Small, Medium, Large, Extra Large)

CHILD: <Small (Medium, Large, Extra Large)>

Finished measurements: 38½ (42, 47, 51, 54½)" (98, 106.5, 119.5, 129.5, 138.5 cm); <20½ (26, 29, 34)" (52, 66, 73.5, 86.5 cm)>

MATERIALS

Montera (50% llama, 50% wool; 100 g = approx. 127 yds/116 m): 8 (9, 9, 10, 11) hanks for tunic; 7 (8, 9, 10, 10) hanks for standard length; <4 (4, 5, 6)> hanks for child's pullover

Equivalent yarn: 1016 (1143, 1143, 1270, 1397) yds (929, 1045, 1045, 1161, 1277 m) of bulky wool for tunic; 889 (1016, 1143, 1270, 1270) yds (813, 929, 1045, 1161, 1161 m) for standard length; <450 (508, 635, 762) yds (411, 464, 581, 697 m)> for child's pullover

Knitting needles: sizes 5 and 8 U.S. (3.75 and 5 mm), 16" (40.5 cm) circular needle in size 5 U.S. (3.75 mm), cable needle (cn)

GAUGE

St st with larger needles: 16 sts and 24 rows = 4" (10 cm)

Cabled ladder pattern: 21 sts and 24 rows = 5" (12.5 cm)

Take time to save time—check your gauge.

PATTERN STITCHES

Stockinette Stitch

Row 1 (RS): K all sts.

Row 2: P all sts.

Garter Stitch Ridge and Ribbing

See charts on page 26.

Cabled Ladder Pattern (over multiple of 18 sts)

See chart on page 26.

BACK

With smaller needles, c.o. 72 (80, 88, 96, 100) <40 (52, 56, 68)> sts.

Work garter st ribbing as follows: For adult's sweater, work rows 1 through 10 twice and end with rows 1 and 2 to give 22 rows in total. <For child's sweater, work rows 1 through 10 once and end with rows 1 through 7 to give a total of 17 rows.>

Garter rib should meas approx. 3" (7.5 cm) <2½" (6.5 cm)>.

In last row of rib, inc 5 (4, 6, 6, 9) <1 (0, 2, 0)> sts evenly across to give 77 (84, 94, 102, 109) <41 (52, 58, 68)> sts.

Change to larger needles and est garter st ridge at side seams: Work 4 sts in garter ridge, pm, work 69 (76, 86, 94, 101) <33 (44, 50, 60)> sts in St st, pm, work rem 4 sts in garter ridge.

Work as est until piece meas 11 (12, 12, 12, 13)" (28, 30.5, 30.5, 30.5, 33 cm) for adult's standard version; 8 (9, 9, 9½, 9½)" (20.5, 23, 23, 24, 24 cm) for tunic <7½ (8½, 8½, 9)" (19, 21.5, 21.5, 23 cm)> for child's version.

In last WSR of St st, inc 5 (6, 6, 6, 7) <3 (2, 4, 4)> sts evenly across to give 82 (90, 100, 108, 116) <44 (54, 62, 72)> sts.

Now est cabled ladder patt as follows: Beg with st 9 (5, 9, 5, 1) <1 (5, 1, 5)>, work to end of graph; then work 4 (4, 5, 5, 6) <2 (2, 3, 3)> rep of patt, ending last rep with st 18 (4, 18, 4, 8) <8 (4, 8, 4)> to give 82 (90, 100, 108, 116) <44 (54, 62, 72)> sts.

Work until piece meas 23 (24, 25, 25, 26)" (58.5, 61, 63.5, 63.5, 66 cm) for adult's standard length; 27 (27, 28, 28, 29)" (68.5, 68.5, 71, 71, 73.5 cm) for tunic; <13 (14, 15, 16)" (33, 35.5, 38, 40.5 cm)> for child's sweater.

B.o. all sts.

FRONT

Work as for back until piece meas 21 (22, 23, 23, 24)" (53.5, 56, 58.5, 58.5, 61 cm) for adult's standard version or 25 (25, 26, 26, 27)" (63.5, 63.5, 66, 66, 68.5 cm) for tunic or <11 (12, 13, 14)" (28, 30.5, 33, 35.5 cm)> for child's version.

SHAPE NECK: Work 30 (33, 38, 41, 44) <12 (17, 20, 24)> sts, join a 2nd ball of yarn, b.o. center 22 (24, 24, 26, 28) <20 (20, 22, 24)> sts, and work to end.

Working each side sep, b.o. 1 st at neck edge every other row 4 <4> times to give 26 (29, 34, 37, 40) <8 (13, 16, 20)> sts at shoulder.

When piece meas same as back at shoulders, b.o. all sts.

SLEEVES

With smaller needles, c.o. 34 (36, 38, 40, 40) <26 (28, 30, 32)> sts.

Work in garter ridge as done on body for 3" (7.5 cm) <2½" (6.5 cm)>.

In last row of ridges, inc 4 <2> sts evenly across to give 38 (40, 42, 44, 44) <28 (30, 32, 34)> sts.

Change to larger needles and est garter ridge at underarm as done on body: Work 4 sts in garter ridge, pm, work 30 (32, 34, 36, 36) <20 (22, 24, 26)> sts in St st, pm, work 4 sts in garter ridge.

At the same time, inc inside the garter ridge as follows: Work 4 sts, inc 1, work across St st, inc 1 before marker, work 4 rem sts.

Cont inc so that 4 sts in garter ridge travel up seam of sweater, inc as follows: Inc 1 st each end every 2nd row 0 (0, 2, 0, 0) <4 (0, 0, 0)> times, every 4th row 0 <8 (13, 14, 15)> times, every 5th row 15 (16, 0, 0, 18) <0> times, then every 6th row 0 (0, 14, 16, 0) <0> times, to give 70 (74, 76, 78, 82) <54 (58, 62, 66)> sts.

When piece meas 16 (17, 18, 19, 19)" (40.5, 43, 45.5, 48.5, 48.5 cm) <10 (11½, 12, 13)" (25.5, 29, 30.5, 33 cm)>, b.o. all sts.

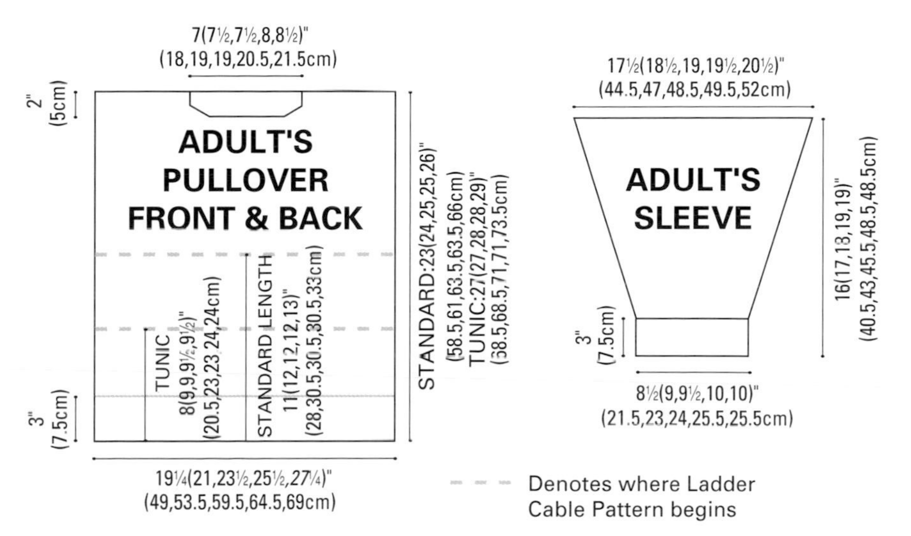

FINISHING

Sew shoulder seams.

With small circular needle, p.u. 76 (78, 80, 82, 84) <74 (76, 78, 80)> sts evenly around neckline.

Work in garter ridge as done on bottom of pullover.

B.o. loosely.

Mark underarm points 8½ (9, 9¾, 9½, 10)" (21.5, 23, 25, 24, 25.5 cm) <6½ (7, 7½, 8)" (16.5, 18, 19, 20.5 cm)> down on front and back from shoulder.

Sew sleeve bet points.

Sew underarm and side seams, leaving a slit at the bottom of the rib, if desired.

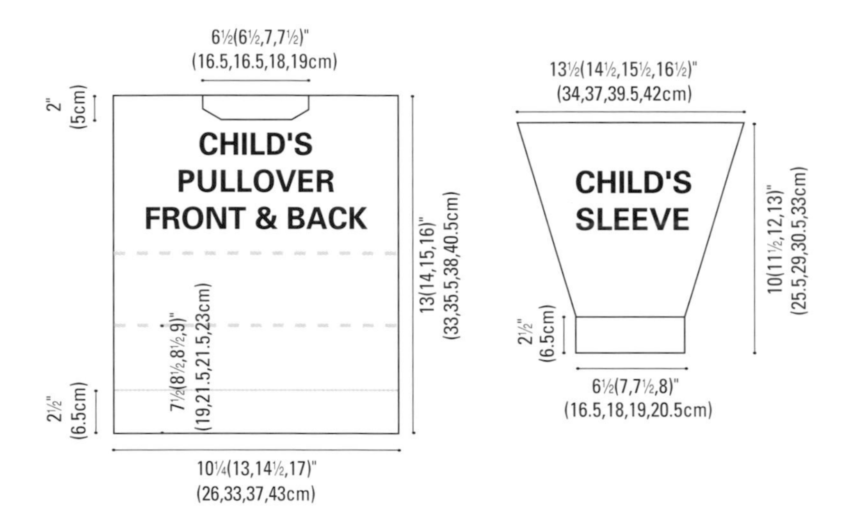

KEY

| = Knit on RS, purl on WS

— = Purl on RS, knit on WS

= PFC: Sl 2 sts to cn and hold in front, p1, k2 from cn

= PBC: Sl 1 st to cn and hold in back, k2, p1 from cn

= FC: Sl 2 sts to cn and hold in front, k2, k2 from cn

■ **Cabled Ladder Pattern** (over multiple of 18 sts)

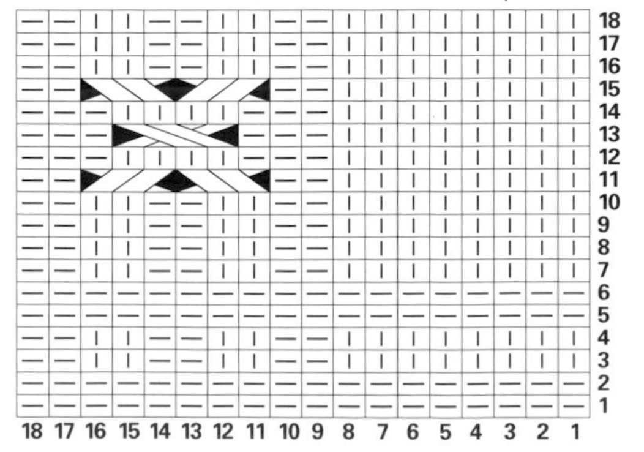

■ **Garter Ridge for Ribbing**

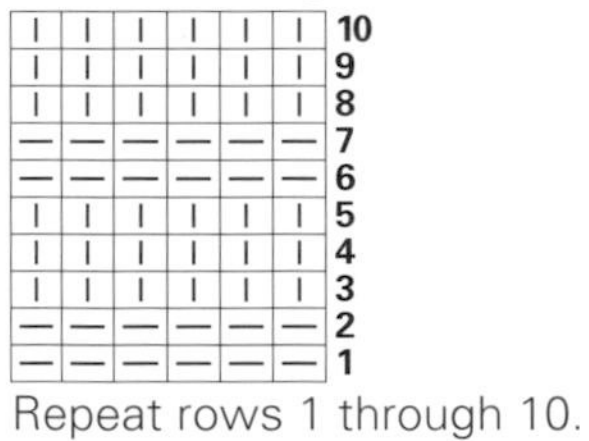

Repeat rows 1 through 10.

■ **Garter Ridge for Side and Sleeve Seams**

					Row
—	—	—	—	—	4
—	—	—	—	—	3
|	|	|	|	|	2
|	|	|	|	|	1
—	—	—	—	—	4
—	—	—	—	—	3
|	|	|	|	|	2
|	|	|	|	|	1

Repeat rows 1 through 4, ending pattern with row 2.

Modern Family

design: **Linda Pratt**
knitting rating: **Intermediate**
photography: **Philip Newton**

As seen in this family portrait of sweaters, reverse stockinette stitch makes a beautiful base for relief cable stitches. An easy, chunky horseshoe cable is divided by an uncommon twist stitch that makes high-relief columns of stitchery. In addition to the pullover sized for the entire family, this design also features an adult's cardigan version.

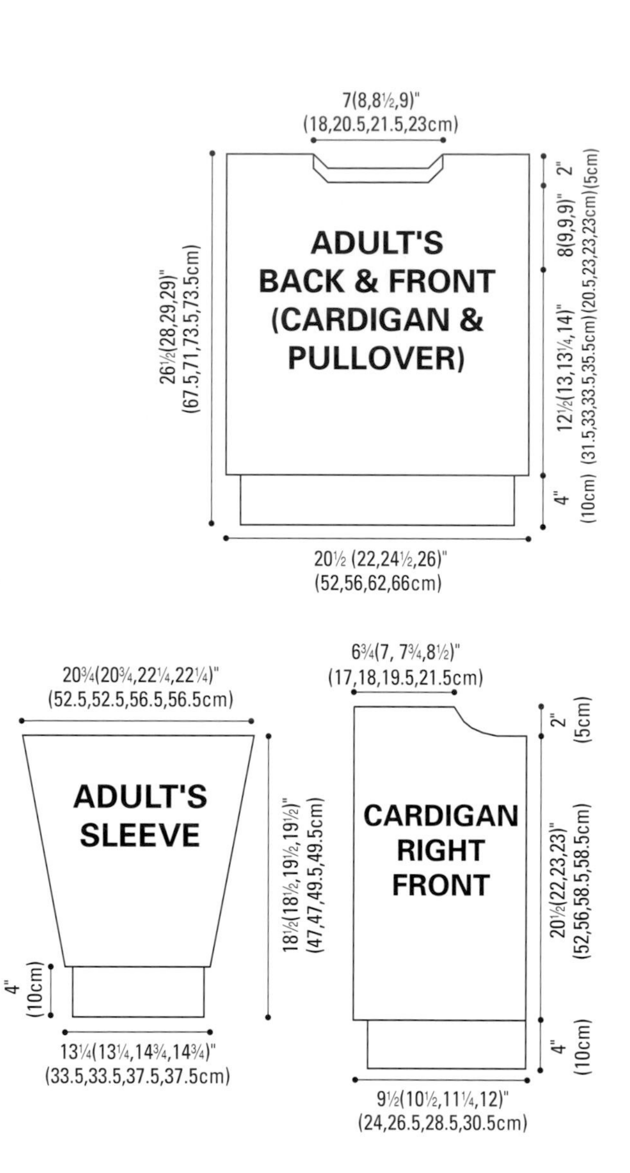

SIZES

ADULT: Small (Medium, Large, Extra Large)

CHILD: <2 (4, 6, 8)>

Finished measurements: 40 (44, 48, 52)" (101.5, 112, 122, 132 cm) <24 (26, 28½, 30½)" (61, 66, 72.5, 77.5 cm)>

NOTE: *Cardigan is sized for adults only.*

MATERIALS

PULLOVER: Montera (50% llama, 50% wool; 100 g = 127 yds/116 m): 10 (10, 11, 12) <3 (3, 4, 4) hanks

Equivalent yarn: 1200 (1270, 1400, 1525) yds (1097, 1161, 1280, 1394 m) <350 (381, 460, 508) yds (320, 348, 421, 465 m)> of bulky wool

CARDIGAN: La Gran (74% mohair, 13% wool, 13% nylon; 1½ oz = 90 yds/82 m): 12 (13, 14, 15) balls

Equivalent yarn: 1080 (1170, 1260, 1350) yds (988, 1070, 1152, 1234 m) of bulky mohair

Knitting needles: sizes 7 and 10 U.S. (4.5 and 6 mm), 16" (40.5 cm) circular needle in size 7 U.S. (4.5 mm), cable needle (cn)

Stitch holders

Five ¾" (2 cm) buttons for cardigan

GAUGE

St st on larger needles: 15 sts and 20 rows = 4" (10 cm)

Wishbone cable = 3¾" (9.5 cm)

Twist 5 = ¾" (2 cm)

Take time to save time—check your gauge.

PATTERN STITCHES

■ **3 x 2 Rib** (over multiple of 5 sts plus 2)

Row 1 (RS): P2, *k3, p2; rep from *.

Row 2: K2, *p3, k2; rep from *.

■ **Reverse Stockinette Stitch** (RSS)

Row 1 (RS): P all sts.

Row 2: K all sts.

■ **Twist 5** (over 5 sts)

Row 1 (RS): K the 5th st from behind the first 4; then k4 and drop all 5 sts off needle.

Row 2: P5.

■ **Wishbone Cable** (over 16 sts)

Rows 1, 3, 7, 9, 11 (RS): K16.

Row 2 and all WS rows: P16.

Row 5: Sl 4 sts to cn and hold in back, k4 , k4 from cn, sl 4 sts to cn and hold in front, k4, k4 from cn.

BACK

With smaller needles, c.o. 82 (87, 92, 97) <42 (46, 52, 52)> sts.

Work in 3 x 2 rib for 4" (10 cm) <2" (5 cm)> and inc 10 (13, 14, 17) <10 (10, 8, 12)> sts evenly across last WSR to give 92 (100, 106, 114) <52 (56, 60, 64)> sts.

Change to larger needles and est patt as follows: Work 3 (4, 4, 5) <6 (7, 8, 10)> sts in RSS, *twist 5, work 3 (4, 5, 6) <7 (8, 9, 9)> sts in RSS, work wishbone cable over 16 sts, work 3 (4, 5, 6) <7 (8, 9, 9)> sts in RSS*; rep bet *s 2 <0> more times, end with twist 5, work 3 (4, 4, 5) <6 (7, 8, 10)> sts in RSS.

ADULT: Work as est in patt until piece meas 16½ (17, 18, 18)" (42, 43, 45.5, 45.5 cm) and pm at each edge to mark for armhole.

When piece meas 25½ (27, 28, 28)" (64.5, 68.5, 71, 71 cm), shape back neck: Work across 30 (32, 34, 37) sts, slip center 32 (36, 38, 38) sts to holder, join another ball of yarn, and work across rem 30 (32, 34, 37) sts.

Working each side sep, b.o. 1 st at neck edge every other row twice to give 28 (30, 32, 35) sts.

B.o. rem sts.

CHILD: Work as est in patt until piece meas <14 (14½, 16, 16½)" (35.5, 37, 40.5, 42 cm)> and b.o. all sts.

PULLOVER FRONT

ADULT: Work as for back.

When piece meas 24½ (26, 27, 27)" (62, 66, 68.5, 68.5 cm), shape neck: Work across 30 (32, 34, 37) sts, sl center 32 (36, 38, 38) sts to holder, join another ball of yarn, and work across rem 30 (32, 34, 37) sts.

Working each side sep, b.o. 1 st at neck edge every other row twice to give 28 (30, 32, 35) sts at each shoulder.

Work even until piece meas the same length as back; then b.o. all sts.

CHILD: Work as for back until piece meas <12½ (13, 14½, 15)" (31.5, 33, 37, 38 cm)>.

To shape neck, work <13 (14, 15, 17)> sts, sl center <26 (28, 30, 30)> sts to holder, join another ball of yarn, and work rem <13 (14, 15, 17)> sts.

Working each side sep, b.o. 1 st at neck edge every other row one time to give <12 (13, 14, 16)> sts at shoulder.

When piece meas same as back to shoulder, b.o. all sts.

CARDIGAN LEFT FRONT

With smaller needles, c.o. 42 (42, 47, 47) sts and work 3 x 2 rib for 4" (10 cm), inc 2 (4, 3, 5) sts across last WSR of rib to give 44 (46, 50, 52) sts.

Change to larger needles and est patt as follows: Work 4 (5, 6, 7) sts in RSS, twist 5, work 5 (5, 6, 6) sts in RSS, work wishbone cable over 16 sts, work 5 (5, 6, 6) sts in RSS, twist 5, and work 4 (5, 6, 7) sts in RSS.

Work as est in patt until piece meas 16½ (17, 18, 18)" (42, 43, 45.5, 45.5 cm); then pm at edge to mark for armhole.

Cont as est until piece meas 24½ (26, 27, 27)" (62, 66, 68.5, 68.5 cm) and shape neck: B.o. every other row at neck edge 6 sts once, 2 sts 5 (5, 6, 5) times, then 1 st 0 (0, 0, 1) time to give 28 (30, 32, 35) sts.

B.o. rem sts.

CARDIGAN RIGHT FRONT

Work as for left front, reversing neck shaping.

SLEEVES

With smaller needles, c.o. 42 (42, 47, 47) <27 (32, 37, 37)> sts.

Work in 3 x 2 rib for 4" (10 cm) <2" (5 cm)> and inc 12 (12, 13, 13) <3 (2, 1, 1)> sts across last WSR to give 54 (54, 60, 60) <30 (34, 38, 38)> sts.

Change to larger needles.

ADULT: Est pattern as follows: Work 6 (6, 9, 9) sts in RSS, twist 5, work 8 sts in RSS, work wishbone cable over 16 sts, work 8 sts in RSS, twist 5, work 6 (6, 9, 9) sts in RSS.

Cont in est patt, and at the same time, inc 1 st each edge in RSS every 4th row 10 times, then every 7th row 4 times to give 82 (82, 88, 88) sts.

When sleeve meas 18½ (18½, 19½, 19½)" (47, 47, 49.5, 49.5 cm), b.o. all sts.

CHILD: Work entire sleeve in RSS and inc 1 st each edge every 4th row <5 (5, 5, 7)> times to give <40 (44, 48, 52)> sts.

Work until piece meas 8 (8½, 8¾, 9)" (20.5, 21.5, 22, 23 cm) and b.o. all sts.

PULLOVER FINISHING

Sew shoulder seams.

With circular needle, p.u. 75 (80, 80, 85) <60 (65, 70, 70)> sts evenly around neck, including the sts from holders at front and back.

Work 3 x 2 rib for 2" (5 cm) <1½" (4 cm)> and b.o. all sts loosely.

Sew in sleeves.

Sew underarm and side seams.

CARDIGAN FINISHING

Sew shoulder seams.

Sew in sleeves.

Sew side and underarm seams.

LEFT BAND: P.u. 94 (98, 102, 102) sts evenly along front edge.

Work in 1 x 1 rib for 1" (2.5 cm) and b.o. all sts loosely.

RIGHT BAND: Work as for left band, placing 5 buttonholes (by yo, k2tog) in 3rd row, spacing them evenly and taking into account that you will be placing a buttonhole in the neck band at top.

NECK BAND: With smaller needles, p.u. 80 (80, 82, 84) sts.

Work 1 x 1 rib for 1" (2.5 cm), placing buttonhole in neck band.

B.o. all sts.

Sew on buttons.

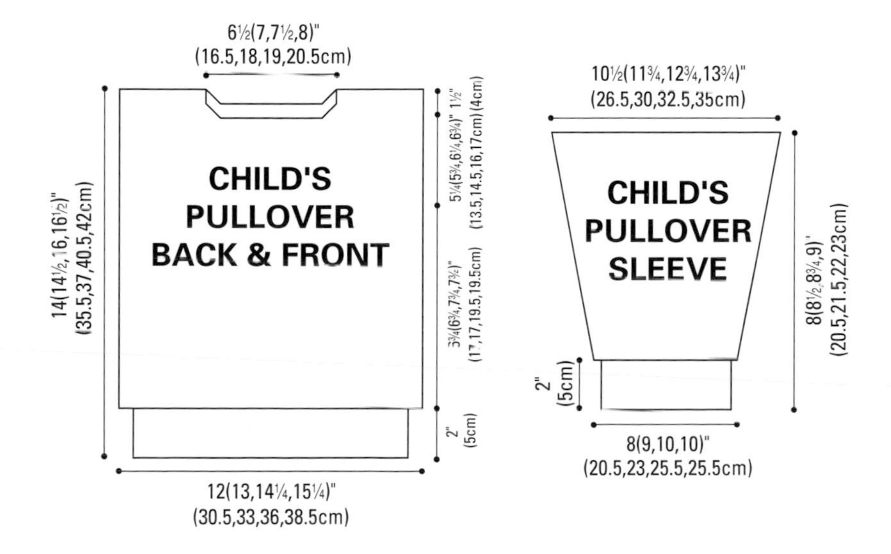

2

Soft Mohair

Mohair is a fabulous fiber for handknitting. It works up quickly on large needles and is available in a vast selection of colors. The richness of its colors results from the fact that mohair responds to commercial dyes like no other fiber. This fiber also reflects the light, giving a luminescent quality to the knitted fabric. Even simple stockinette stitch looks elegant in mohair, and well-chosen cables show off the texture and shine of this soft fiber. Another advantage of mohair, especially for beginners, is that it hides uneven tension and dropped stitches. The designs included in this chapter are easy and quick to execute and will become favorite items in anyone's wardrobe.

Bonnet Point Braids

design: **Cathy Payson**

knitting rating: **Intermediate**

photography: **Philip Newton**

An easy braided cable is repeated over the body of this comfortably sized pullover for women and children. The sleeves and bottom of the body are edged in a two-by-two rib, and the neckline is worked on circular needles in the same cable as in the body of the sweater. Although this design can be easily completed by intermediate knitters, the total effect is of technical prowess.

SIZES

ADULT: Small (Medium, Large, Extra Large)

CHILD: <2/4 (6/8)>

Finished measurements: 40 (45½, 50½, 56½)" (101.5, 115.5, 128.5, 143.5 cm) <25 (31¾)" (63.5, 80.5 cm)>

MATERIALS

La Gran (74% mohair, 13% wool, 13% nylon; 1½ oz = approx. 90 yds/82 m): 13 (14, 15, 16) <9 (10)> balls

Equivalent yarn: 1170 (1260, 1350, 1440) yds (1070, 1152, 1234, 1317 m) <810 (900) yds (741, 823 m)> of bulky mohair

Knitting needles: sizes 9 and 10 U.S. (5.5 and 6 mm), 16" (40.5 cm) circular needles in sizes 9 and 10 U.S. (5.5 and 6 mm), cable needle (cn)

GAUGE

Plaited cable patt on larger needles: 19 sts and 22 rows = 4" (10 cm)

Take time to save time—check your gauge.

PATTERN STITCHES

■ **2 x 2 Rib** (over multiple of 4 sts plus 2)

Row 1 (RS): *K2, p2*; rep bet *s, end k2.

Row 2: Work sts as they appear.

■ **Plaited Cable** (over multiple of 12 sts plus 3)

Rows 1 and 5 (RS): *P3, k9*; rep bet *s, end p3.

Row 2 and all WSR: *K3, p9*; rep bet *s, end k3.

Row 3: *P3, sl next 3 sts to cn, hold in front, k3, k3 from cn, k3*; rep bet *s, end p3.

Row 7: *P3, k3, sl next 3 sts to cn, hold in back, k3, k3 from cn*; rep bet *s, end p3.

■ **1 x 1 Rib**

Row 1 (RS): K1, p1 across row.

Row 2: Work sts as they appear.

BACK

With smaller needles, c.o. 68 (74, 82, 90) <34 (46)> sts.

Work in 2 x 2 rib for 3" (7.5 cm) <2" (5 cm)>, inc 31 (37, 41, 45) <29 (29)> sts in last row to give 99 (111, 123, 135) <63 (75)> sts.

Change to larger needles and work in plaited cable patt until piece meas 26 (27, 28, 29)" (66, 68.5, 71, 73.5 cm) <16 (18)" (40.5, 45.5 cm)> from beg.

B.o. all sts.

FRONT

Work as for back.

When piece meas 24 (25, 26, 27)" (61, 63.5, 66, 68.5 cm) <14 (16)" (35.5, 40.5 cm)>, shape neck: Work 35 (41, 47, 53) <18 (24)> sts, join a 2nd ball of yarn and b.o. center 29 <27> sts, work to end.

Working each side sep, b.o. 1 <1> st at neck edge every other row 5 times to give 30 (36, 42, 48) <13 (19)> sts at shoulder.

When piece meas same as back at shoulders, b.o. all sts.

SLEEVES

With smaller needles c.o. 30 (30, 46, 46) <26> sts.

Work 2 x 2 rib for 2" (5 cm), inc 13 (13, 5, 5) <1> sts in last row to give 43 (43, 51, 51) <27> sts.

Change to larger needles and set up patt as follows: k2 (2, 0, 0) sts, work plaited cable patt over 39 (39, 51, 51) <27> sts, end k2 (2, 0, 0) <0> sts.

Inc 1 st each end in plaited cable patt every 2nd row <5 (10)> times, every 4th row 19 (20, 16, 19) <10> times, and every 6th row 0 (0, 4, 3) times to give 81 (83, 91, 95) <57 (67)> sts.

When piece meas 16 (17¼, 18, 19)" (40.5, 43, 45.5, 48.5 cm) <12 (14)" (30.5, 35.5 cm)>, b.o. all sts.

FINISHING

Sew shoulder seams.

With larger circular needle and RS facing, p.u. 14 <10> sts from left neck edge, 29 <27> sts from center front, 14 <10> sts from right neck edge and 39 <37> sts from center back to give 96 <84> sts.

Turn sweater inside out and work RS of the neck with the WS of the body facing you.

Est row 1 of plaited cable patt in the round as follows: Pm, *p3, k9*; repeat bet *s, ending at the marker.

Work plaited cable patt in the round for 9" (23 cm).

Change to smaller circular needle and work in 1 x 1 rib for 1" (2.5 cm).

B.o. all sts loosely.

Set in sleeves.

Sew underarm and side seams.

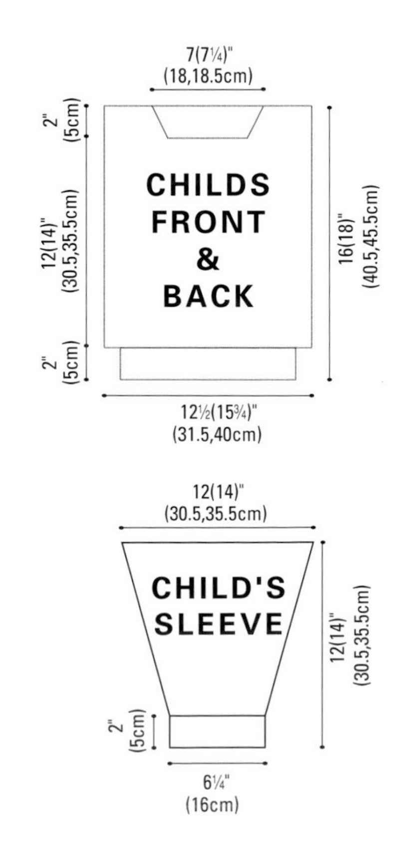

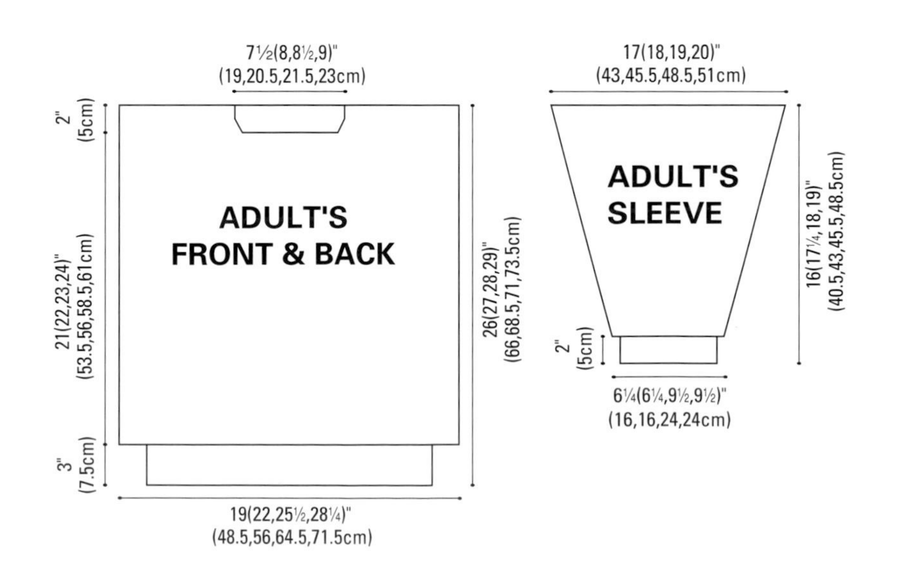

Maggie Rennard Jacket

design: **Deborah Newton**
knitting rating: **Intermediate**
photography: **Peter Ogilvie**

Given that mohair is the most classic of fibers for handknitting, what could be more useful than a cabled mohair cardigan with jacket detailing? Elegantly shaped with set-in sleeves and a shawl collar, this jacket has pockets at the side seams. The sleeves are set into the jacket with enough ease at the shoulders to fit comfortably over a loose blouse or turtleneck.

SIZES

Small (Medium, Large, Extra Large)

Finished measurements: 38 (40, 44, 48)" (96.5, 101.5, 112, 122 cm)

MATERIALS

La Gran (74% mohair, 13% wool, 13% nylon; 1½ oz = approx. 90 yds/82 m): 12 (13, 13, 14) balls

Equivalent yarn: 1080 (1120, 1170, 1260) yds (988, 1024, 1070, 1152 m) of bulky mohair

Knitting needles: sizes 5 and 7 U.S. (3.75 and 4.5 mm), cable needle (cn)

Four ¾" (2 cm) buttons

GAUGE

St st on larger needles: 17 sts and 23 rows = 4" (10 cm)

Double cable = 2½" (6.5 cm)

Take time to save time—check your gauge.

PATTERN STITCHES

■ 1 x 1 Rib

All rows: K1, p1.

■ Stockinette Stitch

Row 1 (RS): K all sts.

Row 2: P all sts.

■ Double Cable (over 16 sts)

Row 1 (RS): P2, k12, p2.

Row 2 and all other WSR: K2, p12, k2.

Row 3: P2, sl next 3 sts to cn and hold in back, k3, k3 from cn, sl next 3 sts to cn and hold in front, k3, k3 from cn, end p2.

Rows 5 and 7: P2, k12, p2.

Rep rows 1 through 8.

BACK

With smaller needles, c.o. 83 (87, 95, 103) sts.

Work in 1 x 1 rib for 3" (7.5 cm), end with a RSR.

Purl across next row, inc 9 sts evenly spaced to give 92 (96, 104, 112) sts.

Change to larger needles.

Next row (RS): K12 (13, 17, 20), work row 1 of cable over next 16 sts, k36 (38, 38, 40) sts, work row 1 of cable over next 16 sts, end k12 (13, 17, 20).

Next row: P12 (13, 17, 20), work row 2 of cable over next 16 sts, p36 (38, 38, 40) sts, work row 2 of cable over next 16 sts, end p12 (13, 17, 20).

Work even as est until piece meas 1" (2.5 cm) above rib, end with a WSR.

FORM POCKET EXTENSIONS: On next row (RS), c.o. 15 sts and k them, pm, slip 1 p-wise, work as est to end.

Next row (WS): C.o. 15 sts and p them, pm, work as est to next marker, end p15.

Next row (RS): K15, sl marker, sl 1, work as est to 1 st before next marker, sl 1, sl marker, end k15.

Work even as est until pocket extensions measure 6" (15 cm), end with a WSR.

B.o. 15 sts at beginning of next 2 rows.

Work even until piece meas 10" (25.5 cm) above rib (13"/33 cm total).

ARMHOLE SHAPING: B.o. 2 sts at beginning of next 6 (6, 8, 8) rows; then dec 1 st at each edge 3 (3, 3, 5) times to give 74 (78, 82, 88) sts.

Work even as est until armhole depth measures 8 (9, 9½,10)" (20.5, 23, 24, 25.5 cm), end with a WSR.

SHOULDER AND BACK NECK SHAPING: Mark center 12 (14, 14, 16) sts.

Work to center sts, join a 2nd ball of yarn, b.o. center 12 (14, 14, 16) sts, and work to end.

Working both sides at the same time with separate balls of yarn, b.o. from each neck edge 4 sts twice, and at the same time, b.o. 8 (8, 9, 9) sts from each shoulder edge twice, then 7 (8, 8, 9) sts once.

LEFT FRONT

With smaller needles, c.o. 41 (43, 47, 51) sts.

Work in 1 x 1 rib for 3" (7.5 cm), end with a WSR.

P across next row, inc 4 sts evenly spaced to give 45 (47, 51, 55) sts.

Change to larger needles.

Next row (RS): K12 (13, 17, 20), work row 1 of cable over 16 sts, k17 (18, 18, 19).

Next row: P17 (18, 18, 19) sts, work row 2 of cable over 16 sts, p12 (13, 17, 20).

Work even as est until piece meas 1" (2.5 cm) above rib, end with a WSR.

To form a pocket extension as for back, c.o. 15 sts at beg of next row.

Work as est until pocket extension meas same as for back, end with a WSR.

B.o. 15 sts at beg of next row.

Work even until piece meas 8" (20.5 cm) above rib (11"/28 cm total), end with a WSR.

NECKLINE SHAPING: Next row, dec row (RS): work to last 3 sts, k2tog, end k1.

Rep dec row after 3 more rows, then alternately every 6th and 4th row thereafter for a total of 13 (14, 14, 15) decs at this edge; at the same time, work even until front meas same as back to armhole, end with a WSR.

ARMHOLE SHAPING: B.o. 2 sts at beg of next 3 (3, 4, 4) RSR; then dec 1 st at armhole edge 3 (3, 3, 5) times.

Work even until front meas same as back to shoulder, end with a WSR to give 23 (24, 26, 27) sts.

SHOULDER SHAPING: B.o. 8 (8, 9, 9) sts at beg of next 2 RSR, then 7 (8, 8, 9) sts at beg of last RSR.

RIGHT FRONT

Work same as for left front, reversing all pattern placement and shaping.

SLEEVES

With smaller needles, c.o. 39 (41, 41, 43) sts.

Work in 1 x 1 rib for 3" (7.5 cm), end with a RSR.

Purl across next row, inc 9 (11, 11, 11) sts evenly spaced to give 48 (52, 52, 54) sts.

Change to larger needles.

Next row (RS): K16 (18, 18, 19), work row 1 of cable, k16 (18, 18, 19).

Next row: P16 (18, 18, 19), work row 2 of cable, p16 (18, 18, 19).

Work even as est for 3 (7, 1, 3) more rows to end with a WSR.

Keeping in patt as est, inc 1 st each end of next row; then for size small, inc 1 st each end alternately every 4th and 6th row thereafter; for all other sizes, incr 1 st each end every 4th row thereafter, making a total of 14 (16, 18, 19) inc sts each end to give 76 (84, 88, 92) total sts.

NOTE: *Work incs as follows: k2, make 1, work to last 2 sts, make 1, end k2.*

Cont until sleeve meas 16 (16½,16½,17)" (40.5, 42, 42, 43 cm) or to desired length, end with WSR.

CAP SHAPING: B.o. 2 sts at the beg of next 8 (12, 14, 16) rows, 3 sts at beg of next 8 rows, then rem 36 sts on the next row.

FINISHING

Sew front to back at shoulders.

NOTE: Left front button band, collar, and buttonhole band are worked in one continuous piece, then sewn onto sweater. Begin with left front button band.

SHAWL COLLAR: With smaller needles, c.o. 7 sts.

Work in 1 x 1 rib until piece, when slightly stretched, meas 11" (28 cm), end with a WSR.

Tie first marker at end of this row.

Change to larger needles.

Work 2 rows in rib.

Inc 1 st at beg of next row, then every other row 30 more times to give 38 sts.

Tie end-of-increases marker on shaped edge.

Work even until shaped edge meas 12½" (31.5 cm) above first marker.

Tie shoulder marker #1 on shaped edge.

Work even for 8½ (9, 9, 9½)" (21.5, 23, 23, 24 cm) more; then tie shoulder marker #2 along shaped edge.

At this point, check the fit by aligning shaped edge of collar with garment and matching markers to shoulder seams.

Work same as for collar between end-of-increases marker and shoulder marker #1; then tie beg-of-decreases marker on shaped edge.

Dec 1 st at neck edge every other row until 7 sts rem; then work 2 rows even.

Sl these sts to holder.

Tie last marker.

Pin collar around jacket, aligning first marker with beg of neck shaping on left front and matching shoulder markers #1 and #2 to shoulder seams.

Match last marker to beg of neck shaping on right front.

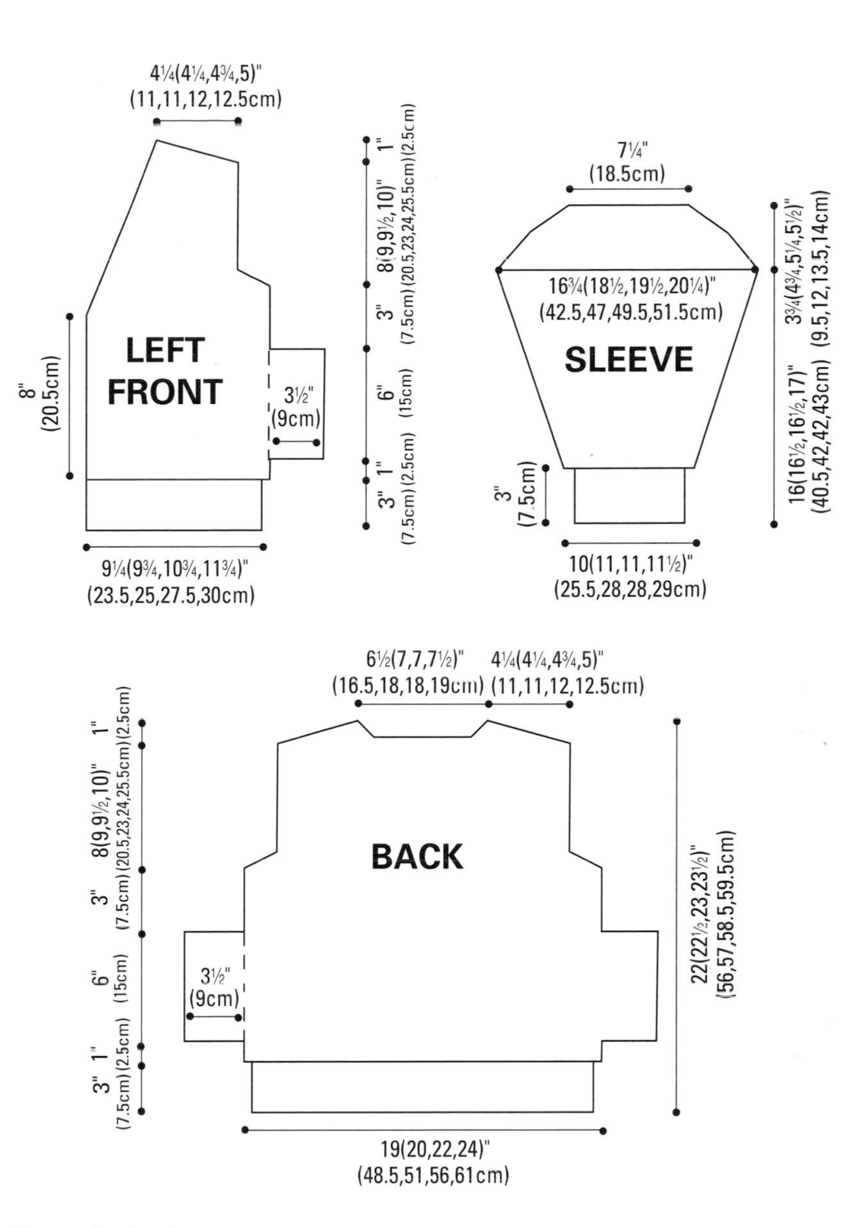

Sew collar in place.

Sew 4 buttons evenly spaced on button band at left front.

Change to smaller needles.

Sl 7 sts from holder and work in rib until piece meas same as for left button band, working a buttonhole opposite each button on left front.

Sew remaining band to right front.

Sew sleeve seams.

Sew sleeve cap in armhole, centering at shoulder seam.

Sew side seams and around pocket extensions, leaving an opening at side.

Trout Fry

designs: **Kristin Nicholas**
knitting ratings: **Experienced** (traveling cable pullover), Beginner (lattice cable pullover), **Beginner** (child's multicolored cardigan)
photography: **Philip Newton**

Soft, warm mohair is a fabulous fiber for adults and children alike. Sized for women and children, the lattice cable pullover will be an interesting challenge for beginning knitters who are just learning cable stitchery. The easy color-block cardigan for children, worked entirely in stockinette stitch, is a great project for using odd skeins of different shades of yarn. Choose fun, brightly colored buttons for closures. The all-over (traveling) cable pattern of the woman's blue pullover grows out of the cables at the ribs.

Traveling Cable Pullover

SIZES

Small (Medium, Large)

Finished measurements: 39 (47, 55)" (99, 119.5, 139.5 cm)

MATERIALS

Montera (50% llama, 50% wool; 100 g = approx. 127 yds/116 m): 10 (11, 12) hanks

Equivalent yarn: 1270 (1397, 1524) yds (1161, 1277, 1394 m) of bulky wool

Knitting needles: sizes 5 and 8 U.S. (3.75 and 5 mm), 16" (40.5 cm) circular needle in size 7 U.S. (4.5 mm), cable needle (cn)

GAUGE

Traveling cable pattern with larger needles: 24 sts and 24 rows = 4" (10 cm)

Rev St st: 16 sts and 24 rows = 4" (10 cm)

PATTERN STITCHES

■ **Reverse Stockinette Stitch** (RSS)

Row 1 (WS): K all sts.

Row 2: P all sts.

■ **Cabled Rib**

See chart on page 38.

■ **Traveling Cable Pattern**

See chart on page 38.

BACK

With smaller needles, c.o. 91 (109, 127) sts.

Work in cabled rib, beginning on WSR at left of chart and noting pattern rep is 18 sts.

Work rows 1 through 4 for 3½" (9 cm), ending with row 2 of cabled rib.

Change to larger needles and work inc row as shown on chart.

Work patt until piece meas 25 (26, 27)" (63.5, 66, 68.5 cm); then b.o. all sts.

FRONT

Work as for back; when piece meas 22 (23, 24)" (56, 58.5, 61 cm), shape neck.

Work 42 (51, 61) sts, join a 2nd ball of yarn and b.o. center 34 (40, 44) sts, work to end.

Working each side sep, b.o. 1 st at neck edge every other row 6 times to give 36 (45, 55) sts at shoulder.

When piece meas same as back at shoulders, b.o. all sts.

SLEEVES

With smaller needles, c.o. 37 sts.

Work in cabled rib exactly as shown on chart for 3" (7.5 cm), ending with row 2 of chart.

Change to larger needles and inc exactly as shown on chart to give 46 sts.

Work in traveling cable patt up center of sleeve, working inc as follows in RSS: Inc 1 st each end every 2nd row 2 (3, 5) times, then every 4th row 18 (19, 20) times to give 86 (90, 96) sts.

When piece meas 16 (17, 18)" (40.5, 43, 45.5 cm), b.o. all sts.

FINISHING

Sew shoulder seams.

With small circular needles, p.u. 108 sts evenly around neckline.

Work in cabled rib for 8 rounds, working sts bet *s for patt in rnd.

In next rnd, work dec rnd as follows: P2tog, p1 p2tog, k4 (or cross cable if on cable rnd).

Work in est patt until neckline meas 3½" (9 cm).

B.o. loosely.

Mark underarm points 9 (9½, 10)" (23, 24, 25.5 cm) down in front and back from shoulder.

Sew sleeve bet points.

Sew underarm and side seams.

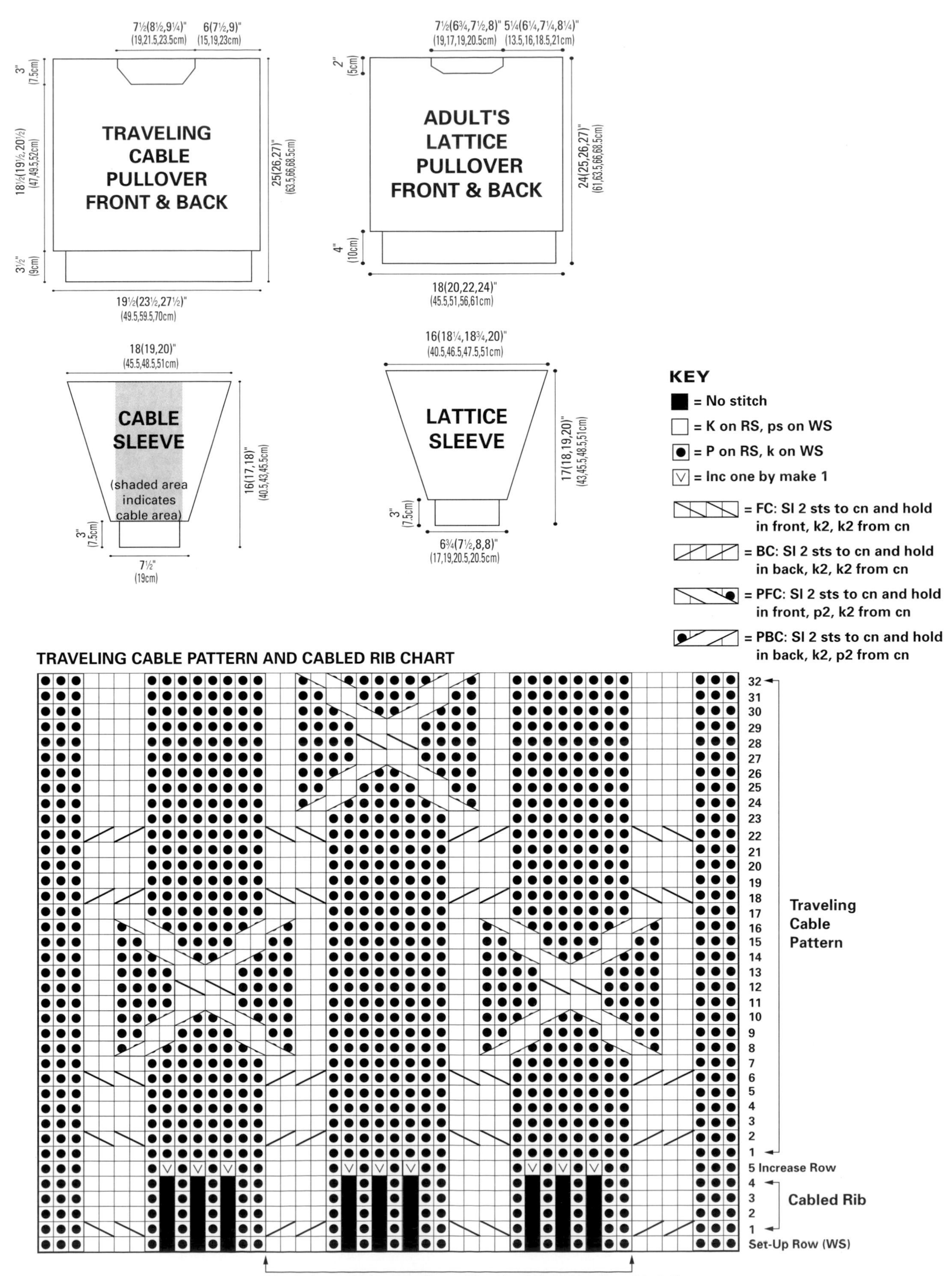

TRAVELING CABLE PULLOVER FRONT & BACK
7½(8½,9¼)" (19,21.5,23.5cm)
6(7½,9)" (15,19,23cm)
3" (7.5cm)
18½(19½,20½)" (47,49.5,52cm)
25(26,27)" (63.5,66,68.5cm)
3½" (9cm)
19½(23½,27½)" (49.5,59.5,70cm)
ADULT'S LATTICE PULLOVER FRONT & BACK
7½(6¾,7½,8)" (19,17,19,20.5cm)
5¼(6¼,7¼,8¼)" (13.5,16,18.5,21cm)
2" (5cm)
24(25,26,27)" (61,63.5,66,68.5cm)
4" (10cm)
18(20,22,24)" (45.5,51,56,61cm)
CABLE SLEEVE
(shaded area indicates cable area)
18(19,20)" (45.5,48.5,51cm)
16(17,18)" (40.5,43,45.5cm)
3" (7.5cm)
7½" (19cm)
LATTICE SLEEVE
16(18¼,18¾,20)" (40.5,46.5,47.5,51cm)
17(18,19,20)" (43,45.5,48.5,51cm)
3" (7.5cm)
6¾(7½,8,8)" (17,19,20.5,20.5cm)
KEY
= No stitch
= K on RS, ps on WS
= P on RS, k on WS
= Inc one by make 1
= FC: Sl 2 sts to cn and hold in front, k2, k2 from cn
= BC: Sl 2 sts to cn and hold in back, k2, k2 from cn
= PFC: Sl 2 sts to cn and hold in front, p2, k2 from cn
= PBC: Sl 2 sts to cn and hold in back, k2, p2 from cn
TRAVELING CABLE PATTERN AND CABLED RIB CHART
32 31 30 29 28 27 26 25 24 23 22 21 20 19 18 17 16 15 14 13 12 11 10 9 8 7 6 5 4 3 2 1
Traveling Cable Pattern
5 Increase Row
4 3 2 1
Cabled Rib
Set-Up Row (WS)
24-stitch repeat for traveling cable, 18-stitch repeat for cabled rib

Lattice Cable Pullover

SIZES

ADULT: Extra Small (Small, Medium, Large)

CHILD: <Small (Medium, Large)>

Finished measurements: 36 (40, 44, 48)" (91.5, 101.5, 112, 122 cm) <25½ (30, 34)" (64.5, 76, 86.5 cm)>

MATERIALS

LaGran (74% mohair, 13% wool, 13% nylon; 1½ oz = approx. 90 yds/82 m): 10 (11, 11, 12) <6 (7, 8)> balls

Equivalent yarn: 900 (990, 990, 1080) yds (823, 905, 905, 988 m) <540 (630, 720) yds (494, 576, 658 m) of bulky mohair

Knitting needles: sizes 8 and 10 U.S. (5 and 6 mm), 16" (40.5 cm) circular needle in size 8 U.S. (5 mm), cable needle (cn)

GAUGE

St st with larger needles: 14 sts and 18 rows = 4" (10 cm)

Adult's cable (32 sts) = 6½" (16.5 cm)

Child's cable (26 sts) = 5¼" (13.5 cm)

Take time to save time—check your gauge.

PATTERN STITCHES

Same as traveling cable pullover except for:

PBC: Sl 1 st to cn and hold in back of work, k2, p1 from cn.

PFC: Sl 2 sts to cn and hold in front of work, p1, k2 from cn.

■ **2 x 3 Rib** (multiple of 5 sts plus 3)

Row 1 (WS): *K3, p2*; rep bet *s, end k3.

Row 2 (RS): *P3, k2*; rep bet *s, end p3.

■ **Stockinette Stitch**

Row 1 (WS): P all sts.

Row 2: K all sts.

■ **Lattice Stitch** (multiple of 6 sts plus 2)

Row 1 (WS): K2, *p4, k2; rep from *.

Row 2: P2, *BC, p2; rep from *.

Row 3 and all WSR: K the k sts and p the p sts.

Row 4: P1, *PBC, PFC; rep from *, end p1.

Row 6: P1, k2, p2, *FC; p2; rep from *, end k2, p1.

Row 8: P1, *PFC, PBC; rep from *, end p1.

Rep rows 1 through 8.

BACK

With smaller needles, c.o. 53 (58, 63, 68) <38 (43, 48)> sts.

Work in 2 x 3 rib for 4" (10 cm) <2" (5 cm)>.

In last RS rows of rib, inc 10 (12, 14, 16) <7 (10, 12)> sts evenly across to give 63 (70, 77, 84) <45 (53, 60)> sts.

Change to larger needles and work in St st until piece meas 24 (25, 26, 27)" (61, 63.5, 66, 68.5 cm) <16 (18, 20)" (40.5, 45.5, 51 cm)>.

B.o. all sts.

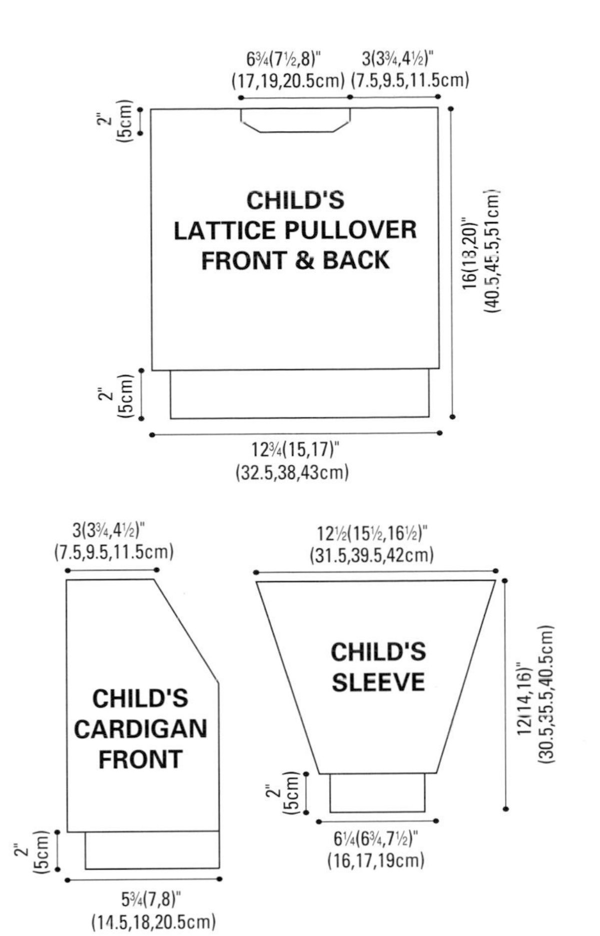

FRONT

With smaller needles, c.o. 53 (58, 63, 68) <38 (43, 48)> sts.

Work in 2 x 3 rib for 4" (10 cm) <2" (5 cm)>.

In last RS rows of rib, inc 19 (20, 23, 24) <16 (17, 18)> sts evenly across to give 72 (78, 86, 92) <54 (60, 66)> sts.

Change to larger needles and est cable as follows: Work 20 (23, 27, 30) <14 (17, 20)> sts in St st, work lattice cable over 32 <26> sts, work to end.

Work cable up center as est until piece meas 22 (23, 24, 25)" (56, 58.5, 61, 63.5 cm) <14 (16, 18)" (35.5, 40.5, 45.5 cm)>.

SHAPE NECK: Work 22 (25, 29, 32) <15 (17, 20)> sts, join a 2nd ball of yarn and b.o. center 28 <24 (26, 26)> sts, work to end.

Working each side sep, b.o. 1 st at neck edge every other row 4 <4> times to give 18 (21, 25, 28) <11 (13, 16)> sts at shoulder.

When piece meas same as back at shoulders, b.o. all sts.

SLEEVES

With smaller needles, c.o. 23 (23, 28, 28) <18 (23, 23)> sts.

Work in 2 x 3 rib for 3" (7.5 cm) <2" (5 cm)>.

In last RS rows of rib, inc 1 (3, 0, 0) <4 (1, 3)> sts evenly across to give 24 (26, 28, 28) <22 (24, 26)> sts.

Change to larger needles and work in St st, inc 1 st at each end every 2nd row 1 (7, 4, 5) <0 (4, 1)> times, then every 4th row 15 (12, 15, 16) <11 (11, 15)> times to give 56 (64, 66, 70) <44 (54, 58)> sts.

When piece meas 17 (18, 19, 20)" (43, 45.5, 48.5, 51 cm) <12 (14, 16)" (30.5, 35.5, 40.5 cm)> or desired length, b.o. all sts.

FINISHING

Sew shoulder seams.

With small circular needles, p.u. 90 <75 (80, 80)> sts evenly around neckline.

Work in 2 x 3 rib in round (p3, k2 all rounds) for 5" (12.5 cm) <3" (7.5 cm)> for T-neck or 2" (5 cm) <1" (2.5 cm)> for crew neck.

B.o. loosely.

Mark underarm points 8 (9, 9½, 10)" (20.5, 23, 24, 25.5 cm) <6½ (7½, 8½)" (16.5, 19, 21.5 cm)> down in front and back from shoulder.

Sew sleeve bet points.

Sew underarm and side seams.

Child's Multicolored Cardigan

SIZES

Small (Medium, Large)

Finished measurements: 25½ (30, 34)" (64.5, 76, 86.5 cm)

MATERIALS

LaGran (74% mohair, 13% wool, 13% nylon; 1½ oz = approx. 90 yds/82 m): 2 (3, 3) balls of color A; 2 balls of B; 2 balls of C;1 (2, 2) balls of D

Equivalent yarn: 180 (240, 270) yds (165, 219, 247 m) of bulky mohair in color A; 180 yds (165 m) of B; 180 yds (165 m) of C; 90 (160, 180) yds (82, 146, 165 m) of D

Knitting needles: sizes 8 and 10 U.S. (5 and 6 mm), 29" (73.5 cm) circular needle in smaller size

Three 1¼" (3 cm) buttons

GAUGE

St st with larger needles: 14 sts and 18 rows = 4" (10 cm)

PATTERN STITCHES

■ **1 x 1 Rib** (over an odd number of sts)

Row 1: *K1, p1; rep from *, end k1.

Row 2: *P1, k1; rep from *, end p1.

BACK

Using color A and smaller needles, c.o. 37 (43, 49) sts.

Work in 1 x 1 rib for 2" (5 cm).

In last RS rows of rib, inc 8 (10, 11) sts evenly across to give 45 (53, 60) sts.

Change to larger needles and work in St st until piece meas 16 (18, 20)" (40.5, 45.5, 51 cm)

B.o. all sts.

RIGHT FRONT

Using color B, c.o. 19 (21, 25) sts.

Work in 1 x 1 rib for 2" (5 cm).

In last RS rows of rib, inc 2 (4, 3) sts evenly across to give 21 (25, 28) sts.

Change to larger needles and work in St st until piece meas 6½ (8½, 10)" (16.5, 21.5, 25.5 cm).

B.o. 1 st at neck edge every other row 10 (12, 12) times to give 11 (13, 16) sts.

When piece meas 16 (18, 20)" (40.5, 45.5, 51 cm), b.o. all sts.

LEFT FRONT

Work same as right front, reversing shaping and using color C.

LEFT SLEEVE

Working in color B, follow instructions for lattice pullover sleeve, above.

RIGHT SLEEVE

Work same as left sleeve, using color D.

FINISHING

Sew shoulder seams.

Mark underarm points 6½ (7½, 8½)" (16.5, 19, 21.5 cm) down in front and back from shoulder.

Sew sleeve bet points.

Sew underarm and side seams.

Mark 3 buttonholes evenly spaced below V-neck shaping on right side for girl's cardigan or left side for boy's cardigan.

Using circular needle and color A, p.u. 139 (145, 151) sts around cardigan opening.

Work 2 rows in 1 x 1 rib.

In next row, where marked on body of cardigan, work buttonholes by yo, k2tog.

When cardigan band is complete (8 rows), b.o. all sts.

Sisters

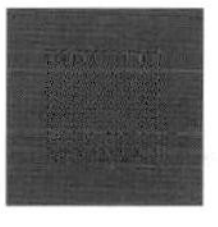

design: **Cathy Payson**
knitting rating: **Beginner**
photography: **Philip Newton**

A simple center cable adds interest to the easy-to-knit pullovers shown on the woman on the left and the child. The base fabric is worked in stockinette stitch, and the edges are done in a two-by-two rib.

The other adult's pullover is worked in a simple variation of the first design: it uses a base of double seed stitch together with the center cable. Double seed stitch makes a very stable fabric that needs no rib. Although they're not shown, children's sizes are also given for this design.

Stockinette Stitch Pullover

SIZES

ADULT: Small (Medium, Large, Extra Large)

CHILD: <2 (4, 6, 8, 10)>

Finished measurements: 40 (44, 48, 52)" (101.5, 112, 122, 132 cm) <22 (24, 26, 28, 30)" (56, 61, 66, 71, 76 cm)

MATERIALS

La Gran (74% mohair, 13% wool, 13% nylon; 1½ oz = approx. 90 yds/82 m): 12 (12, 12, 13) <5 (5, 5, 6, 6)> skeins

Equivalent yarn: 1080 (1080, 1080, 1170) yds (988, 988, 988, 1070 m) <450 (450, 450, 540, 540) yds (411, 411, 411, 494, 494 m)> of bulky mohair

Knitting needles: sizes 8 and 9 U.S. (5 and 5.5 mm), 16" (40.5 cm) circular needle in size 8 U.S. (5 mm), cable needle (cn)

GAUGE

St st on larger needles: 16 sts and 20 rows = 4" (10 cm)

Double cable on larger needles = 3½" (9 cm)

Take time to save time—check your gauge.

PATTERN STITCHES

■ 2 x 2 Ribbing

Row 1: K2, p2.

Row 2: K the k sts, p the p sts.

■ Stockinette Stitch

Row 1 (RS): K all sts.

Row 2: P all sts.

■ Double Cable (over 18 sts)

Row 1: P2, k14, p2.

Rows 2, 4, 6, and 8: K2, p14, k2.

Row 3: P2, sl next 4 sts to cn and hold in front, k3, k4 from cn, sl next 3 sts to cn and hold in back, k4, k3 from cn, p2.

Rows 5 and 7: Rep row 1.

Rep rows 1 through 8.

BACK

With smaller needles, c.o. 80 (88, 96, 104) <40 (44, 48, 52, 56)> sts.

Work in 2 x 2 rib for 2" (5 cm) <1½" (4 cm)>, inc 4 <8> sts evenly across last row to give 84 (92, 100, 108) <48 (52, 56, 60, 64)> sts.

Change to larger needles and work St st over first 33 (37, 41, 45) <15 (17, 19, 21, 23)> sts, work double cable over 18 sts, work in St st to end.

Cont until piece meas 25 (26, 27, 28)" (63.5, 66, 68.5, 71 cm) <12 (13, 14, 15, 16)" (30.5, 33, 35.5, 38, 40.5 cm)>.

B.o. all sts.

FRONT

Work as for back until piece meas 23 (24, 25, 26)" (58.5, 61, 63.5, 66 cm) <10½(11½, 12½, 13½, 14½)" (26.5, 29, 31.5, 34, 37 cm)>.

SHAPE NECK: Work across first 32 (35, 38, 41) <17 (18, 19, 20, 21)> sts, b.o. center 20 (22, 24, 26) <14 (16, 18, 20, 22)> sts, work to end.

Working each side sep, b.o. 1 st at neck edge every other row 4 <3> times to give 28 (31, 34, 37) <14 (15, 16, 17, 18)> sts.

When piece meas same as back to shoulders, b.o. all sts.

SLEEVES

With smaller needles, c.o. 30 (32, 34, 36) <28 (28, 30, 32, 32)> sts.

Work in 2 x 2 rib for 2" (5 cm) <1½" (4 cm)>.

In last row of rib, inc 6 (6, 4, 4) <0> sts evenly across to give 36 (38, 38, 40) <28 (28, 30, 32, 32)> sts.

Change to larger needles and work in St st, inc 1 st every 2nd row 9 (0, 4, 2) times, then every 4th row 13 (22, 19, 21) times to give 80 (82, 84, 86) sts <inc 1 st each end this row and every 4th row 8 (10, 11, 12, 14) times to give 44 (48, 52, 56, 60) sts>.

When piece meas 18½ (19, 19½, 20)" (47, 48.5, 49.5, 51 cm) <11½ (12, 12½, 13, 13½)" (29, 30.5, 31.5, 33, 34 cm)>, b.o. all sts.

FINISHING

Sew shoulder seams.

With small circular needles, p.u. 104 (104, 108, 108) <64 (64, 68, 68, 72)> sts evenly around neckline.

Work in 2 x 2 rib for 3" (7.5 cm) <1½" (4 cm)>.

B.o. all sts.

Sew in sleeves.

Sew underarm and side seams.

Moss Stitch Pullover

SIZES

Same as for stockinette stitch version

MATERIALS

Montera (50% wool, 50% llama; 100 g = approx. 127 yds/116 m): 9 (10, 10, 10) <3 (3, 4, 4, 5)> hanks

Equivalent yarn: 1143 (1270, 1270, 1270) yds (1045, 1161, 1161, 1161 m) <381 (381, 508, 508, 635) yds (348, 348, 465, 465, 581 m)> of bulky wool

Knitting needles: sizes 8 and 9 U.S. (5 and 5.5 mm), 16" (40.5 cm) circular needle in size 8 U.S. (5 mm), cable needle (cn)

GAUGE

Moss stitch patt on larger needles: 18 sts and 22 rows = 4" (10 cm)

Double cable = 2¾" (7 cm)

Take time to save time—check your gauge.

PATTERN STITCHES

Same as stockinette stitch version except:

■ Moss Stitch Pattern

Row 1: K1, p1.

Rows 2 and 4: K the k sts, p the p sts.

Row 3: P1, k1.

Rep rows 1 through 4.

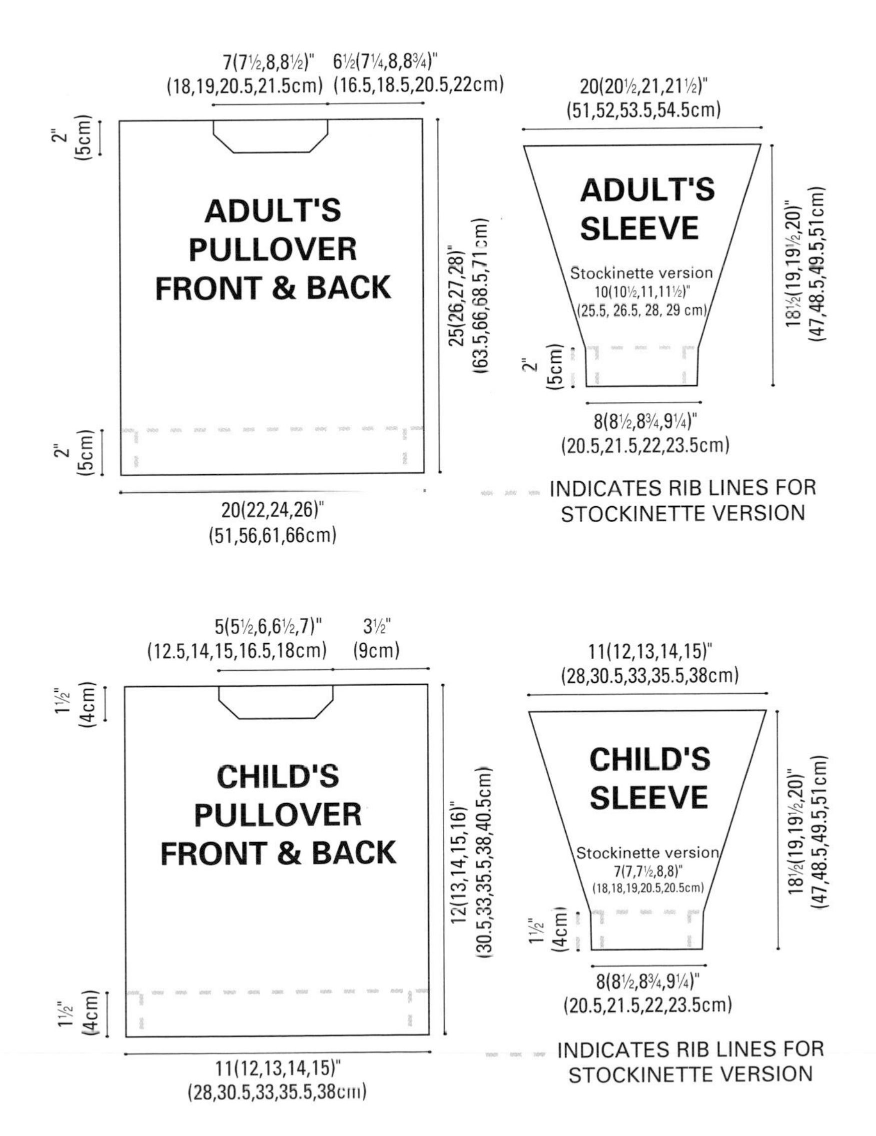

BACK

With smaller needles, c.o. 94 (102, 110, 120) <52 (58, 62, 66, 70)> sts.

Work moss st patt over first 38 (42, 46, 51) <17 (20, 22, 24, 26)> sts, work double cable over next 18 sts, work moss st to end.

Cont as est until piece meas 2" (5 cm) <1" (2.5 cm)>.

Change to larger needles and cont working as est until piece meas 25 (26, 27, 28)" (63.5, 66, 68.5, 71 cm) <9 (10, 11, 12, 13)" (23, 25.5, 28, 30.5, 33 cm)>.

B.o. all sts.

FRONT

Work as for back until piece meas 23 (24, 25, 26)" (58.5, 61, 63.5, 66 cm) <7 (8, 9, 10, 11)" (18, 20.5, 23, 25.5, 28 cm)>.

SHAPE NECK: Work across first 36 (39, 42, 46) <21 (23, 24, 25, 26)> sts, join a 2nd ball of yarn, b.o. center 22 (24, 26, 28) <10 (12, 14, 16, 18)> sts, and work to end.

B.o. 1 st every other neck edge 5 <4> times to give 31 (34, 37, 41) <17 (19, 20, 21, 22)> sts each side.

When piece meas same as back, b.o. all sts.

SLEEVES

With smaller needles c.o. 36 (38, 40, 42) <25 (27, 29, 31, 33)> sts.

Work moss st patt for 2" (5 cm) <1" (2.5 cm)>.

Change to larger needles and work in moss st patt, inc 1 st each end every 3rd row to give 90 (92, 94, 96) <49 (51, 53, 55, 57)> sts.

When piece meas 18 (18½, 19, 19½)" (45.5, 47, 48.5, 49.5 cm) <11½ (12, 12½, 13, 13½)" (29, 30.5, 31.5, 33, 34 cm)>, b.o. all sts.

FINISHING

Sew shoulder seams.

With circular needles, p.u. 76 (76, 80, 84) <64 (68, 68, 72, 72)> sts around neck edge and work 2 x 2 rib patt for 2" (5 cm) <1½" (4 cm)>.

B.o. all sts.

Sew underarm and side seams.

Broken Rib Family

design: **Kristin Nicholas**

knitting rating: **Beginner**

photography: **John Goodman**

Mohair is an extremely lightweight fiber that works up beautifully in simple stitches. A broken rib stitch, the easiest of all rib stitches, is used for the body in both the cardigan and pullover designs. The right side row is worked in knit 1, purl 1 rib, and the wrong side of the fabric is purled. Any of these sweaters makes a very relaxing knitting project. In adult sizes, both a pullover and a cardigan are included, and a pullover is given for children.

Adult's Pullover

SIZES

Small (Medium, Large, Extra Large)

Finished measurements: 36 (40, 44, 48)" (91.5, 101.5, 112, 122 cm)

MATERIALS

La Gran (74% mohair, 13% wool, 13% nylon; 1½ oz = approx. 90 yds/82 m): 8 (9, 10, 11) balls for cropped pullover shown on woman in back; 10 (11, 11, 12) balls for long pullover shown on man

Equivalent yarn: 720 (810, 900, 990) yds (658, 741, 823, 905 m) of bulky mohair for cropped version; 900 (990, 990, 1080) yds (823, 905, 905, 988 m) for longer version

Knitting needles: sizes 8 and 10½ U.S. (5 and 7 mm), double-pointed needles (dpn) in size 8 U.S. (5 mm)

GAUGE

Broken rib stitch on larger needles: 11 sts and 13½ rows = 3" (7.5 cm)

Take time to save time—check your gauge.

PATTERN STITCHES

■ **1 x 1 Ribbing** (over an even number of sts)

All rows: K1, p1.

■ **Broken Rib Stitch** (over multiple of 2 sts plus 1)

Row 1: *K1, p1; rep from *, end k1.

Row 2: P all sts.

KNITTING TIP: To make edge of garment and center front band look neat, on each last st of every row, slip last st as if to purl, ending with yarn in front of work. On first st of next row, knit the stitch.

BACK

Using smaller needles, c.o. 58 (64, 72, 80) sts.

Work in 1 x 1 ribbing for 4" (10 cm).

In last row of rib, inc 9 sts evenly across to give 67 (73, 81, 89) sts.

Change to larger needles and beg broken rib stitch.

Cont evenly until back meas 23 (24, 25, 26)" (58.5, 61, 63.5, 66 cm), including rib, or 20 (21, 22, 23)" (51, 53.5, 56, 58.5 cm) for cropped version.

B.o. all sts.

FRONT

Work same as for back.

When piece meas 20½ (21½, 22½, 23½)" (52, 54.5, 57, 59.5 cm) or 18 (19, 20, 21)" (45.5, 48.5, 51, 53.5 cm) for cropped version, shape neck: Work across 26 (29, 32, 35) sts, join a 2nd ball of yarn and b.o. center 15 (15, 17, 19) sts, work to end.

Working both sides at the same time, b.o. in pattern stitch at neck edge 1 st 5 times to give 21 (24, 27, 30) sts at each shoulder.

Work until front meas same as back to shoulders.

B.o. all sts.

SLEEVES

With smaller needles, c.o. 28 (30, 32, 34) sts.

Work in 1 x 1 rib for 3" (7.5 cm).

Change to larger needles and inc 1 st at each end every 3rd row 17 (18, 19, 20) times to give 62 (66, 70, 74) sts.

Work evenly until sleeve meas 16½(17, 17½, 18)" (42, 43, 44.5, 45.5 cm); then b.o.

FINISHING

Sew shoulder seams.

Mark armhole as shown on diagram.

Sew sleeve cap between markers.

Sew side and sleeve seams.

With right side facing and dpn, p.u. 70 (74, 80, 84) sts evenly around neck and work in 1 x 1 rib for 3" (7.5 cm).

B.o. loosely.

Adult's Cardigan

SIZES

Same as for pullover

MATERIALS

La Gran (74% mohair, 13% wool, 13% nylon; 1½ oz = approx. 90 yds/82 m): 10 (11, 11, 12) balls

Equivalent yarn: 900 (990, 990, 1080) yds (823, 905, 905, 988 m) of bulky mohair

Knitting needles: sizes 8 and 10½ U.S. (5 and 7 mm)

Four stitch holders

Six 1" (2.5 cm) buttons

BACK

Work same as pullover.

POCKET BACKS (make 2)

Using larger needles, c.o. 21 sts and work in broken rib st.

When piece meas 5" (12.5 cm), sl all sts to holder.

RIGHT FRONT

Using smaller needles, c.o. 34 (38, 42, 46) sts.

Work in 1 x 1 rib for 4" (10 cm).

In 5th row, work buttonhole: On RS, work 4 sts, b.o. next st, and work to end.

On next row, work across rib to b.o. st, m1 to replace st.

Cont working buttonholes every 1½" (4 cm).

When rib meas 4" (10 cm) and you are on a WS, inc 6 sts evenly across first 25 (29, 33, 37) sts to give 31 (35, 39, 43) sts; sl rem 9 sts to st holder to use for buttonhole band later.

Change to larger needles and work cardigan front sts in broken rib patt, working as est until piece measures 7" (18 cm).

Insert pocket back as follows: Beg at center front, work 8 sts, sl next 21 sts to holder, work to end.

Next row: Work across and replace slipped sts with pocket back.

When piece meas 8 (9, 10, 11)" (20.5, 23, 25.5, 28 cm), beg shaping right front.

B.o. 1 st every other row 0 (1, 2, 3) times, then 1 st every 6th row 10 times to give 21 (24, 27, 30) sts at shoulder.

When piece meas same as back at shoulder, b.o. all sts.

NOTE: *For man's sweater, work buttonholes on left side.*

LEFT FRONT

Work same as right front, omitting buttonholes on band and reversing neckline shaping.

SLEEVES

Work same as pullover.

FINISHING

To make pocket ribs, use smaller needles to p.u. 21 sts on holder at body of sweater and work in 1 x 1 twisted rib for 1" (2.5 cm).

B.o. all sts neatly.

Sew inside pocket and ribs down neatly.

Sew shoulder seams.

For buttonhole band: P.u. 9 sts on holder and work a buttonhole every 1½" (4 cm) as done before.

When piece meas 8 (9, 10, 11)" (20.5, 23, 25.5, 28 cm) including rib, work band without buttonholes.

Cont working rib piece until it meets center back of neck; then b.o.

On left side, p.u. the 9 sts held and work in 1 x 1 twisted rib until piece meets other rib at back of neck when slightly stretched (remember to sl last stitch as given in knitting tip).

Sew band neatly around cardigan opening.

Mark armhole 8¼ (9, 9½, 10)" (21, 23, 24, 25.5 cm) down in front and back.

Sew sleeve bet markers.

Sew side and sleeve seams.

Sew buttons on left front (or right front if making man's sweater).

Child's Ribbed Pullover

SIZES

2 (4, 6, 8, 10)

Finished measurements: 25 (27, 29, 31, 33)" (63.5, 68.5, 73.5, 78.5, 84 cm)

MATERIALS

La Gran (74% mohair, 13% wool, 13% nylon; 1½ oz = approx. 90 yds/82 m): 4 (4, 4, 5, 5) balls

Equivalent yarn: 360 (360, 360, 450, 450) yds (329, 329, 329, 411, 411 m) of bulky mohair

Knitting needles: sizes 8 and 10½ U.S. (5 and 7 mm), double-pointed needles (dpn) in size 8 U.S. (5 mm)

BACK

Using smaller needles, c.o. 40 (44, 48, 52, 56) sts.

Work in 1 x 1 rib for 2" (5 cm).

In last WSR of rib, inc 5 sts evenly across to give 45 (49, 53, 57, 61) sts.

Change to larger needles and beg broken rib stitch.

Work as est in patt until piece meas 14 (14½, 15, 15½, 16½)" (35.5, 37, 38, 39.5, 42 cm).

B.o. all sts.

FRONT

Work same as back.

When piece measures 12 (12½, 13, 13½, 14½)" (30.5, 31.5, 33, 34, 37 cm), shape neck: Work 16 (17, 18, 19, 20) sts, join a 2nd ball of yarn and b.o. center 13 (15, 17, 19, 21) sts, work to end.

Working both sides at the same time, b.o. 1 st at neck edge every other row 4 times to give 12 (13, 14, 15, 16) sts at shoulder.

When piece meas same as back to shoulder, b.o. shoulder sts.

SLEEVES

Using smaller needles, c.o. 22 (22, 24, 26, 28) sts.

Work in 1 x 1 rib for 2" (5 cm).

In last WSR of rib, inc 3 sts evenly across to give 25 (25, 27, 29, 31) sts.

Change to larger needles and beg broken rib stitch.

Inc 1 st each end every 6th (5th, 6th, 5th, 5th) row 6 (8, 8, 9, 10) times to give 37 (41, 43, 47, 51) sts.

When piece meas 12 (12½, 13, 13½, 14)" (30.5, 31.5, 33, 34, 35.5 cm), b.o. all sts.

FINISHING

Sew shoulder seams.

Mark armhole 5 (5½, 6, 6½, 7)" (12.5, 14, 15, 16.5, 18 cm) down in front and back.

Sew sleeve bet markers.

Sew underarm and side seams.

Using smaller dpn, p.u. 68 (70, 74, 76, 78) sts evenly around neckline and work in 1 x 1 ribbing for 1½" (4 cm).

B.o. loosely.

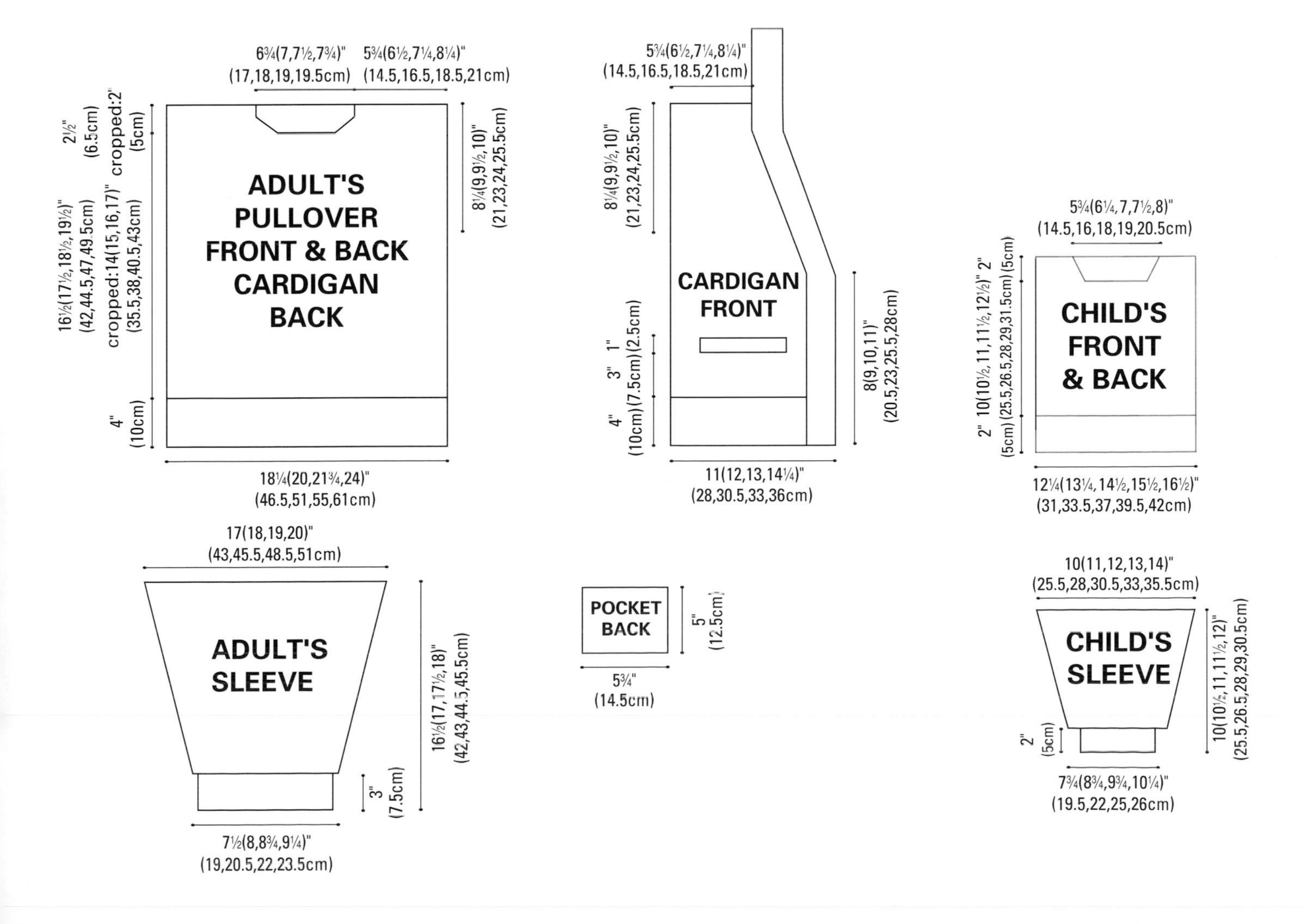

3

Textural Stitchery

The possibilities are endless for creating texture in knitting. Stitches can be twisted to build flat, interlacing patterns; you can use cable needles to create delicate or chunky rows and columns of rope motifs; ribs can grow into cables that travel across the face of the fabric in intricate patterns. To form pictorial images or geometric shapes, you can manipulate simple seed stitch or combinations of knit and purl stitches. Novelty and brushed yarns can simply be knit in stockinette stitch to form interesting lumpy-bumpy or hairy surfaces. This section shows texture at its finest in designs that are suitable for many figure types and lifestyles.

Pete & April

designs: **Kristin Nicholas**

knitting ratings: **Experienced** (cardigan)
Intermediate (vest)

photography: **Philip Newton**

The woman's cabled cardigan combines two easy ribbed cables with a more intricate diamond cable. The large diamond cables, positioned at the front sides and center back of the sweater, contain smaller diamonds within them. In place of traditional ribs, the button bands are also knit in a cable stitch, and the buttonholes are inset in the centers of selected cables.

The man's loose-fitting vest is knit in an easy stitch that combines ribs and garter stitches. Both the button band and the armhole edges are worked with the body of the sweater for minimal finishing. Set-in pockets on the front make the vest more versatile and add interest to the design. The choice of a beautiful and rustic yarn—an irregularly spun silk and wool—adds texture and appeal to both designs.

Cabled Aran Cardigan

SIZES

Small (Medium, Large)

Finished measurements: 46 (48, 52)" (117, 122, 132 cm)

MATERIALS

Mackenzie (70% wool, 30% silk; 100 g = approx. 176 yds/161 m): 9 (10, 10) hanks

Equivalent yarn: 1550 (1580, 1760) yds (1417, 1445, 1609 m) of bulky-weight yarn

Knitting needles: sizes 5 and 7 U.S. (3.75 and 4.5 mm), cable needle (cn)

Nine ¾" (2 cm) buttons

GAUGE

Rev St st: 16 sts and 25 rows = 4" (10 cm)

Diamond cable = 4½" (11.5 cm)

Ribbed cable = 2½" (6.5 cm)

Square cable = 1¾" (4.5 cm)

Take time to save time—check your gauge.

PATTERN STITCHES

T4L: Sl next 3 sts to cn and hold in front of work, p1, k3 from cn

T4R: Sl next st to cn and hold in back of work, k 3 sts from left-hand needle, p1 from cn

T7F: Sl next 4 sts to cn and hold in front, k3, sl last st from cn to left needle and p it, k3 from cn

■ **Reverse Stockinette Stitch** (RSS)

Row 1 (WS): K all sts.

Row 2: P all sts.

■ **Diamond Cable** (over 27 sts)

Row 1 (WS): K10, p3, k1, p3, k10.

Row 2: P10, T7F, p10.

Row 3 and all WSR: Work all sts as they appear.

Rows 4 and 6: P10, k3, p1, k3, p10.

Rows 7 through 18: Rep rows 1 through 6 twice.

Rows 19 and 20: Rep rows 1 and 2.

Row 21: K10, p3, k1, p3.

Row 22: P9, T4R, p1, T4L, p9.

Row 23: K9, p3, k3, p3, k9.

Row 24: P8, T4R, p3, T4L, p8.

Row 25: K8, p3, k2, p1, k2, p3, k8.

Row 26: P7, T4R, p2, k1, p2, T4L, p7.

Row 27: K7, p3, k2, p3, k2, p3, k7.

Row 28: P6, T4R, p2, k3, p2, T4L, p6.

Row 29: K6, p3, k2, p5, k2, p3, k6.

Row 30: P5, T4R, p2, k5, p2, T4L, p5.

Row 31: K5, p3, k2, p7, k2, p3, k5.

Row 32: P4, T4R, p2, T7F, p2, T4L, p4.

Row 33 and all rem WSR: Work all sts as they appear, unless otherwise stated.

Row 34: P3, T4R, p2, T4R, p1, T4L, p2, T4L, p3.

Row 36: P2, T4R, p2, T4R, p3, T4L, p2, T4L, p2.

Row 38: P1, T4R, p2, T4R, p5, T4L, p2, T4L, p1.

Row 40: T4R, p2, T4R, p7, T4L, p2, T4L.

Row 42: T4L, p2, T4L, p7, T4R, p2, T4R.

Row 44: P1, T4L, p2, T4L, p5, T4R, p2, T4R, p1.

Row 46: P2, T4L, p2, T4L, p3, T4R, p2, T4R, p2.

Row 48: P3, T4L, p2, T4L, p1, T4R, p2, T4R, p3.

Row 50: P4, T4L, p2, T7F, p2, T4R, p4.

Row 51: K5, p3, k2, p7, k2, p3, k5.

Row 52: P5, T4L, p2, k5, p2, T4R, p5.

Row 54: P6, T4L, p2, k3, p2, T4R, p6.

Row 56: P7, T4L, p2, k1, p2, T4R, p7.

Row 58: P8, T4L, p3, T4R, p8.

Row 60: P9, T4L, p1, T4R, p9.

Rep rows 1 through 6, then 1 and 2, then 21 through 60 for pattern (total of 48 rows for rep).

Cont rep rows 1 through 60 for remainder of design

■ **Square Cable** (over 8 sts).

Row 1 (WS): P2, k4, p2.

Rows 2, 6, 8: K2, p4, k2.

Row 4: Sl 2 sts to cn and hold in front, k2, p2 from cn, sl 2 to cn and hold in back, p2, k2 from cn.

Rep rows 1 through 8.

■ **Ribbed Cable** (over 13 sts).

Row 1 (WS): P2, k2, p2, k1, p2,k2, p2.

Rows 2, 6, 8, 10, 12, 14: K2, p2, k2, p1, k2, p2, k2.

Row 4: Sl 4 sts to cn and hold in back, k2, sl last 2 sts from cn to left needle and p2, k2 from cn, p1, sl 4 sts to cn and hold in front, k2, sl last 2 sts from cn to left needle and p2, k2 from cn.

Rep rows 1 through 14.

BACK

With smaller needles, c.o. 115 (119, 127) sts.

Est cable sequence as follows: Work 4 (5, 7) in RSS, work ribbed cable over 13 sts, work 2 (2, 3) in RSS, work ribbed cable over 13 sts, work 2 (2, 3) in RSS, work square cable over 8 sts, work 2 (3, 3) in RSS, work diamond cable over 27 sts, work 2 (3, 3) in RSS, work square cable over 8 sts, work 2 (2, 3) in RSS, work ribbed cable over 13 sts, work 2 (2, 3) in RSS, work ribbed cable over 13 sts, work 4 (5,7) in RSS.

Work 12 rows of diamond, square, and ribbed cables as given in pattern instructions.

Change to larger needles and work in est patt until piece meas 25½ (26½, 27½)" (64.5, 67.5, 70 cm).

SHAPE NECK: Work 44 (46, 50) sts, b.o. center 27 sts, work to end.

B.o. 2 (2, 3) sts at neck edge every other row twice to give 40 (42, 44) sts at shoulder.

When piece meas 27 (28, 29)" (68.5, 71, 73.5 cm), b.o. all sts.

LEFT FRONT

With smaller needles, c.o. 54 (56, 60) sts.

Est cable sequence as follows: Work 2 (2, 4) sts in RSS, work ribbed cable over 13 sts, work 1 (2, 3) in RSS, work square cable over 8 sts, work 1 (2, 3) in RSS, work diamond cable over 27 sts, work 2 in RSS.

Work 12 rows of diamond, square, and ribbed cables as given in pattern instructions.

Change to larger needles and work in est patt until piece meas 20 (20½, 21)" (51, 52, 53.5 cm).

SHAPE V-NECK: Dec 1 st at neck edge alternately every other row 4 (2, 4) times, then every 4 rows 10 (12, 12) times to give 40 (42, 44) sts at shoulder.

When piece meas same as back, b.o. all shoulder sts.

RIGHT FRONT

Work same as for left front, reversing cable placement and V-neck shaping.

To place cables: Work 2 sts in RSS, work diamond cable over 27 sts, work 1 (2, 3) sts in RSS, work square cable over 8 sts, work 1 (2, 3) in RSS, work 13 in ribbed cable, work 2 (2, 4) in RSS.

FINISHING

Sew shoulder seams.

Meas down 9 (9½, 10)" (23, 24, 25.5 cm) in front and back and mark.

Sew sleeves bet markers.

Sew side and sleeve seams.

CABLE BAND: Using smaller needles, c.o. 14 sts.

Work in cabled button band patt as follows:

All WSR: K2, p3, k4, p3, k2.

Rows 2, 6, 8, 10: P2, k3, p4, k3, p2.

Row 4: P2, slip 3 sts to cn and hold in front, k2, sl last st on cn to left needle and k it, p2 from cn; sl 2 sts to cn and hold in back, p2, k1, k2 from cn, p2.

Work two pieces, each equal in length to meas from bottom of sweater to center back of neck when slightly stretched.

Work 9 evenly spaced buttonholes on one piece, beg 1" (2.5 cm) up from bottom of sweater (on the 8th row) to V-neck shaping and placing buttonhole every 16th row.

BUTTONHOLE ROW: On row 8 (RS), p2, k3, p1, b.o. 2 sts, p1, k3, p2.

Row 9: C.o. 2 sts where b.o. was done to complete buttonhole.

Attach front bands to sweater, joining them at center back of neck.

Sew on 9 buttons.

SLEEVES

With smaller needles, c.o. 49 (49, 51) sts.

Est cables as follows: Work 2 in RSS, work square cable over 8 sts, work 1 (1, 2) in RSS, work diamond cable over 27 sts, work 1 (1, 2) in RSS, work square cable over 8 sts, work 2 in RSS.

Work 12 rows of diamond and square cables as given in pattern instructions.

Change to larger needles and beg inc out in RSS as follows: Inc 1 st each end every 4 rows 10 (12, 11) times, then every 5 rows 9 (9, 11) times to give 87 (91, 95) sts.

When piece meas 16½ (17, 18)" (42, 43, 45.5 cm), b.o. all sts.

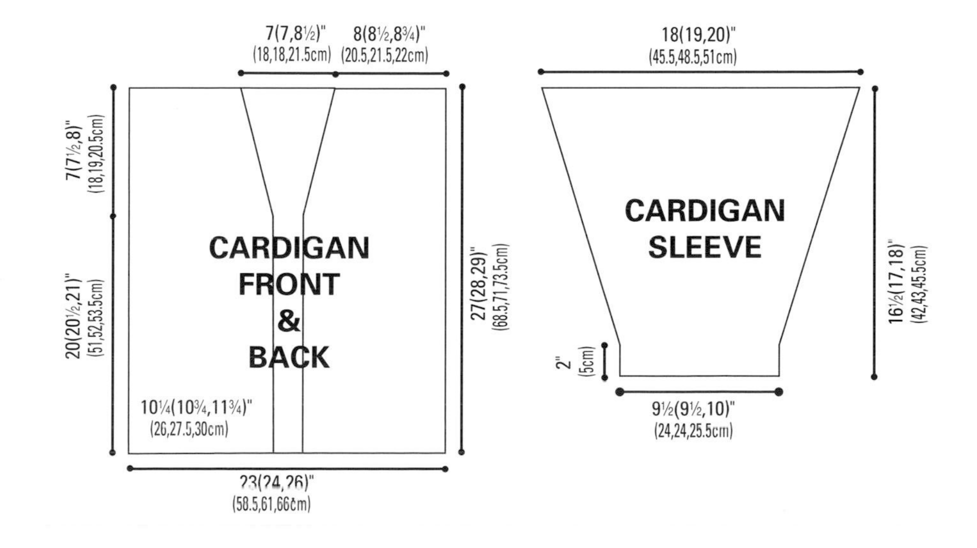

Unisex Loose-Fitting Vest with Pockets

SIZES

Small (Medium, Large, Extra Large)

Finished measurements: 40 (44, 48, 52)" (101.5, 112, 122, 132 cm)

MATERIALS

Mackenzie (70% wool, 30% silk; 100 g = approx. 176 yds/161 m): 4 (5, 5, 6) hanks

Equivalent yarn: 704 (880, 880, 1056) yds (644, 805, 805, 966 m) of bulky-weight yarn

Knitting needles: size 8 U.S. (5 mm)

Five 1" (2.5 cm) buttons

GAUGE

Rib st: 15 sts and 27 rows = 4" (10 cm).

PATTERN STITCHES

■ Garter Rib Stitch

Row 1 (RS): K2, p4, *k2, p3; rep from *, end k2, p4, k2.

Row 2: Sl first st as if to p with yarn in front, p across row, sl last st as if to p, ending with yarn in front.

■ Full-Fashioned Decreases

In order to make a decorative shaping detail at neckline and armhole shaping, follow the instructions below. Always work dec on RSR.

RIGHT-LEANING DECREASES: On RS, work to specified number of sts, k2tog, work to end of row or until next dec should be worked.

LEFT-LEANING DECREASES: On RS, k specified number of sts, ssk, k to end of row or until next dec should be worked.

■ SSK

Sl the first and 2nd sts one at a time knitwise, then insert the tip of the left-hand needle into the fronts of these 2 sts and k them tog from this position.

BACK

C.o. 74 (84, 89, 94) sts.

Work in garter rib until piece meas 14½ (15, 15, 15½)" (37, 38, 38, 39.5 cm) and you have completed a WSR.

B.o. 6 sts at beg of next 2 rows, ending with a WSR.

Beg full-fashioned dec: On every RSR, work 6 sts as est in patt, work left-leaning dec, work across in patt until 8 sts rem, work right-leaning dec, and work to end.

Cont to work dec every RSR until 6 sts total have been dec in full-fashioned method to give 50 (60, 65, 75) sts rem.

When piece meas 24 (24½, 25, 25½)" (61, 62, 63.5, 64.5 cm), beg working in garter st (knit all rows).

Work until piece meas 25 (25½, 26, 26½)" (63.5, 64.5, 66, 67.5 cm).

B.o. all sts.

RIGHT FRONT

C.o. 39 (44, 49, 54) sts.

Work in garter rib until piece meas 7" (18 cm).

INSERT POCKET: On RS, work across 12 sts, place marker (pm), work next 20 sts, pm, sl last 20 sts just k back onto left needle and work them in scrap yarn, cont working in MC to end of row.

Work in garter rib until piece meas 14½ (15, 15, 15½)" (37, 38, 38, 39.5 cm).

Beg shaping underarm and neckline: On WS, b.o. first 6 sts and work to end.

Next row: At neckline edge, work 6 sts as est in patt, work left-leaning dec, work across until 8 sts rem, work right-leaning dec.

Cont working dec every RSR, making a total of 6 full-fashioned dec at armhole.

At neckline dec every other row 1 (2, 3, 0) times, then every 8 rows 8 (8, 8, 0) times, then every 6 rows 0 (0, 0, 12) times to give 18 (22, 26, 30) sts at shoulder.

When piece meas same as back, b.o. all sts.

LEFT FRONT

Work same as right front, but work buttonholes into front band.

Work first buttonhole when piece meas 1" (2.5 cm), then every 3⅜ (3½, 3½, 3⅝)" (8.6, 9, 9, 9.2 cm).

To work buttonhole: Work until 5 sts rem, b.o. next 2 sts, complete row.

Next row: c.o. 2 sts over b.o. sts.

Work total of 5 buttonholes evenly from bottom to beg of neck shaping.

POCKET OPENING: When piece meas 7" (18 cm), work pocket row.

At RS, work across 8 (13, 18, 24) sts, pm, work 20 sts, sl last 20 sts back to right-hand needle and work 20 sts with contrast color scrap yarn, work in MC to end.

Cont as est until piece meas 14½ (15, 15, 15½)" (37, 38, 38, 39.5 cm) and you have completed WSR.

SHAPE ARMHOLE AND NECKLINE: B.o. 6 sts and work to end.

Work 1 WSR.

Next row: At armhole edge, work 6 sts as est in garter rib, work left-leaning dec at armhole, work across until 8 sts rem, work right-leaning dec.

Cont dec at armhole every RSR for 6 times total.

At neckline dec every other row 1 (2, 3, 0) times, then every 8 rows 8 (8, 8, 0) times, then every 6 rows 0 (0, 0, 12) times to give 18 (22, 26, 30) sts at shoulder.

When piece meas same as back, b.o. all sts.

FINISHING

Sew shoulder and side seams.

To finish pocket, unravel contrast yarn.

P.u. bottom sts and b.o. neatly in patt.

P.u. top sts and work into patt or St st as desired.

Work until piece meas 5" (12.5 cm); then b.o.

Sew to underside of garment to complete pocket.

Sew on buttons.

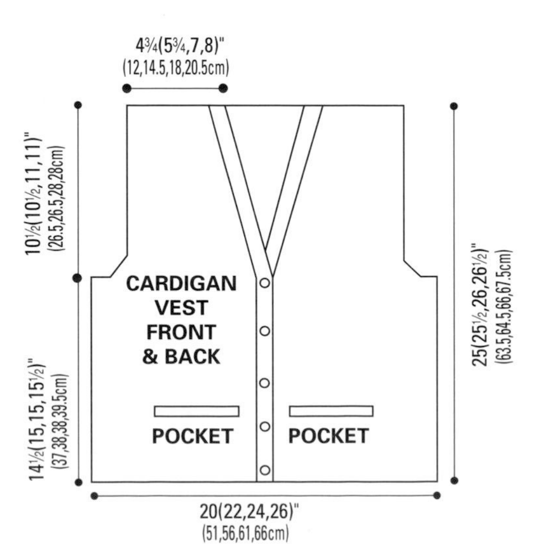

Viridescent Diamond Cardigan

This cropped cardigan with drop shoulders is knit in panels of reflecting triangular twist stitches. The finished look of a twist stitch resembles a closely woven cable, but no cable needle is used. The rounded and shaped collar gives a cosmopolitan finish to the smart-looking cardigan.

design: **Norah Gaughan**
knitting rating: **Advanced**
photography: **John Goodman**

SIZES

Small (Medium, Large)

Finished measurements: 41½ (44, 47)" (105.5, 112, 119.5 cm)

MATERIALS

Paisley (50% wool, 50% rayon; 50 g = approx. 90 yds/82 m): 17 (18, 20) skeins

Equivalent yarn: 1530 (1620, 1800) yds (1399, 1481, 1646 m) of worsted-weight yarn

Knitting needles: sizes 7 and 9 U.S. (4.5 and 5.5 mm)

Stitch markers

Five 1" (2.5 cm) buttons

GAUGE

Pattern stitch with larger needles: 22 sts and 20 rows = 4" (10 cm)

Take time to save time—check your gauge.

PATTERN STITCHES

RT (RIGHT TWIST): K2tog, leaving sts on left-hand needle, insert right-hand needle from the front bet the 2 sts ktog and k the first st again, slip both sts from the needle tog

LT (LEFT TWIST): With right-hand needle behind left-hand needle, skip the first st and k the 2nd st in the back loop; then insert the right-hand needle into the backs of both sts and k2tog

■ **1 x 1 Twisted Rib** (over an even number of sts)

Row 1 (WS): *K1-b, p1; rep from *.

Row 2: *K1, p1; rep from *.

■ **Right Triangle Stitch** (over 16 sts)

Row 1: P6, k6, RT twice.

Rows 2, 4, 6, 8, 10, 12 and 14: P10, k6.

Row 3: P6, k5, RT twice, k1.

Row 5: P6, k4, RT twice, LT once.

Row 7: P6, k3, RT 3 times, k1.

Row 9: P6, k2, RT twice, LT twice.

Row 11: P6, k1, RT 4 times, k1.

Row 13: P6, RT twice, LT 3 times.

Row 15: P5, RT 5 times, k1.

Row 16: P11, k5.

Row 17: P4, RT twice, LT 4 times.

Rows 18 and 20: P12, k4.

Row 19: P3, LT twice, RT 4 times, k1.

Row 21: P4, LT 6 times.

Row 22: P11, k5.

Row 23: P5, LT twice, RT 3 times, k1.

Rows 24, 26, 28, 30, 32, 34 and 36: P10, k6.

Row 25: P6, LT 5 times.

Row 27: P6, k1, LT twice, RT twice, k1.

Row 29: P6, k2, LT 4 times.

Row 31: P6, k3, LT twice, RT once, k1.

Row 33: P6, k4, LT 3 times.

Row 35: P6, k5, RT twice, k1.

Row 37: P6, k6, LT twice.

Row 38: P10, k6.

■ **Left Triangle Stitch** (over 16 sts)

Row 1: LT twice, k6, p6.

Rows 2, 4, 6, 8, 10, 12 and 14: K6, p10.

Row 3: K1, LT twice, k5, p6.

Row 5: RT once, LT twice, k4, p6.

Row 7: K1, LT 3 times, k3, p6.

Row 9: RT twice, LT twice, k2, p6.

Row 11: K1, LT 4 times, k1, p6.

Row 13: RT 3 times, LT twice, p6.

Row 15: K1, LT 5 times, p5.

Row 16: K5, p11.

Row 17: RT 4 times, LT twice, p4.

Rows 18 and 20: K4, p12.

Row 19: K1, LT 4 times, RT twice, p3.

Row 21: RT 6 times, p4.

Row 22: K5, p11.

Row 23: K1, LT 3 times, RT twice, p5.

Rows 24, 26, 28, 30, 32, 34 and 36: K6, p10.

Row 25: RT 5 times, p6.

Row 27: K1, LT twice, RT twice, k1, p6.

Row 29: RT 4 times, k2, p6.

Row 31: K1, LT once, RT twice, k3, p6.

Row 33: RT 3 times, k4, p6.

Row 35: K1, LT twice, k5, p6.

Row 37: RT twice, k6, p6.

Row 38: K6, p10.

BACK

With smaller needles, c.o. 96 (104, 112) sts.

Work in 1 x 1 twisted rib for 2½" (6.5 cm), ending with a RSR.

Next row (WS): P and inc 18 sts evenly across row to give 114 (122, 130) sts.

Change to larger needles and set up patt as follows: Row 1: K7 (11, 15), pm, work row 1 of right triangle patt 3 times over the next 48 sts, pm, p4, pm, work row 1 of left triangle patt 3 times over the next 48 sts, pm, k7 (11, 15) sts.

Row 2: P7 (11, 15) sts, work row 2 of left triangle patt to next marker, k4, work row 2 of right triangle patt to next marker, p7 (11, 15) sts.

Work in est patt and when piece meas 11 (11½, 12)" (28, 29, 30.5 cm), pm at each edge to mark for armholes.

When piece meas 8 (8½, 9)" (20.5, 21.5, 23 cm) above markers, b.o. all sts.

LEFT FRONT

With smaller needles, c.o. 48 (52, 56) sts.

Work in 1 x 1 twisted rib as for back for 2½" (6.5 cm), ending with a RSR.

Next row (WS): P and inc 10 sts evenly spaced across row to give 58 (62, 66) sts.

Change to larger needles and set up patt as follows: Row 1 (RS): K7 (11, 15) sts, pm, work row 1 of right triangle patt 3 times over the next 48 sts, pm, p3.

Row 2: K to marker, work row 2 of right triangle patt 3 times to next marker, and p to end of row.

Work in est patt and when piece meas 11 (11½, 12)" (28, 29, 30.5 cm), pm at armhole edge.

Continue to work even until piece meas 3 (3½, 4)" (7.5, 9, 10 cm) above armhole marker ending with a RSR.

SHAPE NECK: B.o. at neck edge 2 sts 3 (4, 5) times, 1 st every other row 4 times, then 1 st every 4th row 3 times.

Work even on 45 (47, 49) sts until piece meas same as back to shoulder, and b.o. all sts in St st.

RIGHT FRONT

Work to correspond to left front through inc row to give 58 (62, 66) sts.

Change to larger needles and set up patt as follows: Row 1 (RS): P3, pm, work row 1 of left triangle patt 3 times over the next 48 sts, pm, k7 (11, 15) sts.

Row 2: P to first marker, work row 2 of left triangle patt 3 times to next marker, k to end of row.

Finish to correspond to left front, reversing all shaping.

SLEEVES

With smaller needles, c.o. 44 (46, 48) sts.

Work in 1 x 1 twisted rib for 1½" (4 cm), ending with a RSR.

P and inc 14 sts evenly across next row to give 58 (60, 62) sts.

Change to larger needles and set patt as follows: Row 1 (RS): P1 (2, 3) sts, k6, RT twice, p6, RT twice (right triangle patt), pm, p4, (left triangle patt) LT twice, k6, p6, LT twice, k6, p1 (2, 3) sts.

Row 2 : K1 (2, 3), p10, k6, p10, k4, p10, k6, p10, k1 (2, 3).

Cont to work in patts as est, and at the same time, inc 1 st each edge every 4th row 7 (9, 11) times, then every 6th row 8 (7, 6) times, working the first 5 (3, 2) inc sts into the patt and working the rem inc sts in St st.

Work even on 88 (92, 96) sts until piece meas 17 (17½, 18)" (43, 44.5, 45.5 cm) and b.o. all sts.

FINISHING

LEFT FRONT BAND: With RS facing and smaller needles, p.u. 81 (85, 89) sts along left front edge.

Row 1 (WS): *K1-b, p1; rep from * to last st, end k1.

Row 2 (RS): K1, *k1-b, p1; rep from * to last 2 sts, k1-b, k1.

Rep these 2 rows until piece meas 1" (2.5 cm) and b.o. in ribbing.

Mark positions in p sts for 5 buttons.

RIGHT FRONT BAND: Work as for left band for 2 rows.

On 3rd row yo, k2tog (p st and k st next to it) for buttonholes opposite markers on left front band.

Work even until rib meas 1" (2.5 cm) and b.o. all sts in ribbing.

Sew shoulder seams.

COLLAR: With smaller needles c.o. 113 (117, 121) sts.

Work in 1 x 1 twisted rib in short rows as follows: *rib to last st, turn, repeat from * once, **rib to last 2 sts, turn, rep from ** once.

Cont in this manner to work 1 st fewer at end of every row 22 (24, 26) times to give 11 (12, 13) sts rem at each end.

Work 1 complete row across all sts.

B.o. all sts in rib.

Sew b.o. edge of collar to neck edge, beg at cast-off edge of front band.

Sew in sleeves bet markers.

Sew underarm and side seams.

Sew on buttons.

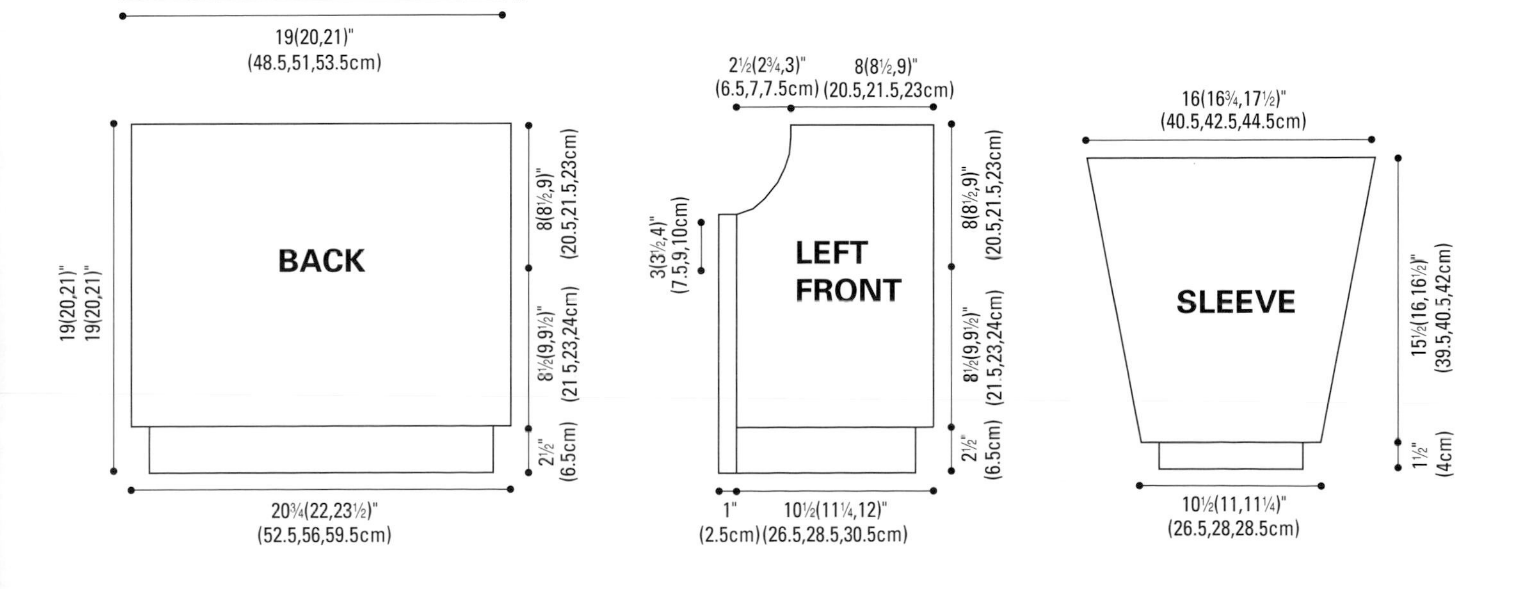

Practical Cardigan

design: **Norah Gaughan**

knitting rating: **Intermediate**

photography: **John Goodman**

The design of this cardigan combines a basket-weave texture and twist stitches in a soothing, repetitive pattern stitch that can be quickly memorized. The cropped silhouette of the cardigan features set-in sleeves, making the design great for both dressy and casual wear. Choose antique or heirloom buttons to finish this sweater, which will become a favorite for years to come.

SIZES

Small (Medium, Large)

Finished measurements: 38½ (42, 46)" (98, 106.5, 117 cm)

MATERIALS

Boston (100% wool; 50 g = approx. 95 yds/87 m): 16 (16, 17) skeins

Equivalent yarn: 1520 (1520, 1615) yds (1390, 1390, 1477 m) of worsted-weight yarn, preferably wool

Knitting needles: sizes 5 and 8 U.S. (3.75 and 5 mm)

Five 1" (2.5 cm) buttons

GAUGE

Pattern stitch with larger needles: 22 sts and 26 rows = 4" (10 cm)

Take time to save time—check your gauge.

PATTERN STITCHES

RT (RIGHT TWIST): K2tog, leaving sts on left-hand needle, insert right-hand needle from the front bet the 2 sts ktog and k the first st again; then slip both sts from the needle tog

LT (LEFT TWIST): With right-hand needle behind left-hand needle, skip the first st and k the 2nd st in the back loop; then insert the right-hand needle into the backs of both sts and k2tog

■ **1 x 1 Rib** (over an even number of sts)

All rows: *K1, p1*; rep bet *s.

■ **Pattern Stitch** (over multiple of 10 sts plus 6)

Row 1 (WS): K1, *p4, k1; rep from *.

Row 2: *P1, k4, p1, LT, RT; rep from * and end p1, k4, p1.

Rows 3 and 5: *P6, k1, RT, k1; rep from * and end p1, k4, p1.

Row 4: *P6, k1, RT, k1; rep from * and end p6.

Row 6: *P1, k4, p1, RT, LT; rep from * and end p1, k4, p1.

Row 7: Rep row 1.

Rows 8 and 10: P1, *k4, p6; rep from * and end k4, p1.

Row 9: K1, *p4, k6; rep from * and end p4, k1.

Repeat rows 1 through 10.

BACK

With smaller needles, c.o. 132 (146, 158) sts.

Work in 1 x 1 rib for 1½" (4 cm), ending with a WSR.

K across next row and dec 26 (30, 32) sts evenly across to give 106 (116, 126) sts.

Change to larger needles and work even in pattern stitch until piece meas 9½ (10, 10½)" (24, 25.5, 26.5 cm).

SHAPE ARMHOLES: Keeping in est patt, b.o. at the beg of row 3 sts twice, then 2 sts 6 times.

Then b.o. each end every other row 3 times, then each end every 4th row 3 times to give 76 (86, 96) sts.

Work even until armhole meas 7 (7½, 8)" (18, 19, 20.5 cm), ending with a WSR.

SHAPE SHOULDERS AND NECK: Work 31 (35, 39) sts, join another ball of yarn, b.o. center 14 (16, 18) sts, and work to end of row.

Working each side sep, b.o. at each neck edge 4 sts twice, 3 sts once and 2 sts once.

At the same time, when armhole meas 7½ (8, 8½)" (19, 20.5, 21.5 cm), b.o. at each shoulder edge 6 (7, 9) sts twice, then 6 (8, 8) sts once.

LEFT FRONT

With smaller needles, c.o. 64 (70, 76) sts.

Work in 1 x 1 rib as for back for 1½" (4 cm), ending with a WSR.

K across next row and dec 13 (14, 15) sts evenly across to give 51 (56, 61) sts.

Change to larger needles and beg working in pattern stitch with row 1.

On row 2 of pattern stitch, for small and large sizes, end row with LT, RT, p1.

Cont to work even in pattern stitch as est, shaping armholes as for back, until armhole meas 5 (5½, 6)" (12.5, 14, 15 cm), ending with a RSR to give 36 (41, 46) sts.

SHAPE NECK: At neck edge, b.o. 4 sts once, 3 sts twice, 2 sts 3 times and 1 st 2 (3, 4) times.

Work even on 18 (22, 26) sts until piece meas the same length as back, shaping shoulder as for back.

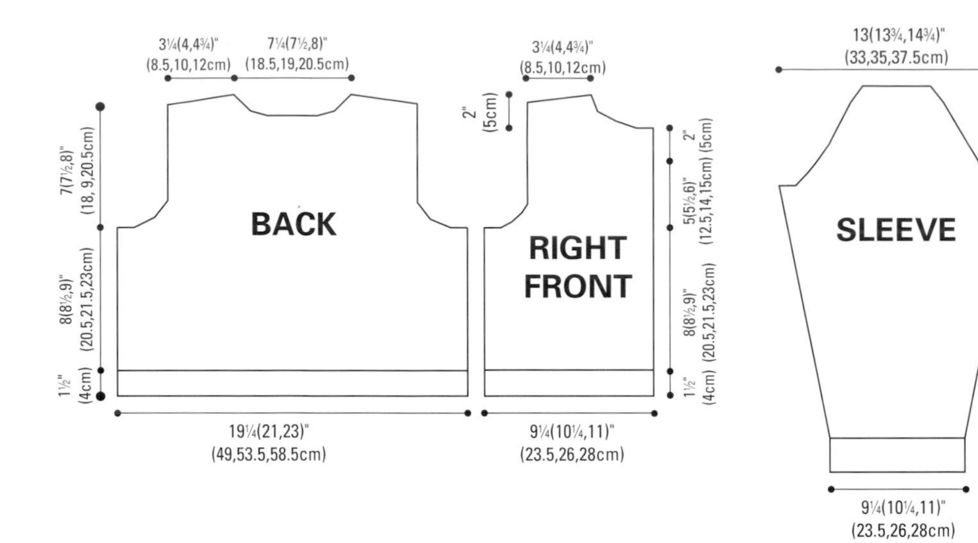

RIGHT FRONT

Work to correspond to left front, reversing all shaping.

(Since pattern will have alternating squares because of row beginning, it is not necessary to place pattern differently.)

SLEEVES

With smaller needles, c.o. 52 (56, 62) sts.

Work in 1 x 1 rib for 2" (5 cm), ending with a RSR.

K across next row and dec 1 (0, 1) sts evenly across to give 51 (56, 61) sts.

Beg pattern stitch as for left front.

Keeping in est pattern, inc 1 st each edge every 8th row 3 (2, 0) times, then every 10th row 7 (8, 10) times.

Work even on 71 (76, 81) sts until piece meas 17 (17½, 18)" (43, 44.5, 45.5 cm).

SHAPE CAP: B.o. 4 sts at the beg of the next 2 rows, 2 (3, 3) sts at beg of next 2 rows, then dec 1 st each edge every other row 9 (10, 11) times.

B.o. 2 sts at beg of next 6 rows, 3 sts at beg of next 2 rows.

B.o. rem 23 (24, 27) sts.

FINISHING

Sew shoulder and side seams.

NECK BAND: With RS facing and smaller needles, p.u. 95 (101, 107) sts evenly around neck.

Work in 1 x 1 rib for 1½" (4 cm).

B.o. in ribbing.

LEFT FRONT BUTTON BAND: With smaller needles and RS facing, p.u. 89 (95, 101) sts along left front edge, including edge of neck band.

Row 1: K1, *p1, k1; rep from *.

Row 2: K2, p1, *k1, p1; rep from * to last 2 sts and k2.

Rep these 2 rows until band meas 1½" (4 cm).

B.o. in ribbing.

Mark positions for 5 buttonholes evenly spaced in p sts of left front band.

RIGHT FRONT BAND: Work as for left front band for ¾" (2 cm).

Work buttonholes opposite markers on left front band by working to marked p st and working yo, k2tog.

Finish to correspond to left front band.

Set in sleeves.

Sew underarm and sleeve seams.

Sew on buttons.

Deborah's Biking Cardigan

design: **Deborah Newton**
Knitting rating: **Intermediate**
Photography: **Clint Clemens**

Simple combinations of knit and purl stitches in diamond and chevron patterns are set between panels of garter rows and seed stitch bands. Three-by-three ribs finish the cardigan except at the button band, which is done in seed stitch for added interest. In addition to the cropped design shown, instructions are also given for an alternative longer length. This sweater is a perfect choice for intermediate knitters who want a challenge that is easily accomplished.

SIZES

Petite (Small, Medium, Large).

Finished measurements: 38¾ (40, 41½, 43½)" (98.5, 101.5, 105.5, 110.5 cm)

MATERIALS

Cambridge (70% cotton, 30% wool; 50 g = approx. 85 yds/78 m): 15 (16, 17, 18) skeins for cropped version shown; 19 (20, 21, 22) skeins for longer version

Equivalent yarn: 1275 (1360, 1445, 1530) yds (1166, 1244, 1321, 1399 m) of worsted-weight yarn for cropped version shown; 1615 (1700, 1785, 1870) yds (1477, 1554, 1632, 1710 m) for longer version

Knitting needles: sizes 6 and 7 U.S. (4 and 4.5 mm)

Five 1" (2.5 cm) buttons

GAUGE

Charted pattern: 20 sts and 32 rows = 4" (10 cm)

Take time to save time—check your gauge.

PATTERN STITCHES

■ **3 x 3 Rib** (over multiple of 6 sts plus 3)

Row 1 (WS): P3, *k3, p3; rep from *.

Row 2: K3, *p3, k3; rep from *.

■ **Seed Band** (over an odd number of sts)

Rows 1, 2, and 3: K all sts.

Row 4: P all sts.

Rows 5, 6, 7, 8, and 9: K1, *p1, k1; rep from *.

Row 10: P all sts.

Rows 11 and 12: K all sts.

■ **Diamond/Zigzag Pattern**

See chart.

■ **Moss Stitch** (over an even number of sts)

Row 1 (WS): *K1, p1; rep from *.

Row 2: K2, *p1, k1; rep from *.

BACK

With larger needles, c.o. 105 (105, 111, 117) sts.

Work in 3 x 3 rib for 1½" (4 cm), ending with a RSR.

P across next row and dec 4 (2, 4, 4) sts evenly across to give 101 (103, 107, 113) sts.

Work 1 rep of seed band.

On RSR, beg diamond/zigzag pattern with row 1 of chart, beg where indicated for size.

Work even until row 24 of chart is complete, then rows 17 through 24 once more, ending with a WSR.

Work 1 rep of seed band.

Cont as est, alternating diamond/zigzag pattern and seed band.

Work even until piece meas 9½" (24 cm) for cropped version or 15" (38 cm) for longer version (adding 44 more rows).

End with WSR 8 of diamond/zigzag pattern.

SHAPE ARMHOLE: B.o. 2 sts at the beg of the next 8 (8, 8, 6) rows, then 3 sts at the beg of the next 0 (0, 0, 2) rows to give 85 (87, 91, 95) sts.

Work even until armhole meas 7½ (8, 8½, 9)" (19, 20.5, 21.5, 23 cm), ending with a WSR.

For shoulder and back neck shaping, work across 35 (35, 37, 38) sts, join another ball of yarn, b.o. center 15 (17, 17, 19) sts, and work to end.

Working each side sep, b.o. at each shoulder edge 8 (8, 9, 9) sts twice, then 9 (9, 9, 10) sts once.

At the same time, b.o. 5 sts at each neck edge twice.

LEFT FRONT

With larger needles, c.o. 51 (51, 57, 57) sts.

Work in 3 x 3 rib as for back, ending with a RSR.

P across next row and dec 4 (2, 6, 4) sts evenly across to give 47 (49, 51, 53) sts.

Work seed band as for back.

Work diamond/zigzag pattern where indicated on chart.

Work same as back to armhole, ending with a WSR.

SHAPE ARMHOLE: B.o. 2 sts at the beg of the next 4 (4, 4, 3) RS rows, then 3 sts at the beg of the next 0 (0, 0, 1) RS rows to give 39 (41, 43, 44) sts.

Work even as est until armhole meas 5½ (6, 6½, 7)" (14, 15, 16.5, 18 cm), ending with a RSR.

SHAPE NECK: B.o. at neck edge 2 (4, 4, 4) sts once, 3 sts once, 2 sts three times; then dec 1 st each RSR 3 times to give 25 (25, 27, 28) sts.

Work even until armhole meas the same as back, ending with a WSR.

To shape shoulder, b.o. 8 (8, 9, 9) sts at the beg of the next 2 (2, 3, 2) RSR, then 9 (9, 0, 10) sts at the beg of next RSR.

RIGHT FRONT

Work as for left front, beg where indicated on diamond/zigzag chart and reversing all shaping.

SLEEVES

With larger needles, c.o. 51 (51, 57, 57) sts.

Work in 3 x 3 rib for 1½" (4 cm), ending with a RSR.

P across next row and inc 12 (12, 8, 10) sts evenly across to give 63 (63, 65, 67) sts.

Beg diamond/zigzag pattern where indicated on chart.

Cont as est until 8 rows are complete, ending with a WSR.

Inc 1 st each end of the next row and every following 10th (8th, 8th, 6th) row 11 (14, 15, 17) times to give 85 (91, 95, 101) sts.

At the same time, cont until row 16 of chart is complete above the rib, ending with a WSR; then work seed band.

Working inc sts into est patterns, cont to alternate 32 rows of chart and seed band.

Work even until piece meas 15½" (39.5 cm) above rib (17"/43 cm total), ending with WSR 8 of chart.

CAP SHAPING: B.o. 2 sts at the beg of the next 24 (26, 28, 30) rows; then b.o. 3 sts at the beg of the next 4 rows.

B.o. rem 25 (27, 27, 29) sts on the next row.

FINISHING

Sew shoulder and side seams.

With RS facing and starting at right front, use smaller needles to p.u. 75 (81, 18, 87) sts evenly around entire neckline edge to left front.

Work in 3 x 3 rib for ¾" (2 cm).

LEFT FRONT BUTTON BAND: With smaller needles, c.o. 8 sts.

Work in moss st until band, when slightly stretched, meas the same as front edge including neckline rib; then b.o.

Sew to left front, stretching slightly to fit.

Sew 5 buttons evenly spaced along band.

RIGHT FRONT BUTTONHOLE BAND: With RS facing and smaller needles, p.u. 105 (108, 111, 114) sts for cropped version or 135 (138, 141, 144) sts for longer version.

Next row (WS): P3 (0, 3, 0) sts, *k3, p3; rep from *.

Work 3 x 3 rib as est for 2 more rows.

On next row, work a 4-st buttonhole opposite each button by b.o. 4 sts on this row and c.o. 4 sts on the next row above the b.o. sts.

Cont rib until band meas 1" (2.5 cm); then b.o. all sts.

Sew sleeve seams.

Sew sleeve cap in armhole, centering it at shoulder seam.

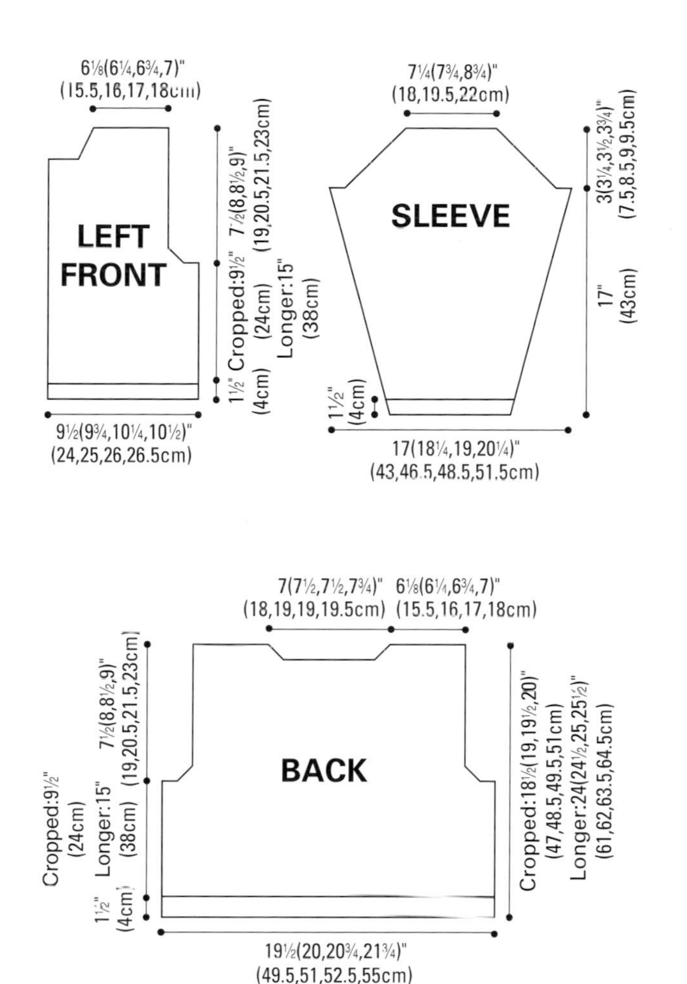

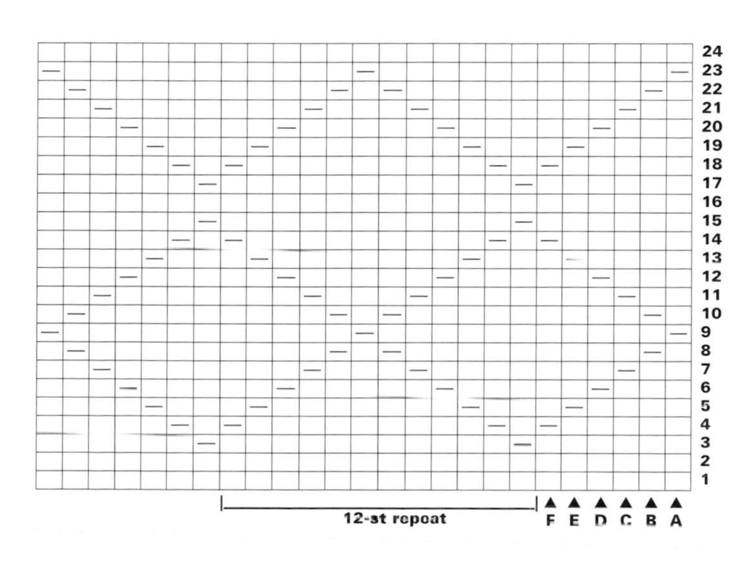

KEY

☐ = Knit on RS, purl on WS

⊟ = Purl on RS, knit on WS

Odd number rows are RSR; read right to left

Even number rows are WSR; read left to right

A: Beg back large, left front small

B: Beg back medium

C: Beg back small

D: Beg back petite, sleeve large

E: Beg sleeve medium, left front large

F: Beg all right fronts, left front medium, sleeve petite and small

designs: **Cathy Payson** (cardigan),
Julie Hoff (pullover)

knitting ratings: **Experienced** (cardigan),
Intermediate (pullover)

photography: **Philip Newton**

The intricately cabled cardigan intersperses bobbled medallion cables and braided cables between columns of knotted ribs. Ribs added after the front edges are finished create a gentle scoop at the V-shaped neckline.

Oak leaves frequently inspire Julie Hoff's designs, and in this pullover the leaves are worked in seed stitch with added center veins made of bobbles. The edging of the sweater continues the bobble motif and adds a simple knit-and-purl chevron stitch border. The design looks more difficult than it really is.

SIZES

Small (Medium, Large)

Finished measurements: 41½ (45½, 49½)" (105.5, 115.5, 125.5 cm)

MATERIALS

Avalon (25% angora, 50% baby alpaca, 25% lambswool; 50 g = approx. 165 yds/151 m): 18 (19, 19) hanks

Equivalent yarn: 2900 (2970, 3135) yds (2652, 2716, 2867 m) of sport-weight yarn

Knitting needles: sizes 5 and 6 U.S. (3.75 and 4 mm), cable needle (cn)

GAUGE

Knotted rib patt with larger needles: 20 sts and 32 rows = 4" (10 cm)

Plaited cable (13 sts) = 1¼" (3 cm)

Medallion cable = 2¼" (5.5 cm)

Take time to save time—check your gauge.

PATTERN STITCHES

FC (FRONT CROSS): Sl 3 sts to cn and hold in front, k3, k3 from cn.

BC (BACK CROSS): Sl 3 sts to cn and hold in back, k3, k3 from cn.

■ Knotted Rib

Row 1 (RS): P1, *K into front and back of next st, p1*; rep bet *s.

Row 2: K1, *p2tog, k1*; rep bet *s.

■ Plaited Cable (over 13 sts)

Row 1 (RS): P2, k9, p2.

Row 2 and all WSR: K2, p9, k2.

Row 3: P2, FC, k3, p2.

Row 5: P2, k9, p2.

Row 7: P2, k3, BC, p2.

■ Medallion Cable (over 17 sts)

Rows 1 and 3 (RS): P2, k13, p2.

Row 2 and all WSR except row 16: K2, p13, k2.

Row 5: P2, FC, k1, BC, p2.

Rows 7, 9, and 11: P2, k13, p2.

Row 13: P2, BC, k1, FC, p2.

Row 15: P2, k6, k into front and back of next st twice (4 sts); turn, p these 4 sts; turn, k these 4 sts; turn, p these 4 sts; turn, k these 4 sts, k next 6 sts, p2.

Row 16: K2, p6, p 4 inc sts tog (to make bobble), p6, k2.

Rep rows 1 through 16.

BACK

With smaller needles, c.o. 147 (157, 167) sts.

Work knotted rib for 2" (5 cm).

Change to larger needles and set up patt as follows: Work 5 (10, 15) sts in knotted rib, *17 sts in medallion cable, 5 sts in knotted rib, 13 sts in plaited cable, 5 sts in knotted rib*; rep bet *s twice, work 17 sts in medallion cable and 5 (10, 15) sts in knotted rib.

Cont as est until piece meas 26 (27, 28)" (66, 68.5, 71 cm).

B.o. all sts.

LEFT FRONT

With smaller needles, c.o. 63 (67, 73) sts.

Work knotted rib for 2" (5 cm), inc 4 (5, 4) sts evenly across last row.

Change to larger needles and work 5 (9, 15) sts in knotted rib, 17 in medallion cable, 5 in knotted rib, 13 in plaited cable, 5 in knotted rib, 17 in medallion cable and 5 in knotted rib.

Cont as est until piece meas 14 (15, 16)" (35.5, 38, 40.5 cm), including rib.

SHAPE NECK: B.o. 1 st at neck edge every 4th row 20 (2, 4) times, then every 6th row 2 (16, 15) times.

When piece meas same as back, b.o. all sts.

RIGHT FRONT

Work rib as for left front.

Next row (RS), work knotted rib for 5 sts, medallion cable for 17, knotted rib for 5, plaited cable for 13, knotted rib for 5, medallion cable for 17, and knotted rib for 5 (9, 15).

Work as for left front, reversing shaping.

SLEEVES

With smaller needles, c.o. 55 sts.

Work knotted rib for 2" (5 cm), inc 8 sts evenly spaced across last row.

Change to larger needles and set up patt as follows: Work knotted rib for 5 sts, plaited cable for 13, knotted rib for 5, medallion cable for 17, knotted rib for 5, plaited cable for 13, and knotted rib for 5.

Cont as est, inc out in knotted rib patt, inc 1 st each end every 4th row 0 (0, 9) times, every 5th row 20 (22, 19) times, and every 6th row 3 (3, 0) times to give 109 (113, 119) sts.

When piece meas 17 (18, 19)" (43, 45.5, 48.5 cm), b.o. all sts.

FINISHING

Sew shoulder seams.

With smaller needles, p.u. 99 (107, 115) sts along right front and work knotted rib for ¾" (2 cm).

Next row: Make 5 buttonholes evenly spaced by yo, k2tog.

Cont working rib for ¾" (2 cm) more.

B.o. all sts.

Work left front band as for right front band but omit buttonholes.

P.u. 201 (209, 217) sts along top of right button band, right front, back neck, left front, and top of left front button band.

Work knotted rib for 1½" (4 cm); then b.o. all sts.

Sew on sleeves.

Sew underarm and side seams.

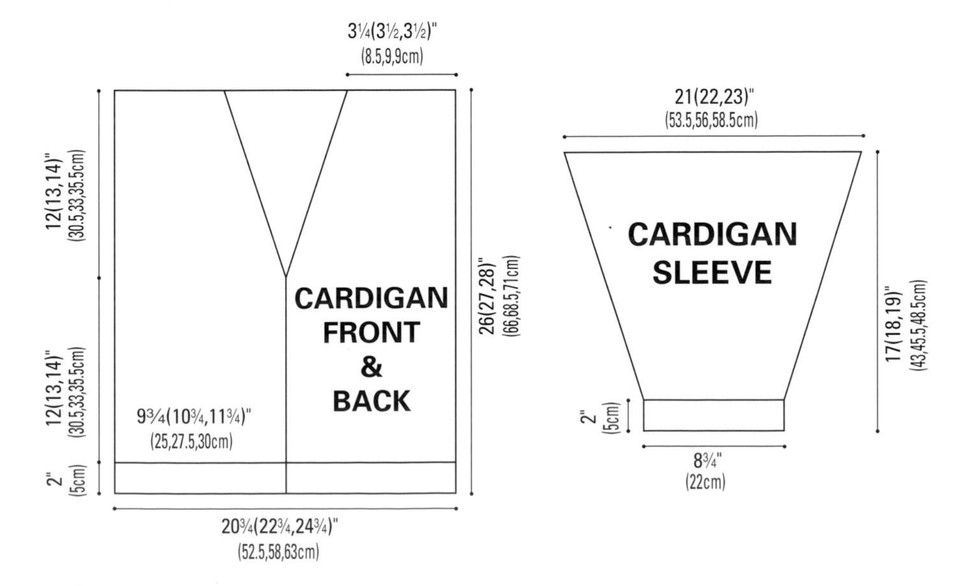

Pullover

SIZES

Small (Medium, Large)

Finished measurements: 45 (47, 49)" (114.5, 119.5, 124.5 cm)

MATERIALS

Paisley (50% wool, 50% rayon; 50 g = approx. 95 yds/87 m): 17 (17, 18) hanks

Equivalent yarn: 1550 (1615, 1710) yds (1417, 1477, 1536 m) of worsted-weight yarn

Knitting needles: size 7 U.S. (4.5 mm), 16" (40.5 cm) circular needle in size 6 U.S. (4 mm)

Six stitch holders

GAUGE

St st on larger needles: 19 sts and 27 rows = 4" (10 cm)

Take time to save time—check your gauge.

PATTERN STITCHES

■ **Stockinette Stitch**

Row 1 (RS): K all sts.

Row 2: P all sts.

■ **Reverse Stockinette Stitch** (RSS)

Row 1 (RS): P all sts.

Row 2: K all sts.

■ **Large Bobble**

(K1, p1, k1, p1) into 1 st.

Turn work, k4; turn, k4; turn, k4.

Pull 2nd st over first st on right needle 3 times; turn, p1.

■ **Small Bobble**

(K1, p1, k1, p1) into 1 st.

Turn work, k4; turn, k4.

Pull 2nd st over first st on right needle 3 times.

BACK

With larger needles, c.o. 95 (101, 107) sts.

Row 1: P5 (1, 4) *make large bobble, p6; rep from *, end last rep p5 (8, 4).

Work 2 rows RSS, then 2 rows St st.

Work chart 1 as indicated.

Work 2 rows St st, 2 rows RSS, ending with a WSR.

Work 10 (12, 14) rows in St st, inc 11 sts evenly across first row to give 106 (112, 118) sts.

Work leaf pattern as follows: on RS k7 (8, 9) sts *pm, work across chart 2, pm, k9 (11, 13); rep from *, ending last rep k9 (10, 11).

Work 17 (19, 21) rows St st, ending with a WSR.

Work leaf pattern as follows: k9 (10, 11); *pm, work chart 3, pm, k9 (11, 13); rep from *, ending last rep k7 (8, 9).

Work leaves as est, removing markers upon completion, and at same time, when piece meas 15½ (16¾, 18)" (39.5, 42.5, 45.5 cm), shape armhole: B.o. 6 sts at beg of next 2 rows to give 94 (100, 106) sts.

Work 17 (19, 21) rows in St st, ending with a WSR.

Work leaf pattern as follows: K1 (2, 3) *pm, work chart 2, pm, k9 (11, 13) rep from *, ending last rep k3 (4, 5).

Work leaves as est, removing markers upon completion and cont in St st.

When piece meas 243/4 (26, 271/4)" (63, 66, 69 cm), shape neck: Work across first 33 (36, 39) sts, join 2nd ball of yarn and b.o. center 28 sts, work to end.

Working each side sep, b.o. at each neck edge 4 sts once.

When piece meas 25½ (26¾, 28)" (64.5, 68, 71 cm), b.o. rem 29 (32, 35) sts.

FRONT

Work as for back until piece meas 22¾ (24, 25¼)" (58, 61, 64 cm).

SHAPE NECK: Work across first 41 (44, 47) sts, join 2nd ball of yarn and b.o. center 12 sts, work to end.

Working each side sep, b.o. at neck edge 3 sts twice, 2 sts once, and 1 st 4 times.

When piece meas 25½ (26¾, 28)" (64.5, 68, 71 cm), b.o. rem 29 (32, 35) sts.

SLEEVES

With larger needles, c.o. 44 sts.

Row 1 (RS): P1, *make large bobble, p6; rep from *, end p1.

Work RSS for 2 rows, then St st for 2 rows, working chart 1 as indicated.

Work St st for 6 (8, 10) rows, inc 1 st each end on next RSR once, every other row 3 (0, 0) times, every 4th row 23 (26, 22) times, then every 6th row 0 (0, 4) times to give 98 sts.

At the same time, work leaf pattern as follows: On 7th (9th, 11th) row (RS): k13 (14, 16) sts, including inc st if applicable, pm, work chart 2, pm, k13 (14, 16) sts, including inc st.

Work leaf as est, removing markers upon completion.

Work St st for 13 (15, 17) rows, ending with a WSR.

Work leaf pattern as follows: K6 (8, 10) sts, including inc st if applicable, *pm, work chart 3, pm*, k12; rep bet *s.

End k6 (8, 10), including inc st.

Work leaves as est, removing markers upon completion.

Cont in St st until piece meas 16¾(17¾, 18¾)" (42.5, 45, 47.5 cm) or desired length.

B.o. all sts.

FINISHING

Block all pieces.

Sew shoulder seams.

COLLAR

With circular needle, p.u. 16 sts from left front, 12 sts from center front, 16 sts from right front, 6 sts from right back, 28 sts from center back, and 6 sts from left back to give 84 sts.

K 1 row, p 2 rows, k 1 row, work chart 1 as indicated, k1 row, p 2 rows.

Work large bobbles on b.o. row as follows: *Work large bobble, b.o. bobble and next 6 sts purlwise; rep from * to end.

Sew on sleeves.

Sew underarm and side seams.

Block collar and seams.

KEY

| = K on RS, p on WS

○ = P on RS, k on WS

● = Make small bobble

|| = Edge st

CHART 1 (14-st repeat plus 2)

CHART 2

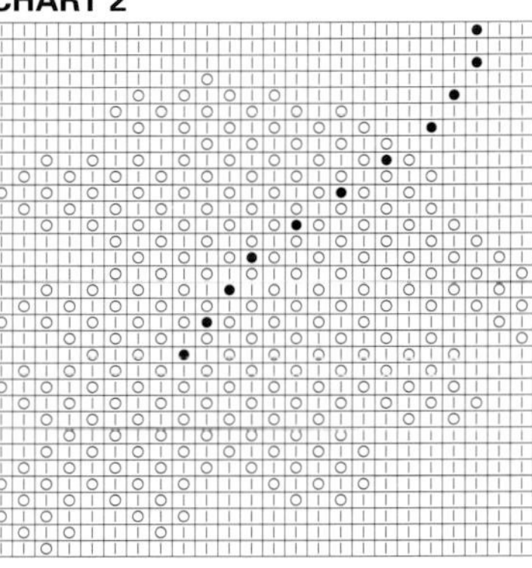

CHART 3

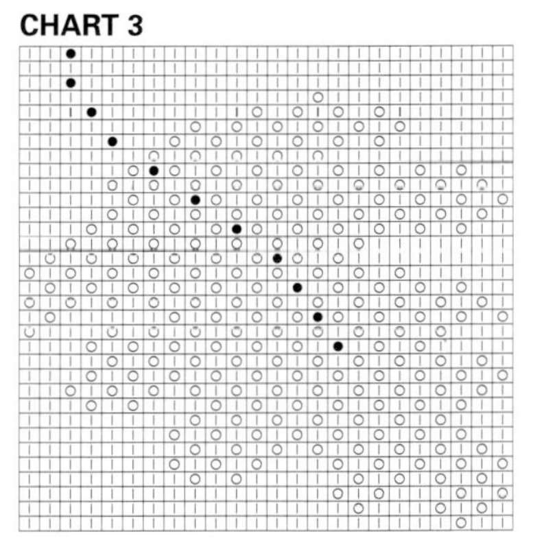

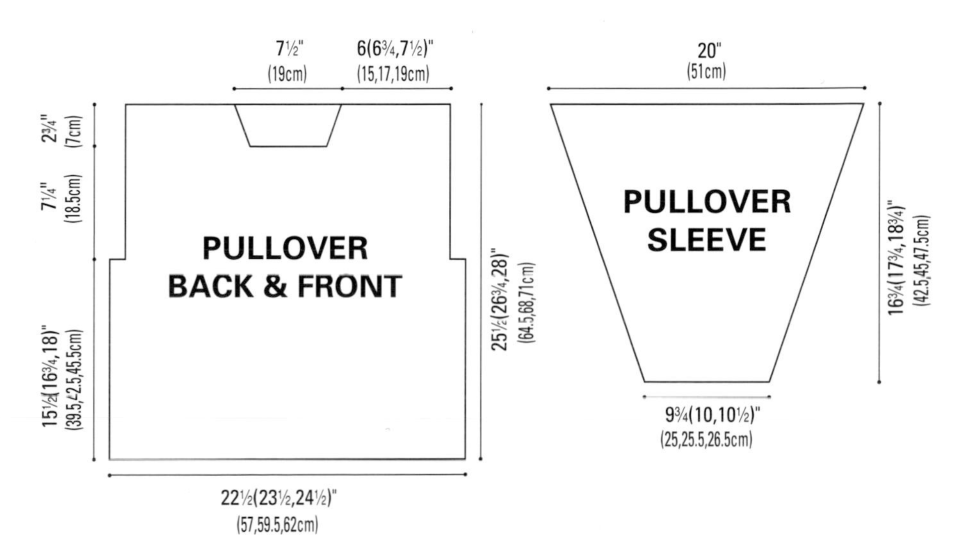

4

Knitting with Color

In the past 10 years, American knitwear has experienced an explosion in the free and unrestrained use of color. Colors are combined much more freely than in the past, and even solid-colored sweaters are knitted in more unusual shades. Working with color is a learning process, and as a knitter's skill increases, more interesting color combinations tend to develop. Many of the designs in this chapter are inspired by nature or antique textiles and combine off-beat colors that aren't usually found in ready-to-wear. Although the intarsia technique is used for some, most of these colorwork designs employ the traditional Fair Isle technique of two-color stranding. Fair Isle is a restful technique for knitters, and it produces an extra-thick fabric that is especially suitable for northern climates.

Camino del Sol

design: **Jodi Berkebile**
knitting rating: **Experienced**
photography: **Philip Newton**

Classic western cowboy gear inspired this colorful striped vest with pointed front edges. Its diamond motif, which repeats across the front in a design reminiscent of southwestern handwoven blankets, adds a dramatic accent to the striped back. A slight gathering at the back is cleverly worked into the knit piece, which is further decorated with an added knit belt. A multicolored rib and western-style silver buttons complete the colorful garment.

SIZES

Small (Medium, Large)

Finished measurements: 40 (42, 44)" (101.5, 106.5, 112 cm)

MATERIALS

Tapestry (75% wool, 25% mohair, 50 g = approx. 95 yds/87 m): 2 (2, 3) hanks each of colors A, D, and E; 2 (3, 3) hanks of B; 4 hanks of C

Equivalent yarn: 190 (190, 270) yds (174, 174, 247 m) each of worsted-weight wool in colors A, D, and E; 190 (270, 270) yds (174, 247, 247 m) of B; 380 yds (347 m) of C

Knitting needles: sizes 4 and 6 U.S. (3.25 and 4 mm), 16" (40.5 cm) circular needle in size 5 U.S. (3.75 mm)

Five 1¼" (3 cm) silver buttons

GAUGE

Color pattern with larger needles: 20 sts and 27 rows = 4" (10 cm)

Take time to save time—check your gauge.

PATTERN STITCHES

■ Stockinette Stitch

Row 1 (RS): K all sts.

Row 2: P all sts.

■ 1 x 1 Rib

Row 1 (RS): K1, p1.

Row 2: Work sts as they appear.

■ Color 1 x 1 Rib

Row 1 (RS): With color A, k all sts.

Row 2: With color B, k1, p1.

Row 3: With color C, work sts as they appear.

Row 4: With color D, work as for row 3.

Row 5: With color E, b.o. in 1 x 1 rib.

LEFT FRONT

With larger needles and color E, c.o. 3 sts.

Follow chart for front, inc as shown.

On center front edge, inc 1 st every other row 10 times, then 1 st every row 2 times.

At the same time, on side edge, inc 2 sts every row 8 times, then 1 st every row 4 times; then c.o. an additional 18 (20, 23) sts to give 53 (55, 58) sts.

Cont to work according to chart, until side straight edge meas 7¼ (7½, 7¾)" (18.5, 19, 19.5 cm).

SHAPE ARMHOLE AND NECK according to chart as follows: At armhole edge, b.o. 9 (10, 11) sts, dec 1 st every row 5 times, then 1 st every other row 5 (6, 6) times.

At neck edge, b.o. 1 st every 3rd and 4th row alternately 9 times each to give 16 (16, 18) sts.

Work until armhole meas 11¼ (11½, 11¾)" (28.5, 29, 30 cm).

B.o. 5 (5, 6) sts at armhole edge 2 times; then b.o. rem 6 sts.

Piece should meas 21 (21½, 22)" (53.5, 54.5, 56 cm) from point of bottom to shoulder.

RIGHT FRONT

Work as for left front, but reverse all shaping and patterning.

BACK

With larger needles and color B, c.o. 96 (100, 106) sts and work in stripe patt for 3¼" (8.5 cm), ending with a WSR.

On next row, keeping in patt, work across 33 (35, 36) sts, k2tog over next 30 (30, 34) sts (for gathered belt area), and cont in patt across last 33 (35, 36) sts to give 81 (85, 89) sts.

Cont as est until piece meas 4½" (11.5 cm).

Keeping in stripe patt, work across 33 (35, 36) sts, inc 15 (15, 17) sts evenly over next 15 (15, 17) sts, and cont across last 33 (35, 36) sts in patt to give 96 (100, 106) sts.

Work even until side straight edge meas same as front.

SHAPE ARMHOLE: B.o. 8 (8, 9) sts each side, then 1 st each side every other row 10 (11, 11) times to give 60 (62, 66) sts.

When armhole meas 3¾" (9.5 cm), beg back motif as follows: Work in stripe patt across 29 (30, 32) sts, work motif patt over next 2 sts, work to end in stripe patt.

Cont working in stripe and motif patt according to graph until armhole meas 10¾ (11, 11¼)" (27.5, 28, 28.5 cm).

SHAPE NECK: Work across first 18 (18, 20) sts, b.o. center 24 (26, 26) sts, and work to end.

Working each side sep, b.o. 1 st at each neck edge 2 times to give 16 (16, 18) sts.

When armhole meas 11¼ (11½, 11¾)" (28.5, 29, 30 cm), work shoulder shaping as for front.

BELT

With smaller needles and color A, c.o. 7 sts and work garter st (knit all rows) for 4 rows.

On next row make a buttonhole by b.o. 2 sts in center of row and c.o. 2 sts to replace them on next row.

Cont in garter st until belt meas 3½" (9 cm).

Work another buttonhole, work 3 more rows in garter st, b.o. all sts.

FINISHING

Gently block all pieces.

Sew shoulder and side seams.

With circular needle, p.u. 143 (148, 152) sts around each armhole and work in color 1 x 1 rib patt.

P.u. 163 (171, 181) sts along bottom edge from left front point along back edge to front point.

Work color 1 x 1 rib patt, inc 1 st each side on rows 2, 3, and 4.

For center and neck edge, p.u. 21 sts from point up center slope, pm, 32 (32, 34) sts along center front, pm, 71 (73, 75) sts along V-neck to shoulder, 42 (46, 50) sts around back, 71 (73, 75) sts down V-neck, pm, 32 (32, 34) sts along other center front, pm, and 21 sts down slope to front point.

Markers designate the center front straight edge area.

Work in color 1 x 1 rib patt, inc 1 st on outside of all four markers on rows 2 and 4 of pattern.

At same time on row 2, make 3 buttonholes (one just inside each marker and 1 centered between the two) on right center front straight area.

Complete rib patt.

Sew buttons in place on left center front to correspond to buttonholes.

Sew a button on each side of gathered belt area on back.

Button belt in place.

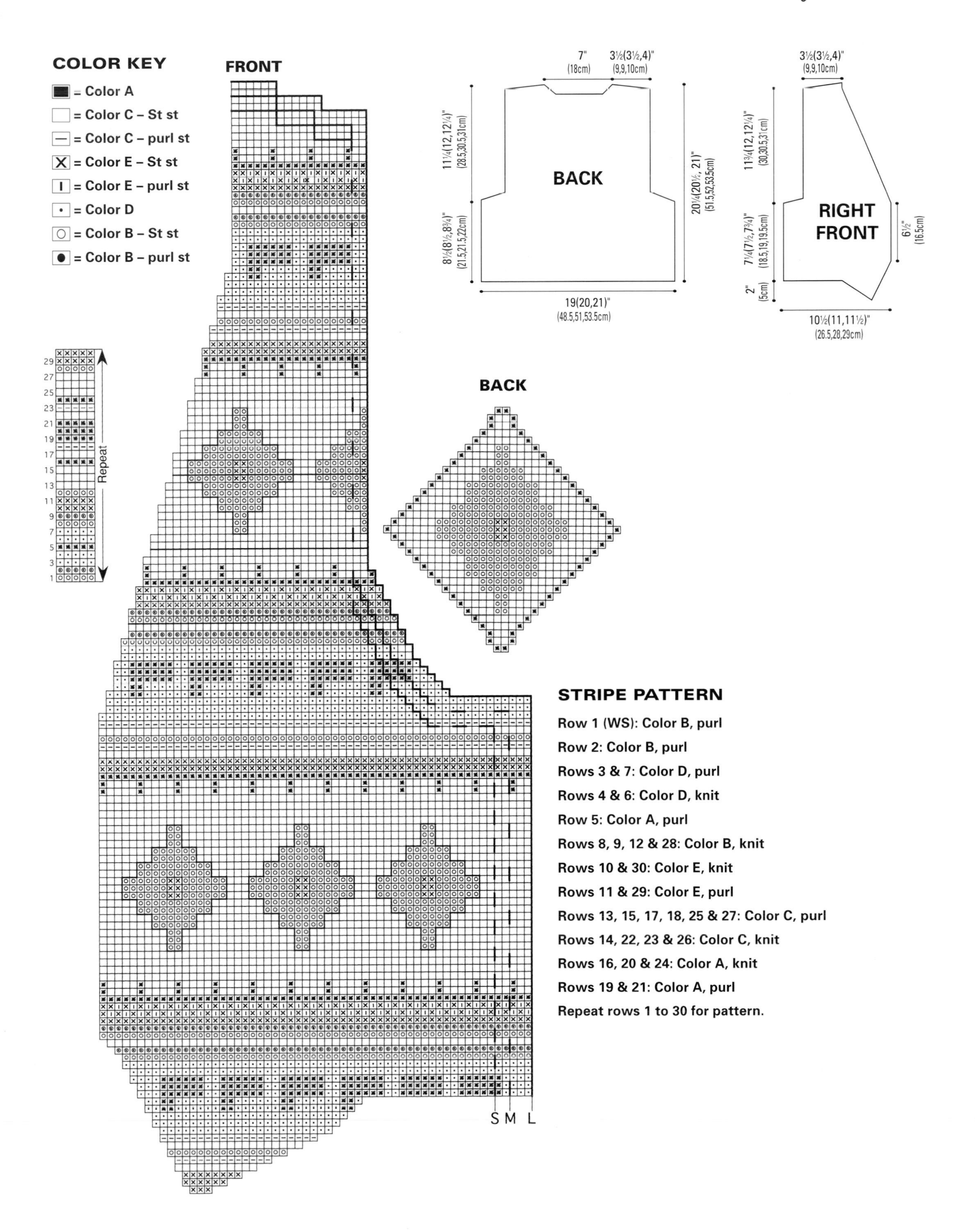

COLOR KEY

- ■ = Color A
- □ = Color C – St st
- — = Color C – purl st
- X = Color E – St st
- I = Color E – purl st
- • = Color D
- ○ = Color B – St st
- ● = Color B – purl st

STRIPE PATTERN

Row 1 (WS): Color B, purl
Row 2: Color B, purl
Rows 3 & 7: Color D, purl
Rows 4 & 6: Color D, knit
Row 5: Color A, purl
Rows 8, 9, 12 & 28: Color B, knit
Rows 10 & 30: Color E, knit
Rows 11 & 29: Color E, purl
Rows 13, 15, 17, 18, 25 & 27: Color C, purl
Rows 14, 22, 23 & 26: Color C, knit
Rows 16, 20 & 24: Color A, knit
Rows 19 & 21: Color A, purl
Repeat rows 1 to 30 for pattern.

Terra-Cotta & Maize Cardigan

design: **Sally Lee**

knitting rating: **Experienced**

photography: **John Goodman**

This classic but colorful cardigan was inspired by the sun-drenched hues of the American southwest. Its delicate panels of lace are knit in a chevron design and are divided by simple Fair Isle color stitchery. For added texture, the edges are worked in simple two-by-two ribs. Mother-of-pearl buttons emphasize the luminescence of the mercerized cotton yarn.

SIZES

Small (Medium, Large)

Finished measurements: 34 (37, 39½)" (86.5, 94, 100.5 cm)

MATERIALS

Newport Light (100% mercerized pima cotton; 50 g = approx. 93 yds/85 m): 6 skeins of color A, 2 skeins of B, 3 skeins each of C and F, 1 skein each of D and E

Equivalent yarn: 500 (525, 560) yds (457, 480, 512 m) of worsted-weight cotton in color A, 165 (175, 185) yds (151, 160, 169 m) of B, 240 (260, 280) yds (219, 238, 256 m) each of C and F, 80 (85, 93) yds (73, 78, 85 m) each of D and E

Knitting needles: sizes 3 and 6 U.S. (3 and 4 mm)

Two small stitch holders

Five ⅞" (2.2 cm) buttons

GAUGE

St st on larger needles: 6 sts and 7 rows = 1" (2.5 cm)

Take time to save time—check your gauge.

PATTERN STITCHES

P2TOG-B: P1 st, sl the st back on left needle, with right needle sl next st over the purled st and off the left needle, and slip the st back to right needle.

SSK: Slip the first and second sts knitwise, one at a time, then insert the tip of the left-hand needle into the fronts of these 2 sts from the left, and k them together.

■ **2 x 2 Rib** (over multiple of 4 sts plus 2)

Row 1: *K2, p2*; rep bet *s, end k2.

Row 2: Work all sts as they appear.

■ **Zigzag Eyelet Pattern** (over multiple of 16 rows and 8 sts plus 6)

Row 1 (RS): K3, *k6, k2tog, yo; rep from *, end k3.

Row 2: P3, *p1, yo, p2tog, p5; rep from *, end p3.

Row 3: K3, *k4, k2tog, yo, k2; rep from *, end k3.

Row 4: P3, *p3, yo, p2tog, p3; rep from *, end p3.

Row 5: K3, *k2, k2tog, yo, k4; rep from *, end k3.

Row 6: P3, *p5, yo, p2tog, p1; rep from *, end p3.

Row 7: K3, *k2tog, yo, k6; rep from *, end k3.

Row 8: P3, *p6, p2tog-b, yo; rep from *, end p3.

Row 9: K3, *k1, yo, ssk, k5; rep from *, end k3.

Row 10: P3, *p4, p2tog-b, yo, p2; rep from *, end p3.

Row 11: K3, *k3, yo, ssk, k3; rep from *, end k3.

Row 12: P3, *p2, p2tog-b, yo, p4; rep from *, end p3.

Row 13: K3, *k5, yo, ssk, k1; rep from *, end k3.

Row 14: P3, *p2tog-b, yo, p6; rep from *, end p3.

Row 15: K all sts.

Row 16: P all sts.

BODY (make in one piece)

With color A and smaller needles, c.o. 214 (230, 246) sts and work back and forth in 2 x 2 rib for ¾" (2 cm).

Buttonhole row (RS only): Work 3 sts, b.o. the next 2 sts, work to end.

Next row: Inc 2 sts to replace the 2 b.o. on previous row.

Work until rib measures 2½" (6.5 cm).

Next row (RS): Work 8 sts and place them on a st holder.

Change to larger needles and work in St st according to chart A until there are 8 sts left on needle; then put them on a st holder.

There should be 198 (214, 230) sts on needle.

Place marker for side seams by working 48 (52, 56) sts, pm, work next 102 (110,

118) sts, pm, work across last 48 (52, 56) sts to end, still working from chart A.

When 10 rows have been completed, work 16 rows zigzag pattern in color F.

Work 10 rows according to chart B, then 16 rows in zigzag pattern in color A.

Cont working in this sequence until 63 (66, 69) rows after rib have been completed.

ARMHOLE SPLIT: Work across until 2 sts before marker, join 2nd ball of yarn, b.o. next 4 sts, work across to 2 sts before next marker, join a 3rd ball of yarn, b.o. the next 4 sts, work to end.

Working with 3 separate pieces, work 1 more row.

Next row: Dec 1 st each side of armhole edge.

Cont working for 43 (46, 49) more rows and beg shaping neck on front edges only: B.o. 4 sts at each neck edge, 3 sts at each neck edge every other row twice, then 1 st every row 4 times.

When decreases have been completed, work 6 more rows and b.o. rem 31 (35, 39) sts.

At the same time, when you begin to shape front neck, work 11 rows on the back following the pattern.

Next row: B.o. center 18 sts for back of neck, then 4 sts from each neck edge every other row twice to give 31 (35, 39) sts.

B.o. all sts.

SLEEVES

With color A and smaller needles, c.o. 38 (40, 42) sts.

Work in 2 x 2 rib for 2¼" (5.5 cm).

In last row of rib, inc 16 (20, 24) sts to give 54 (60, 66) sts.

Change to larger needles and work in St st, starting with 10 rows of chart B; then cont working in sequence as for body.

Work 3 (6, 9) rows; then inc 1 st each edge and cont to do this every 5th row until there are 92 (98, 104) sts on needle.

Work evenly until 17 (17½, 18)" (43, 44.5, 45.5 cm) above rib.

SHAPE CAP: B.o. 3 sts at beg of next 2 rows.

Work 1 more row and b.o. 1 st each edge at beg of next 7 rows.

B.o. all sts.

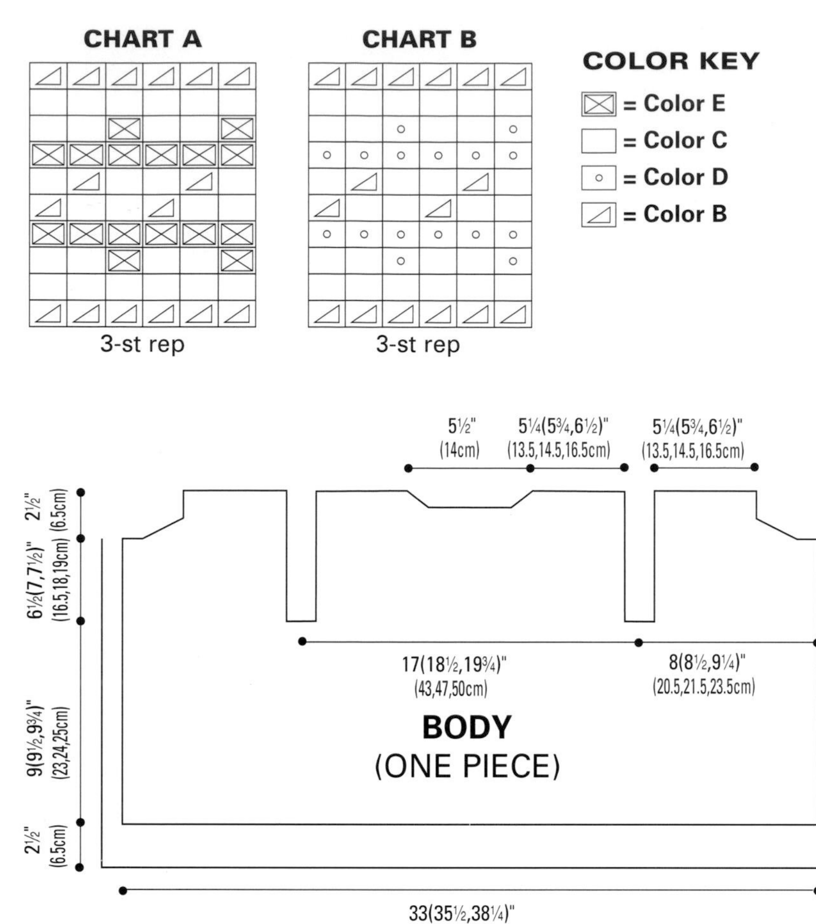

FINISHING

LEFT SIDE: With smaller needles, p.u. the 8 sts from holder and work in 2 x 2 rib until band measures 1" (2.5 cm) shorter than entire front.

Put sts back on st holder.

RIGHT SIDE: With smaller needles, p.u. 8 sts from holder and work 2 x 2 rib until right band measures same as left band, making 3 more buttonholes evenly spaced.

Put 8 sts back on st holder.

Sew shoulder seams and set in sleeves.

Sew underarm seams.

With smaller needles and color A, p.u. 8 sts from first st holder, 15 sts from front neck, 30 sts from back neck, 15 sts from other front neck, and 8 sts from the 2nd st holder (76 sts in all).

Work in 2 x 2 rib for ½" (1.5 cm) and make 5th buttonhole.

Cont in rib until neck band measures 1" (2.5 cm).

B.o. all sts.

Stitch down front bands.

Sew on 5 buttons.

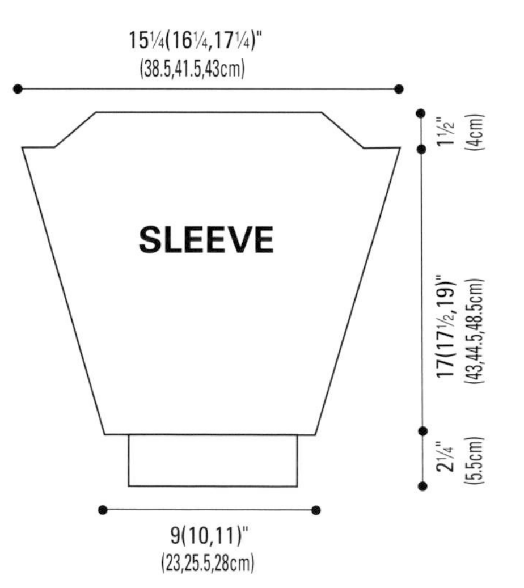

Adamsville Arabesque

design: **Sally Lee**

knitting rating: **Experienced**

photography: **Philip Newton**

Blankets woven in the western United States during the 1930s often combined geometric and plaid motifs in one piece. This colorful but sophisticated shawl collar jacket was derived from these beautiful textiles. To give the jacket a very tailored appearance, the collar is worked in stockinette stitch rather than a more conventional rib.

SIZES

Small (Medium, Large)

Finished measurements: 46 (48, 50)" (117, 122, 127 cm)

MATERIALS

Paisley (50% rayon, 50% wool; 50 g = approx. 95 yds/87 m): 13 hanks of color A (MC), 4 hanks of B, 1 hank of C, 7 hanks of D

Equivalent yarn: 1200 (1220, 1235) yds (1097, 1115, 1129 m) of bulky/worsted-weight wool in color A (MC); 320 (360, 380) yds (293, 329, 347 m) of B; 95 yds (87 m) of C; 620 (645, 665) yds (567, 590, 608 m) of D

Knitting needles: sizes 5, 8, and 9 U.S. (3.75, 5, and 5.5 mm)

Stitch holders

Five 1¼" (3 cm) buttons

GAUGE

St st on larger needles: 18 sts and 22 rows = 4" (10 cm)

Take time to save time—check your gauge.

PATTERN STITCHES

■ Stockinette Stitch

Row 1 (RS): K all sts.

Row 2: P all sts.

■ 2 x 2 Ribbing

Row 1 (RS): K2, p2.

Row 2: Work sts as they appear.

POCKET BACKS (make 2)

With color A and largest needles, c.o. 22 sts.

Work in St st for 6" (15 cm).

Place on holder.

BODY (make in one piece)

HEM: With medium-sized needles and color A, c.o. 216 (232, 248) sts.

Work in St st until piece meas 1½" (4 cm).

FRONT FACINGS: Next row, c.o. 10 sts at the beg and end of the row to give 236 (252, 268) sts.

Change to largest needles; then follow graph for color changes and buttonhole placement.

Work buttonholes as follows (WS): Work to last 18 sts.

B.o. next 4 sts, work next 8 sts, b.o. next 4 sts, work 2 sts.

Next row: C.o. 4 sts over each b.o. st on previous row.

POCKET ROW: Work 31 (35, 39) sts, place the next 22 sts on holder, work 22 sts of pocket back, work to last 53 (57, 61) sts, place next 22 sts on holder, work 22 sts of pocket back, work to end.

Follow graph for color changes, neck, and armhole shaping.

SLEEVES

With smallest needles and color A, c.o. 44 (46, 48) sts.

Work 2 x 2 rib for 5" (12.5 cm).

In last row inc 6 (6, 8) sts evenly across.

Change to largest needles and work in St st, following graph for color changes and shaping.

POCKET TOPS (make 2)

With smallest needles and color A, p.u. 22 sts from holder and work in 2 x 2 rib for 1" (2.5 cm).

B.o. all sts.

Sew pocket backs and tops carefully in place.

FINISHING

Sew shoulder seams.

Turn up hem and stitch down.

Sew collar tog at center back.

Set in neckline.

Set in sleeves and sew underarm seams.

Stitch down front neckline and facing.

Sew on buttons.

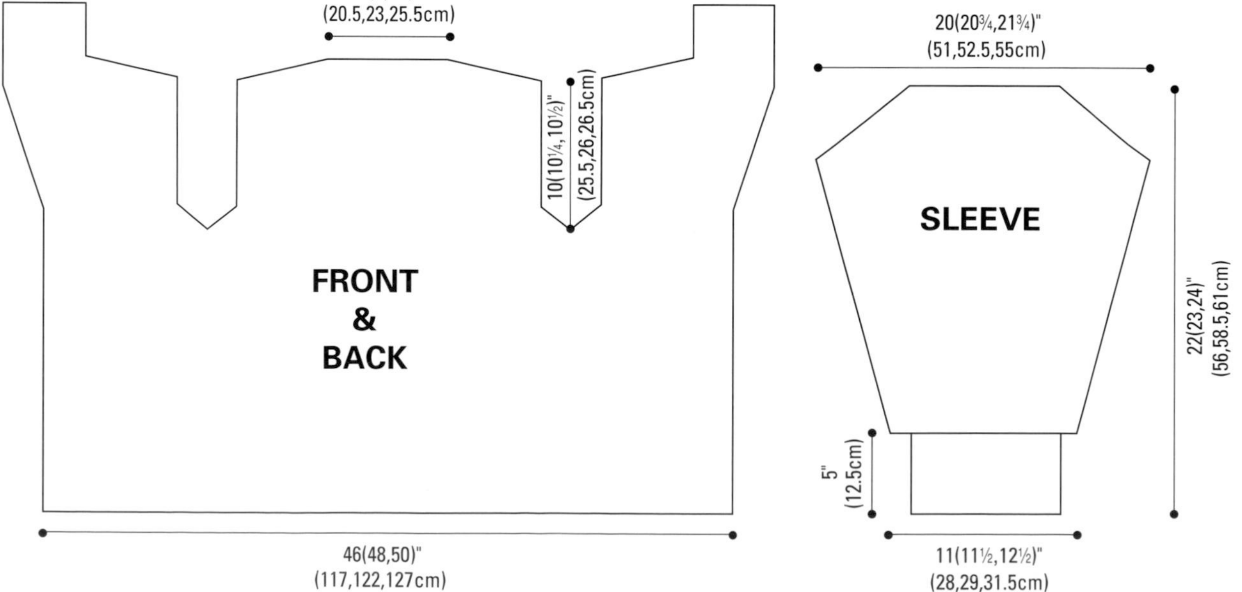

SLEEVE

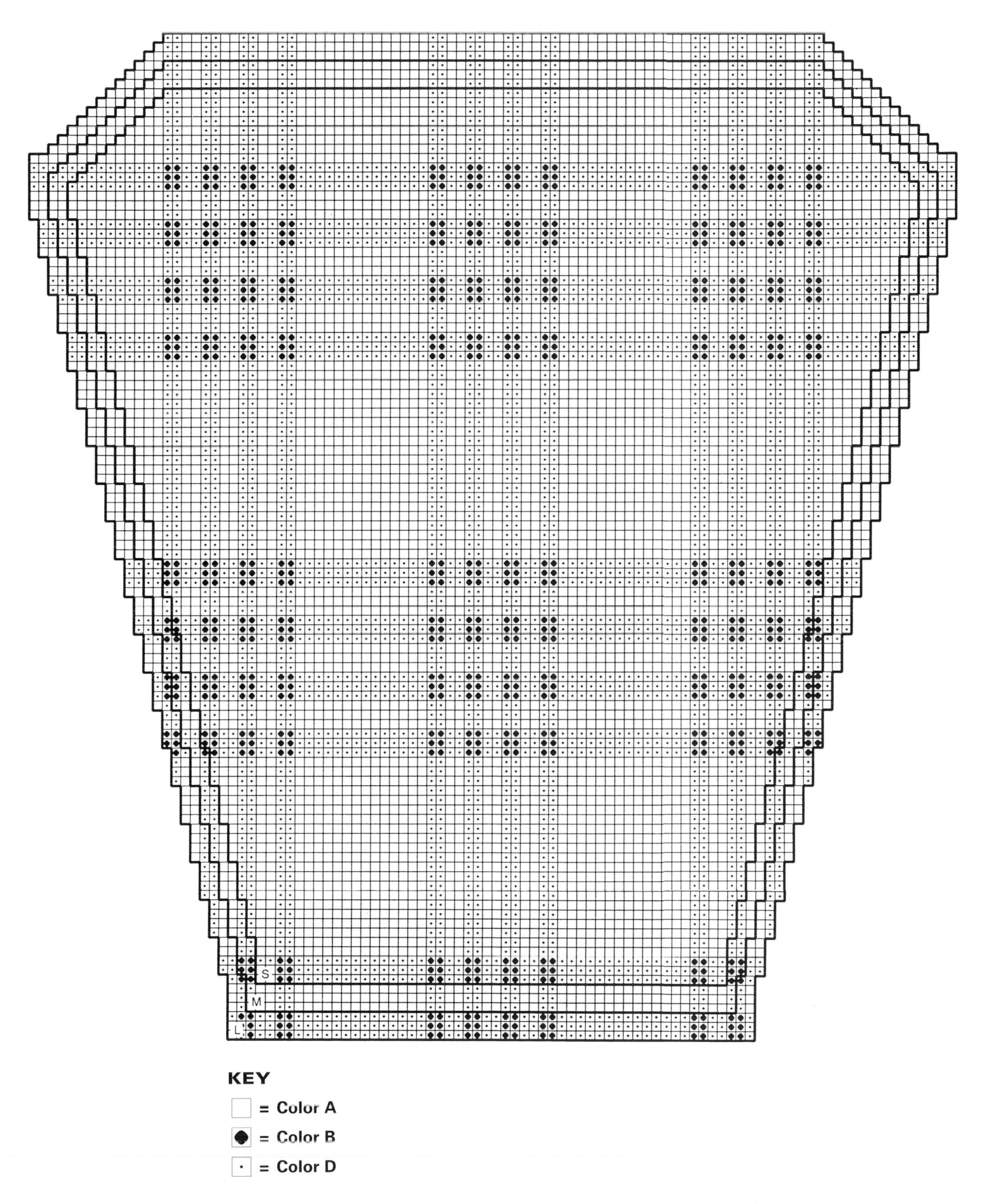

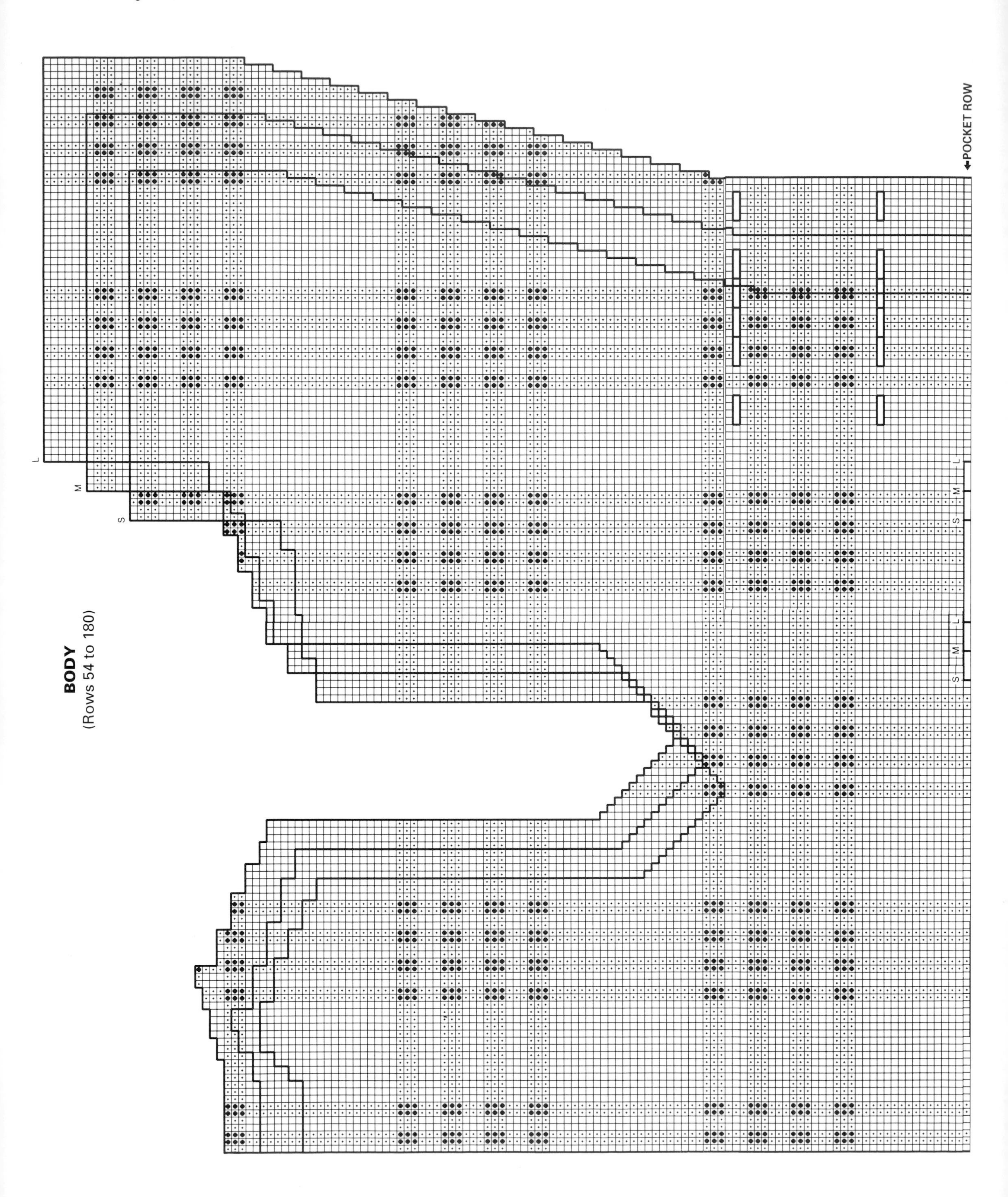

BODY
(Rows 54 to 180)
POCKET ROW
L
M
S

BODY
(Rows 1 to 53)

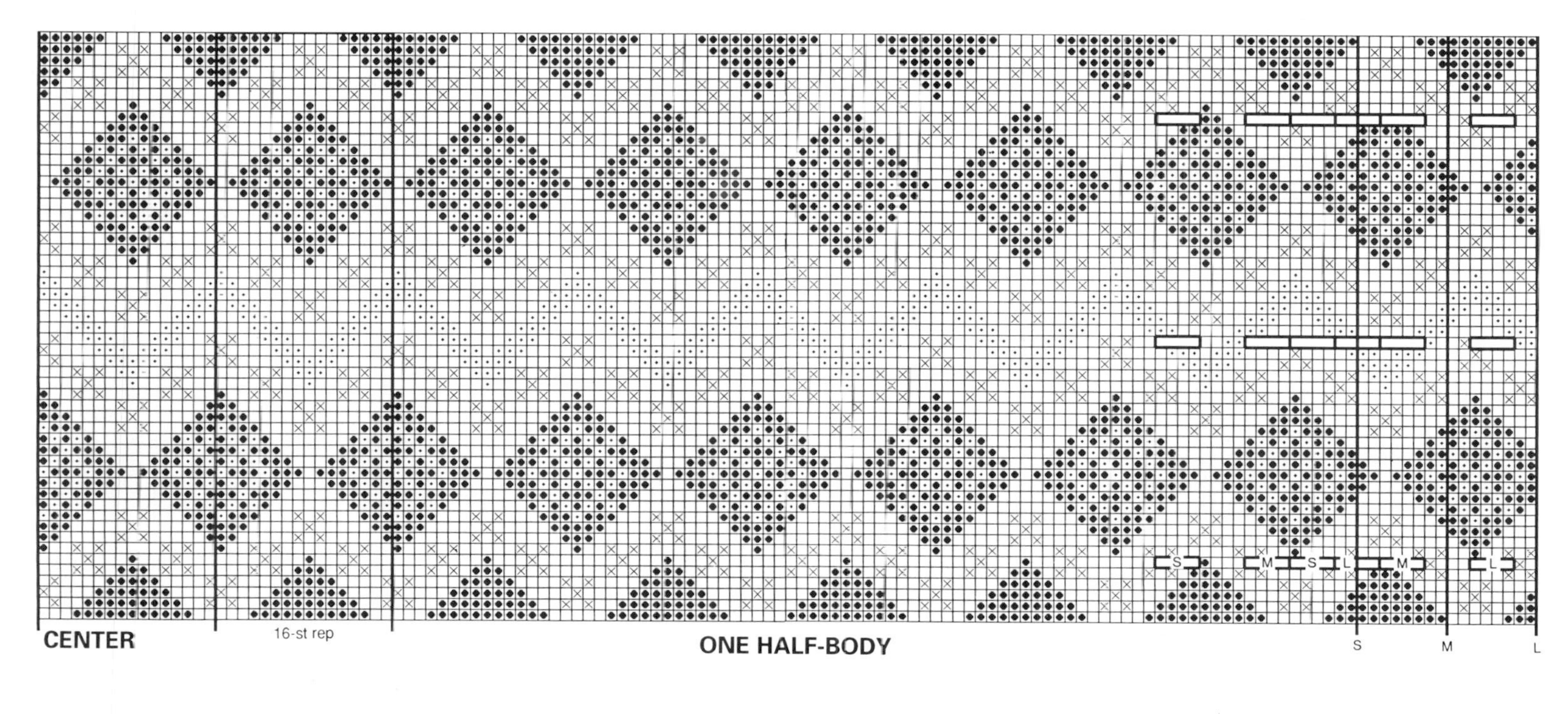

KEY

= Color A

= Color B

= Color C

= Color D

= 4-st buttonhole

NOTE: *For body chart, work rows 1 to 53 as follows: work to center; then cont working 16-st rep to end of row, ending with same st as you began and omitting buttonholes. Work rows 54 to 180 as follows: work to center; then work chart in reverse, beg at center, from left to right, omitting buttonholes.*

Prince of Wales Blazer

design: **Sally Lee**
knitting Rating: **Experienced**
photography: **Peter Ogilvie**

The traditional Prince of Wales tartan plaid is asymmetrically exploded onto the body of this striking mohair cardigan. The sleeves are worked in a miniature overall houndstooth pattern, and two-color corrugated ribs frame the design and pockets. This is a superb cardigan for city or country.

SIZES

Small (Medium, Large)

Finished measurements: 42 (45, 48)" (106.5, 114.5, 122 cm)

MATERIALS

La Gran (74% mohair, 13% wool, 13% nylon; 1½ oz = approx. 90 yds/82 m): 12 skeins of color A; 3 skeins of B; 2 skeins of C; 1 skein of D

Equivalent yarn: 1000 (1040, 1080) yds (914, 951, 988 m) of bulky brushed mohair in color A, 230 (240, 270) yds (210, 219, 247 m) of B, 160 (170, 180) yds (146, 155, 165 m) of C, 90 yds (82 m) of D

Knitting needles: 36" (91.5 cm) circular needles in sizes 6 and 9 U.S. (4 and 5.5 mm)

Stitch holders

Five 1" (2.5 cm) buttons

Shoulder pads

GAUGE

St st on larger needles: 16 sts and 20 rows = 4" (10 cm)

Take time to save time—check your gauge.

PATTERN STITCHES

■ **Two-Color Rib** (over multiple of 4 sts plus 2)

Row 1 (RS): K2 in color A, p2 in color B, carrying yarn behind sts. (The first and last 2 sts must be in color A.)

Row 2: Work all sts as they appear.

POCKET BACKS (make 2)

With larger needles and color A, c.o. 20 sts.

Work in St st for 5" (12.5 cm) and place sts on holder.

BODY (make in one piece)

With color A and smaller needles, c.o. 158 (174, 186) sts.

Work in 2-color rib for 3" (7.5 cm), inc 2 (0, 2) sts in last row to give 160 (176, 188) sts.

Change to larger needles and work in St st according to graph.

POCKET ROW (row 31 (33, 35)): Work 9 (13, 17) sts, place next 20 sts on holder, work until 29 (33, 37) sts rem, place next 20 sts on holder, work to end.

Next row: Put pocket backs in place of sts placed on holders in previous row.

Work until row 76 (73, 72) of graph and b.o. for V-neck shaping as follows: B.o. 1 st each neck edge every 5th row 9 (11) times for the small and medium sizes and every 4th row 14 times for the large size.

At the same time, split work for armhole openings at row 78 (79, 80) by working across 37 (40, 43) sts, join a 2nd ball of yarn, work across next 84 (90, 96) sts, join another ball of yarn, work to end.

Fronts: Keep armhole edges straight and cont neck dec.

When rows 126 (129, 132) have been completed, b.o. rem 28 (30, 31) sts for shoulders.

Cont on back section until row 121 (124, 127); then b.o for back neck by working across 37 (39, 41) sts, join 2nd ball of yarn, b.o. center 10 (12, 14) sts, and work to end.

B.o. at each neck edge every other row 4 (4, 5) sts once and 5 sts once.

B.o. rem 28 (30, 31) sts for shoulders.

SLEEVES

With color A and smaller needles, c.o. 30 (34, 34) sts.

Work in 2-color rib for 2½" (6.5 cm), inc 16 (14, 16) sts evenly across last rib row to give 46 (48, 50) sts.

Change to larger needles and work in St st according to graph, inc 1 st each end every 4th row 15 (16, 17) times to give 76 (80, 84) sts.

When piece meas 17 (17½, 18)" (43, 44.5, 45.5 cm), b.o. all sts.

FINISHING

With smaller needles, p.u. 20 sts from holders and work 2-color rib over 18 sts on pocket tops (dec 2 sts on first row) for 2½" (6.5 cm).

B.o. all sts and sew pocket tops and backs into place.

Sew shoulder seams.

With smaller circular needle, color A, and RS facing, p.u. 84 (87, 88) sts from right front to beg of V-shaping, 58 (62, 67) sts to shoulder, 22 (24, 28) sts around back neck, 58 (62, 67) sts down from shoulder to V-shaping, and 84 (87, 88) sts to bottom to give 306 (322, 338) sts.

Work in 2-color rib for 4 rows.

BUTTONHOLE ROW (RS): work 6 (5, 6) sts, b.o. 2 sts *work 17 (18, 18), b.o. 2 sts*; rep bet *s 3 more times.

Row 5: Work as est, c.o. 2 sts to replace b.o. sts on previous row.

After 8 rows total have been worked, b.o. in color A.

Set in sleeves and sew underarm and side seams.

Sew on buttons.

SHOULDER PADS (make 2): With larger needles, c.o. 24 sts and work St st for 6" (15 cm).

B.o. all sts.

Fold diagonally over foam pad and sew edges; tack in place.

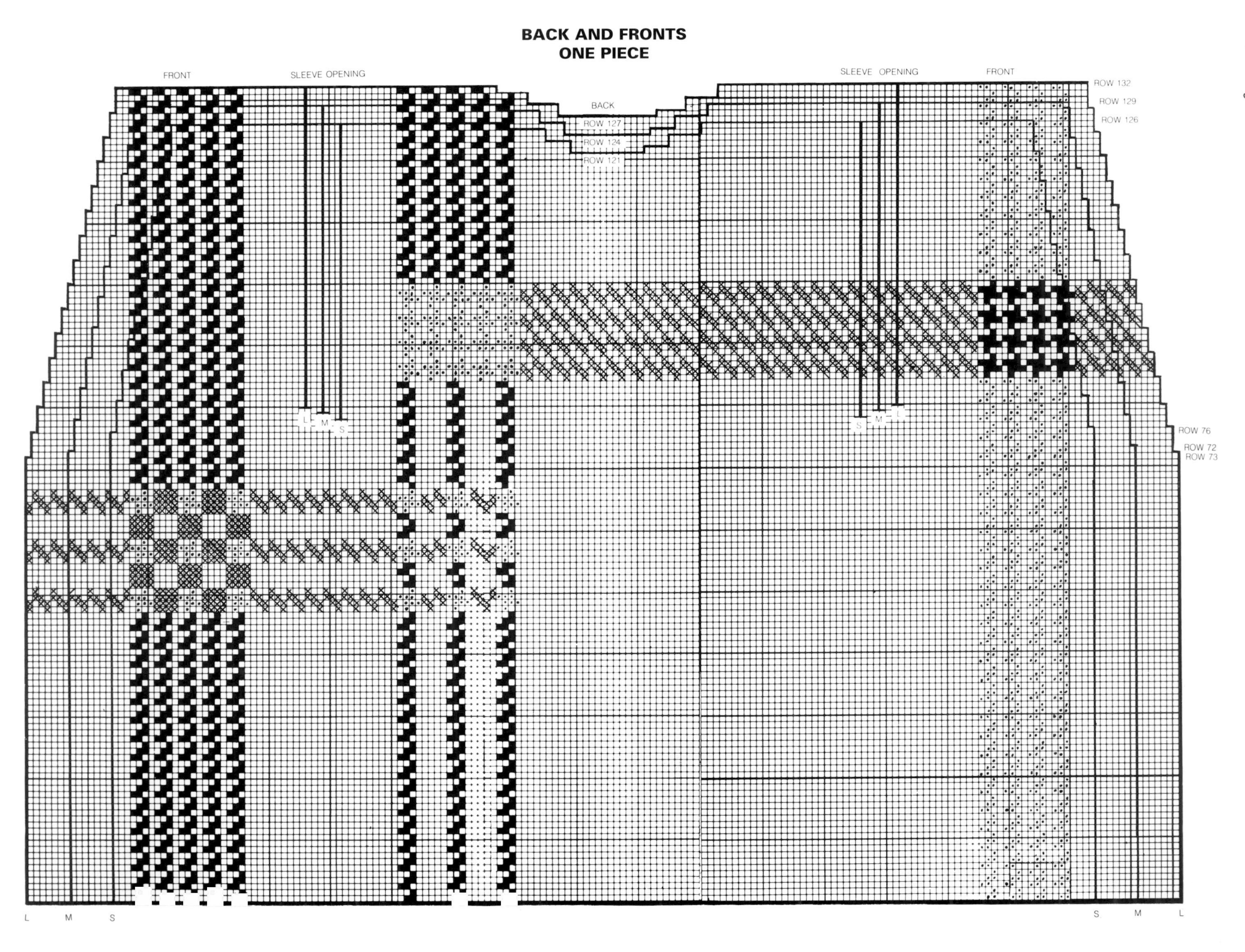
BACK AND FRONTS
ONE PIECE
FRONT
SLEEVE OPENING
BACK
ROW 127
ROW 124
ROW 121
SLEEVE OPENING
FRONT
ROW 132
ROW 129
ROW 126
ROW 76
ROW 72
ROW 73
L
M
S
S
M
L

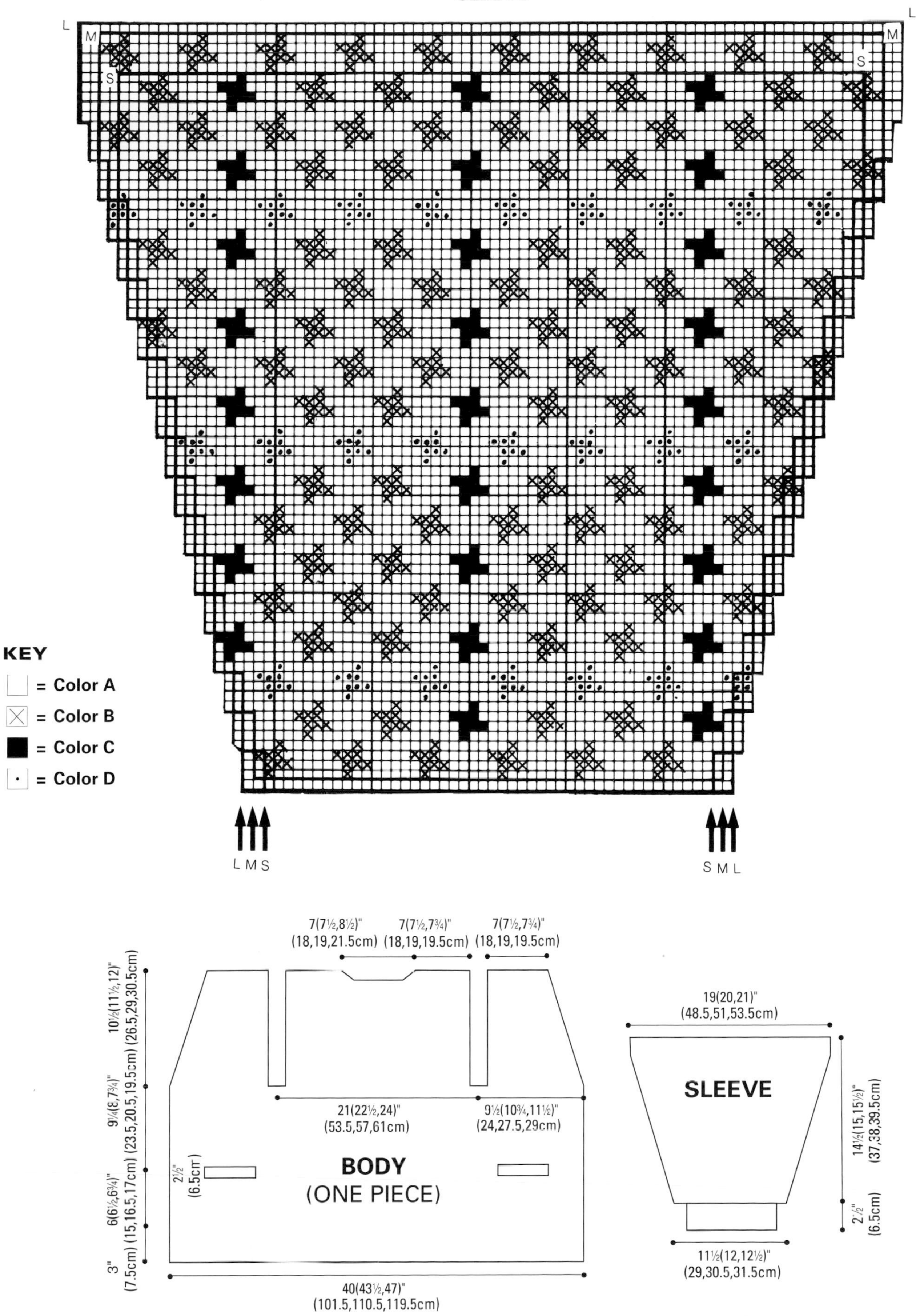
SLEEVE
L
M
S
L
M
S
KEY
= Color A
= Color B
= Color C
= Color D
L M S
S M L
7(7½,8½)" (18,19,21.5cm)
7(7½,7¾)" (18,19,19.5cm)
7(7½,7¾)" (18,19,19.5cm)
10½(11½,12)" (26.5,29,30.5cm)
9¼(8,7¾)" (23.5,20.5,19.5cm)
6(6½,6¾)" (15,16.5,17cm)
3" (7.5cm)
21(22½,24)" (53.5,57,61cm)
9½(10¾,11½)" (24,27.5,29cm)
2½" (6.5cm)
BODY
(ONE PIECE)
40(43½,47)" (101.5,110.5,119.5cm)
19(20,21)" (48.5,51,53.5cm)
SLEEVE
14½(15,15½)" (37,38,39.5cm)
2½" (6.5cm)
11½(12,12½)" (29,30.5,31.5cm)

5

A Journey to Great Britain

American knitters frequently look to the knitting traditions of Great Britain for stimulation and inspiration. The history of knitting in England is like that of no other country. There, knitwear has survived in portraiture and flourished in life, and many British museums have pieces of knitted fabric in their collections. In Great Britain it seems that everyone knows how to knit. It's this common thread winding through the British culture that drew our cameras to the pastoral settings of Northumberland. With its muted undertones of moss and bracken, the British countryside makes a beautiful backdrop for the intricately designed American knitwear in this chapter.

The Sheep Dog Trail

Photographed in the courtyard of Eglingham Hall Farm in Eglingham, Northumberland, England

designs: **Susan Mills** (striped pullover)
Linda Pratt (solid pullover)
Susan Mills (ombre pullover)

knitting ratings: **Intermediate** (striped pullover)
Beginner (solid and ombre pullovers)

photography: **Philip Newton**

This trio of pullovers was designed for the casual lifestyle Americans so enjoy. Very simple stockinette and reverse stockinette stitches are used in all the sweaters, and minimal finishing is necessary.

The natural-colored yarn used in both the solid and the striped sweaters is a very thick and very thin wool yarn, which provides interest without adding difficulty to the knitting. In the solid pullover, the uneven texture is accented by changing from stockinette to reverse stockinette stitch whenever a thick spot in the yarn is encountered. In the striped pullover, it is combined with two different colors of a thick, single-ply yarn to produce narrow, wavy stripes. A two-color corrugated rib accents the collar, cuffs, and hem.

In the ombre pullover, classic brushed mohair is double stranded with a thick-and-thin two-color nub yarn. The ombre effect is achieved by changing the mohair to create a gradual shift in color. Make sure to choose four distinct shades—light, medium, dark, and very dark—or the desired effect won't be created.

Striped Pullover

SIZES

Small (Medium, Large)

Finished measurements: 40 (48, 56)" (101.5, 122, 142 cm)

MATERIALS

Montera (50% llama, 50% wool; 100 g = approx. 128 yds/117 m): 2 (2, 3) skeins each of colors A and B; Kilimanjaro (90% wool, 10% nylon; 50 g = approx. 77 yds/70 m): 4 (4, 5) skeins

Equivalent yarn: 254 (254, 381) yds (232, 232, 348 m) of bulky wool in each of two colors; 308 (308, 385) yds (282, 282, 352 m) of novelty thick-and-thin wool

Knitting needles: size 10 U.S. (6 mm), 16" (40.5 cm) circular knitting needle in size 10 U.S. (6 mm)

GAUGE

2 x 2 corrugated rib with larger needles: 16 sts = 4" (10 cm)

St st with larger needles: 12 sts = 4" (10 cm)

Take time to save time—check your gauge.

PATTERN STITCHES

■ **2 x 2 Corrugated Rib** (over multiple of 4 sts)

Row 1 (RS): *K2 with color B, p2 with color A; rep from *.

Row 2: *K2 with color A, p2 with color B; rep from *.

BACK

With color A, c.o. 80 (96, 112) sts.

Work 2 x 2 corrugated rib with colors A and B for 3" (7.5 cm).

With color A, work dec row as follows: *K2, k2tog; rep from * across row to give 60 (72, 84) sts.

With color A, p 1 row.

Beg stripe pattern: *With Kilimanjaro, k 2 rows; with color B, k 1 row, p 1 row; with Kilimanjaro, k 2 rows; with color A, k 1 row, p 1 row; rep from * for stripe sequence.

Work in stripe sequence until back meas 25 (27, 29)" (63.5, 68.5, 73.5 cm).

B.o. all sts.

FRONT

Work as for back until piece meas 2" (5 cm) less than length of back.

SHAPE NECK: Maintaining est stripe patt, work across 20 (26, 32) sts, join another ball of yarn, b.o. center 20 sts, and work across rem 20 (26, 32) sts.

Working each shoulder sep, b.o. 1 st at each neck edge every other row twice to give 18 (24, 30) sts rem on each shoulder.

When piece meas same length as back, b.o. all sts.

SLEEVES

With color A, c.o. 32 (36, 36) sts.

Work in 2 x 2 corrugated rib with colors A and B for 3" (7.5 cm).

With color A, work dec row as follows: *K2, k2tog; rep from * across row to give 24 (27, 27) sts.

With color A, p 1 row.

Beg stripe patt as for back, and at the same time, inc 1 st each edge every 4 rows 15 (15, 17) times to give 54 (57, 61) sts.

When sleeve meas 15 (16, 17)" (38, 40.5, 43 cm), b.o. all sts.

FINISHING

Sew shoulder seams.

With circular needle and A, p.u. 60 (64, 68) sts around neck.

Work 2 x 2 corrugated rib for 2" (5 cm).

With color A, b.o. all sts loosely.

Set in sleeves.

Sew side and sleeve seams.

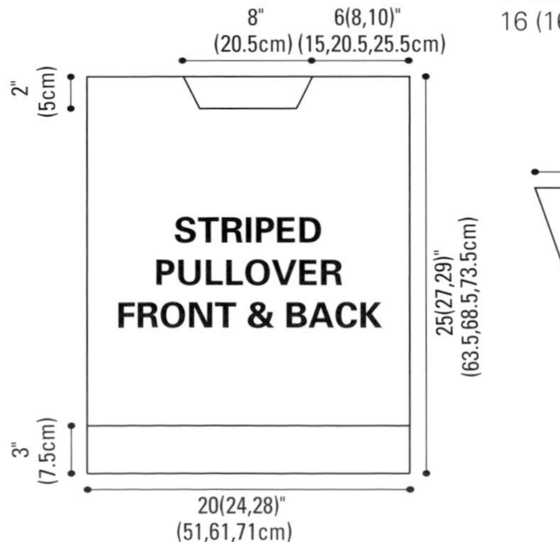

Textured Solid Pullover

SIZES

Small (Medium, Large)

Finished measurements: 43½ (52½, 61)" (110.5, 133.5, 155 cm)

MATERIALS

La Gran (74% mohair, 13% wool, 13% nylon; 1½ oz = approx. 90 yds/82 m): 8 (9, 10) skeins; Kilimanjaro (90% wool, 10% nylon; 50 g = approx. 77 yds/70 m): 10 (11, 12) skeins

Equivalent yarn: 720 (810, 900) yds (658, 741, 823 m) of brushed bulky mohair; 720 (810, 900) yds (658, 741, 823 m) of novelty thick-and-thin wool

Knitting needles: size 10½ U.S. (7 mm), 16" (40.5 cm) circular needle in size 10½ U.S. (7 mm)

GAUGE

Patt st on larger needles: 11 sts and 16 rows = 4" (10 cm)

Take time to save time—check your gauge.

PATTERN STITCHES

■ **Naturally Textured Stitch**

With one strand of each yarn held tog, work in St st until you reach a "bump" in the Kilimanjaro. Work the sts through the "bump" in rev St st. When the yarn becomes thinner again, work in St st. Should your work beg to show an undesired pattern, join another skein of the novelty yarn and alternate every other row.

BACK

With 2 strands of the mohair, c.o. 60 (72, 84) sts.

Change to one strand of each yarn and work in naturally textured stitch until piece meas 16 (16½, 17)" (40.5, 42, 43 cm).

18(19,20)" (45.5,48.5,51cm)

STRIPED PULLOVER SLEEVE

15(16,17)" (38,40.5,43cm)

8" (20.5cm)

Mark for armholes.

Cont until piece meas 25 (26, 27)" (63.5, 66, 68.5 cm).

B.o. all sts.

FRONT

Work as for back until piece meas 23½(24½, 25½)" (59.5, 62, 64.5 cm).

SHAPE NECK: Work across 22 (27, 33) sts, place center 16 (18, 18) sts on holder, join a double strand of yarn, and work rem 22 (27, 33) sts.

Working each shoulder sep, b.o. 1 st at each neck edge every other row 2 (3, 3) times to give 20 (24, 30) sts rem on each shoulder.

When front meas same length as back, b.o. all sts.

SLEEVES

With 2 strands of mohair, c.o. 34 (36, 36) sts.

Change to one strand of each yarn.

Work in naturally textured stitch, inc 1 st each side every 6th row 8 (9, 12) times to give 50 (54, 60) sts.

When piece meas 16 (17, 17)" (40.5, 43, 43 cm), b.o. all sts.

FINISHING

Sew shoulder seams.

With RS facing and circular needle, p.u. 38 (42, 46) sts around neck.

Work in naturally textured stitch for 3½" (9 cm).

B.o. all sts loosely.

Set in sleeves.

Sew side and sleeve seams.

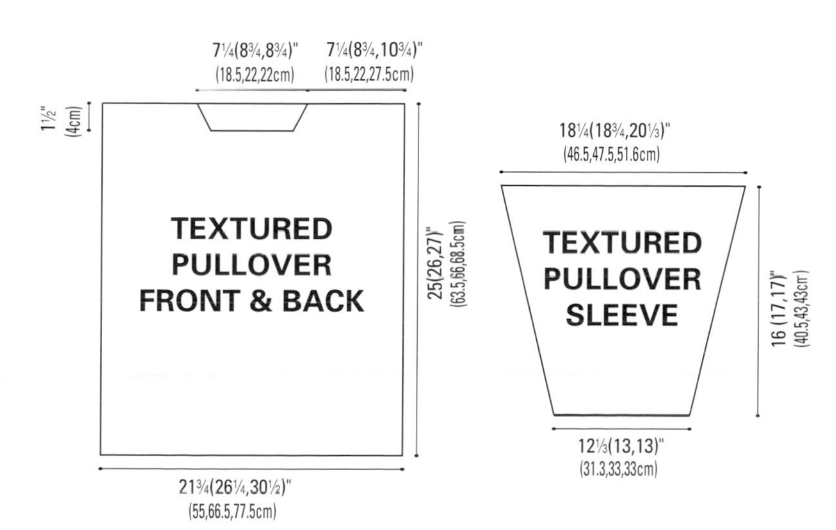

Ombre Pullover

SIZES

Small (Medium, Large, Extra Large)

Finished measurements: 40 (44, 48, 52)" (101.5, 112, 122, 132 cm)

MATERIALS

La Gran (74% mohair, 13% wool, 13% nylon; 1½ oz = approx. 90 yds/82 m): 5 (5, 6, 6) balls of #6575; 4 (5, 5, 5) balls of #6587; 2 (2, 2, 3) balls of #6591; 1 (2, 2, 2) balls of #6513; Granite (100% cotton; 100 g = approx. 220 yds/201 m): 4 (4, 5, 5) skeins of #5573

Equivalent yarn: 450 (450, 540, 540) yds (411, 411, 494, 494 m) of light-colored brushed bulky mohair; 360 (450, 450, 450) yds (329, 411, 411, 411 m) of medium-colored brushed bulky mohair; 180 (180, 180, 270) yds (165, 165, 165, 247 m) of dark-colored brushed bulky mohair; 90 (180, 180, 180) yds (82, 165, 165, 165 m) of very dark-colored brushed bulky mohair; 880 (880, 1100, 1100) yds (805, 805, 1006, 1006 m) of novelty seed cotton yarn

Knitting needles: sizes 9 and 10 U.S. (5.5 and 6 mm), 16" (40.5 cm) circular knitting needle in size 9 U.S. (5.5 mm)

GAUGE

Rev St st with larger needles: 13 sts and 18 rows = 4" (10 cm)

Take time to save time—check your gauge.

PATTERN STITCHES

■ **Stockinette Stitch**

Row 1 (RS): K all sts.

Row 2: P all sts.

Reverse Stockinette Stitch (RSS)

Row 1 (RS): P all sts.

Row 2: K all sts.

NOTE: *Use two strands for each color as follows.*

Color A = 1 strand La Gran 6575 and 1 strand Granite

Color B = 1 strand La Gran 6587 and 1 strand Granite

Color C = 1 strand La Gran 6591 and 1 strand Granite

Color D = 1 strand La Gran 6513 and 1 strand Granite

BACK

With smaller needles and color A, c.o. 65 (72, 78, 85) sts.

Work in St st for 1½" (4 cm).

Change to larger needles and work in RSS and color A for 8 (12, 8, 10) rows.

Cont in RSS as follows: *4 rows color B, 2 rows color C, 2 rows color D, 2 rows color C, 4 rows color B, 8 rows color A.

Rep from * 5 (5, 6, 6) times total, end last rep with 8 (11, 8, 10) rows of color A.

Next row: B.o. 19 (22, 24, 27) sts, work center 27 (28, 30, 31) sts and place on holder for neck, b.o. rem 19 (22, 24, 27) sts.

FRONT

Work as for back until 0 (3, 0, 2) rows of last rep of color A have been completed.

SHAPE NECK: Work across 22 (25, 27, 30) sts, place center 21 (22, 24, 25) sts on holder; then join color A and work across rem 22 (25, 27, 30) sts.

Working each shoulder sep, b.o. 1 st at each neck edge every other row 3 times to give 19 (22, 24, 27) sts rem on each shoulder.

When front meas same length as back, b.o. rem sts.

SLEEVES

With smaller needles, c.o. 26 (26, 29, 29) sts.

Work in St st for 1½" (4 cm).

Change to larger needles and work in RSS and color A for 6 (8, 10, 12) rows.

Work RSS stripe sequence as for back 3 times, end last rep with 6 (8, 10, 12) rows of color A, and at the same time, inc 1 st each edge every 4 rows 14 (13, 11, 14) times, then every 6 rows 2 (3, 5, 4) times to give 58 (58, 61, 65) sts.

When sleeve meas 15½ (16½, 17¼, 18¼)" (39.5, 42, 43, 46.5 cm), b.o. all sts.

FINISHING

Sew shoulder seams.

With RS facing and circular needle, p.u. 27 (28, 30, 31) sts from back neck holder, 7 sts from side of front neck, 21 (22, 23, 24) sts from front neck holder, and 7 sts from side of front neck to give 62 (64, 67, 69) sts.

Work in St st for 3" (7.5 cm).

B.o. all sts loosely.

Set in sleeves.

Sew side and sleeve seams.

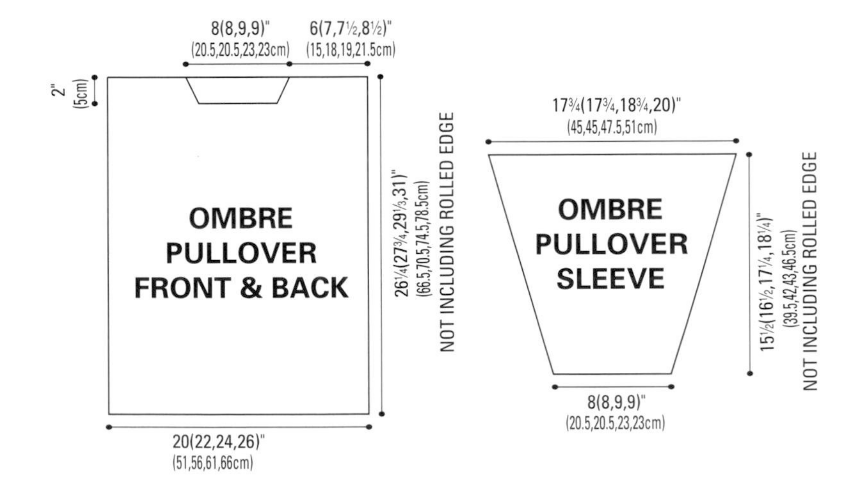

The Ladies of Chillingham Castle

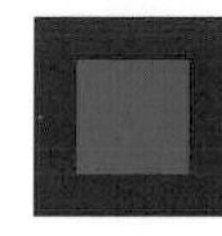

Photographed on the grounds of Chillingham Castle, Northumberland, England

designs: **Susan Mills** (pullover), **Kristin Nicholas** (cardigan)
knitting ratings: **Experienced** (pullover), **Beginner** (cardigan)
photography: **Philip Newton**

The moss, bracken, and heather colors of Great Britain inspired this mohair duo. The colorful pullover features a different colorwork pattern on each piece of the sweater: the front is a derivation of a classic British argyle, and the edges are trimmed in a multicolored garter stitch rib.

The cardigan is very easy to knit, with the main body worked completely in reverse stockinette stitch. A border of large nine-by-nine rib finishes the edges, and two inset pockets add convenience and versatility.

Argyle Pullover

SIZES

One size

Finished measurement: 47" (119.5 cm)

MATERIALS

La Gran (74% mohair, 13% wool, 13% nylon; 1½ oz = approx. 90 yds/82 m): 2 skeins each of colors A, D, E, and F; 4 skeins each of B and C

Equivalent yarn: 180 yds (165 m) each of bulky brushed mohair in colors A, D, E, and F; 360 yds (329 m) each of B and C

Knitting needles in size 9 U.S. (5.5 mm), 16" (40.5 cm) circular knitting needle in size 9 U.S. (5.5 mm)

GAUGE

St st with larger needles: 10 sts = 3" (7.5 cm)

NOTE: *It is very important that your gauge remain consistent throughout the sweater. Knit a swatch for each sweater piece and adjust your needle size accordingly.*

PATTERN STITCHES

See charts.

BACK

With smaller needles and color B, c.o. 74 sts and work rib as follows:

Row 1 (RS): K2 with color B, *k3 with color D, k3 with color B; rep from *, end last rep k2 with color B.

Row 2: P2 with color B, *p3 with color D, p3 with color B; rep from *, end p2 with color B.

Rep these 2 rows, changing color D every 2 rows to colors E, C, A, and F in that order until rib meas 3½" (9 cm).

Inc 4 sts across last row of rib to give 78 sts.

Change to larger needles and work diamond chart for back.

When piece meas 30" (76 cm), b.o. all sts.

FRONT

Work as for back, except work argyle chart.

When piece meas 28" (71 cm), shape neck: Keeping in pattern, b.o. center 24 sts.

Working each side sep, b.o. 1 st at neck edge every other row 3 times to give 24 sts rem for each shoulder.

When front meas same as back, b.o. all sts.

SLEEVE

With smaller needles, c.o. 32 sts and work rib as for back for 3" (7.5 cm).

Change to needles sized to obtain gauge and beg working appropriate chart.

Keeping in patt, inc 1 st each side every 3 rows 20 times to give 72 sts.

When each sleeve meas 18" (45.5 cm), b.o. all sts.

FINISHING

Sew right shoulder seam.

With smaller needles, p.u. 62 sts around neck with color B and work rib as for back.

Sew neck and left shoulder seam.

Sew side and sleeve seams.

Cardigan

SIZES

Extra Small (Small, Medium, Large)

Finished measurements: 36 (42, 48, 54)" (91.5, 106.5, 122, 137 cm)

MATERIALS

La Gran (74% mohair, 13% wool, 13% nylon; 1½ oz = approx. 90 yds/82 m): 10 (11, 11, 12) balls

Equivalent yarn: 900 (950, 1000, 1100) yds (823, 869, 914, 1006 m) of brushed bulky mohair

Knitting needles: sizes 7 and 10 U.S. (4.5 and 6 mm)

Nine 1" (2.5 cm) buttons

GAUGE

9 x 9 rib and rev St st: 12 sts and 20 rows = 4" (10 cm)

Take time to save time—check your gauge.

PATTERN STITCHES

■ **Reverse Stockinette Stitch** (RSS)

Row 1 (WS): K all sts.

Row 2: P all sts.

■ **9 x 9 Rib** (over multiple of 18 sts plus 1)

Row 1 (RS): *P5, k9, p4; rep from *, end p5.

Row 2: *K5, p9, k4; rep from *, end K5.

NOTE: *Body is knit in one piece until armholes; then each section is worked separately.*

POCKET (make 2)

C.o. 15 sts.

Work in St st until piece meas 6" (15 cm); then place sts on holder.

BODY

C.o. 109 (127, 145, 163) sts with smaller needles.

Work in 9 x 9 rib for 8" (20.5 cm), ending with a WSR.

INSERT POCKETS: Work 4 sts, b.o. in rib next 15 sts, replace 15 sts just b.o. with pocket sts, having p side of fabric facing WS of garment; then work across until 19 sts rem, rep pocket placement, and work last 4 sts.

Now work cardigan in RSS.

When piece meas 18 (17½, 18½, 19)" (45.5, 44.5, 47, 48.5 cm), split work for armholes.

Work 27 (32, 36, 41) sts, join another ball of yarn, work back 55 (63, 73, 81) sts, join a 3rd ball of yarn, and work rem 27 (32, 36, 41) sts.

Cont as est, working each section sep.

When piece meas 20 (20, 21, 22)" (51, 51, 53.5, 56 cm), beg shaping neckline fronts.

At neck edge, b.o. 1 st every other row 0 (2, 2, 6) times, then every 4 rows 9 (8, 8, 6) times to give 18 (22, 26, 29) sts at shoulder.

When piece meas 27 (27, 28, 29)" (68.5, 68.5, 71, 73.5 cm), b.o. all shoulder sts.

Work back straight until piece meas 27 (27, 28, 29)" (68.5, 68.5, 71, 73.5 cm).

B.o. all sts.

SLEEVES

C.o. 37 sts on larger needles.

Work in 9 x 9 rib for 4" (10 cm).

Change to smaller needles and work for 4" (10 cm) more (to make the cuff snug and allow it to accommodate the foldover portion).

Change to larger needles and beg working in RSS.

Inc 1 st each end every 4 rows 0 (0, 0, 4) times, every 6 rows 6 (9, 9, 8) times, and every 8 rows 3 (1, 2, 0) times to give 55 (57, 57, 61) sts.

When piece meas 21 (21½, 22, 22)" (53.5, 54.5, 56, 56 cm), b.o. all sts.

FINISHING

Sew shoulder seams.

Sew sleeves into openings.

Sew pockets to secure to main body of sweater.

LEFT CARDIGAN BAND: With smaller needles, c.o. 9 sts.

On RS, p3, k2, p2, k2.

On WS, p2, k2, p2, k2, sl as if to p, bringing yarn toward you.

Work as est until piece meas entire length of cardigan to back of neck; then b.o. all sts.

RIGHT CARDIGAN BAND: With smaller needles, c.o. 9 sts.

On RS, k2, p2, k2, p2, sl last st as if to p with yarn toward you.

Next row (WS): K3, p2, k2, p2.

Work as est, placing 9 buttonholes up center front: Beg 1" (2.5 cm) into length of band and evenly space buttonholes until V-neck shaping begins.

To work buttonhole: On RS, work 4 sts, b.o. next 2 sts, work to end.

On next row, c.o. 2 sts where sts were b.o.

Sew bands onto edge of garment and seam them at back of neck.

NOTE: *It may be easier to apply edging as you go. The trick is to make edging slightly shorter than length of garment so that band doesn't stretch out of shape.*

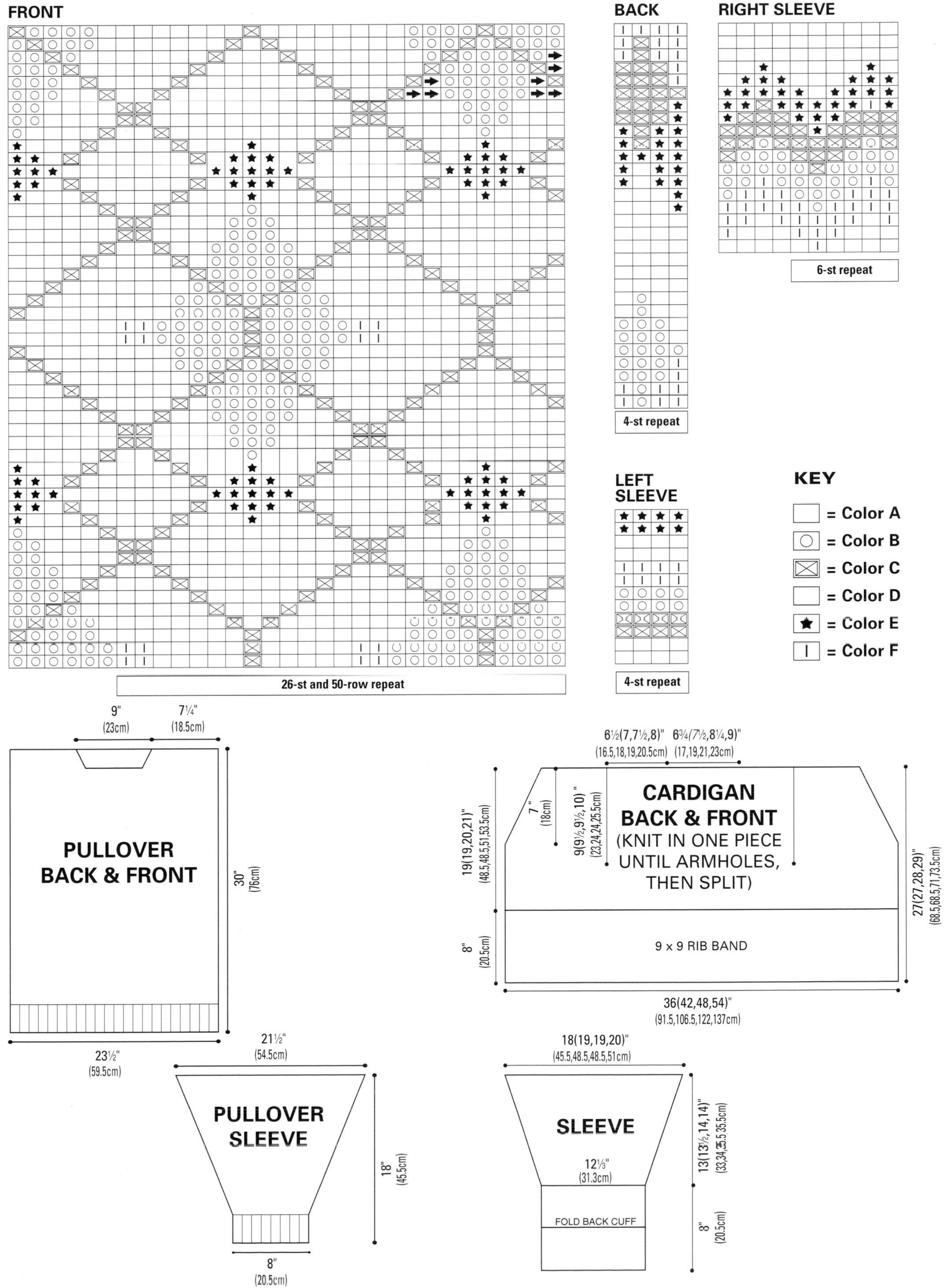

FRONT
26-st and 50-row repeat
BACK
4-st repeat
RIGHT SLEEVE
6-st repeat
LEFT SLEEVE
4-st repeat
KEY
= Color A
= Color B
= Color C
= Color D
= Color E
= Color F
9" (23cm)
7¼" (18.5cm)
PULLOVER BACK & FRONT
30" (76cm)
23½" (59.5cm)
21½" (54.5cm)
PULLOVER SLEEVE
18" (45.5cm)
8" (20.5cm)
6½(7,7½,8)" (16.5,18,19,20.5cm)
6¾(7½,8¼,9)" (17,19,21,23cm)
CARDIGAN BACK & FRONT
(KNIT IN ONE PIECE UNTIL ARMHOLES, THEN SPLIT)
7" (18cm)
9(9½,9½,10)" (23,24,24,25.5cm)
19(19,20,21)" (48.5,48.5,51,53.5cm)
27(27,28,29)" (68.5,68.5,71,73.5cm)
8" (20.5cm)
9 x 9 RIB BAND
36(42,48,54)" (91.5,106.5,122,137cm)
18(19,19,20)" (45.5,48.5,48.5,51cm)
SLEEVE
12⅓" (31.3cm)
FOLD BACK CUFF
13(13½,14,14)" (33,34,35.5 35.5cm)
8" (20.5cm)

The English Gardeners

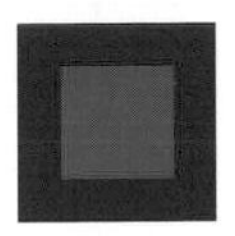

Photographed at Eglingham Hall Farm, Eglingham, Northumberland, England

designs: **Julie Hoff** (cardigan)
Kathy Zimmerman (pullover)

knitting rating: **Experienced**

photography: **Philip Newton**

Fine alpaca is used in the woman's cardigan, which combines intarsia leaves in autumnal tones and cables knit in leaf shapes. This design is a fun challenge for the experienced knitter.

The man's pullover features an overall cable pattern on front and back, and the raglan sleeves have an interesting treatment that emphasizes the diagonal seamline.

Autumn Leaves Cardigan

SIZES

Small (Medium, Large)

Finished measurements: 42 (46, 50)" (106.5, 117, 127 cm)

MATERIALS

Inca (100% alpaca; 50 g = approx. 115 yds/105 m): 15 (15, 16) skeins of main color (MC), 1 skein each of colors A, B, C, D, and E

Equivalent yarn: 1725 (1725, 1840) yds (1577, 1577, 1682 m) of sportweight alpaca in main color, 115 yds (105 m) each of sport-weight alpaca in five leaf colors

Knitting needles: size 5 U.S. (3.75 mm), 36" (91.5 cm) circular needle in size 2 U.S. (2.75 mm)

Seven ⅜" (1 cm) buttons.

GAUGE

St st with larger needles: 23 sts = 4" (10 cm)

Take time to save time—check your gauge.

PATTERN STITCHES

See charts for main stitches.

■ **Reverse Stockinette Stitch** (RSS)

Row 1 (RS): P all sts.

Row 2 (WS): K all sts.

■ **Moss Stitch** (over an odd number of sts)

Row 1: *K1, p1; rep from *, end k1.

Rows 2 and 3: *P1, k1; rep from *, end p1.

Row 4: *K1, p1; rep from *, end k1.

■ **Twisted Rib**

Row 1: *K1-b, p1-b; rep from *.

Row 2: P the p sts through the back loops, and k the k sts through the back loops.

BACK

C.o. 118 (130, 142) sts.

Work twisted rib for 1" (2.5 cm), ending with a WSR.

Using the intarsia method, work leaves chart through row 50 as follows: K3 (4, 5) sts, leaf 1 (17 sts), k3 (5, 7) sts, leaf 2 (12 sts), k3 (5, 7) sts, leaf 3 (19 sts), leaf 4 (20 sts), k2 (4, 6) sts, leaf 5 (12 sts), k2 (4, 6) sts, leaf 6 (19 sts), k3 (4, 5) sts.

Next row (RS): K across, adding 20 sts evenly spaced to give 138 (150, 162) sts.

Next row (WS): Est cable patterns as follows: Work 11 (17, 23) sts in moss st, [*work 4-st cable, 5 sts acorn chart, 4-st cable*, 9 sts leaf chart, rep bet *s once], work 46 sts diamond cable, rep bet [ ]s, work 11 (7, 23) sts in moss st.

Cont as est until piece meas 12½ (12, 11½)" (31.5, 30.5, 29 cm).

SHAPE ARMHOLES: B.o. 6 sts at the beg of the next 2 rows.

Cont until the 8th rep of acorn has been worked.

SHAPE SHOULDERS AND BACK OF NECK: On RSR, b.o. 13 (15, 17) sts; then work across 31 (35, 39) sts in est patt.

Working this shoulder only, b.o. 13 (15, 17) sts once more, 14 (16, 18) sts once, and at the same time, b.o. 4 sts once at neck edge.

B.o. center 38 sts and work the other shoulder to match.

NOTE: *When finishing shoulders, do not beg new acorn or leaf patterns.*

LEFT FRONT

C.o. 59 (65, 71) sts.

Work twisted rib for 1" (2.5 cm), ending with a WSR.

Using the intarsia method, work leaves chart through row 50 as follows: K3 (4, 6) sts, leaf 1 (17 sts), k3 (5, 7) sts, leaf 2 (12 sts), k3 (5, 7) sts, leaf 3 (19 sts), k2 (3, 3) sts.

Next row (RS): K, inc 13 sts evenly spaced to give 72 (78, 84) sts.

Next row (WS): Est cable patterns as follows: Work 26 sts of front diamond cable chart, *4-st cable, 5 sts acorn chart, 4-st cable*, 9 sts leaf chart; rep bet *s once more, and work 11 (17, 23) sts in moss st.

When piece meas 12", (30.5 cm), shape neck: Dec 1 st at neck edge every 4 rows 12 times, then every other row 14 times.

At the same time, shape armholes and shoulders as for back.

RIGHT FRONT

Work as for left front, reversing all shaping and cable charts and working leaf chart as follows: K2 (2, 3), leaf 4 (20 sts), k2 (4, 6) sts, leaf 5 (12 sts), k2 (4, 6) sts, leaf 6 (19 sts), k2 (4, 5) sts.

SLEEVES

C.o. 52 (52, 56) sts.

Work twisted rib for 1" (2.5 cm), ending with a WSR.

Work rows 1 to 4 of leaves chart (for the second sleeve, work rows 47 to 50).

Next row (RS): K, inc 12 sts evenly spaced to give 64 (64, 68) sts.

Next row (WS): Est cable patterns as follows: Work 4 (4, 6) sts in RSS, 4-st cable, 46 sts in diamond cable, 4-st cable, and 4 (4, 6) sts in RSS.

Add 1 st each edge in the next and every 4 rows 18 times, then every 6 rows 3 (6, 7) times.

At the same time, when sleeve meas 3½ (3½, 4)" (9, 9, 10 cm), beg leaf chart over RSSs.

As more sts are added, work another 4-st cable, 5 sts acorn chart, 4-st cable, 4 (7, 10) sts in moss st.

NOTE: *Beg acorn chart only in row 1 or 15 of leaf chart so that the 2 charts will end together at the top of the sleeve. When 4 leaf charts have been worked, do not start another leaf or acorn chart.*

When sleeve meas 17½ (18, 18½)" (44.5, 45.5, 47 cm), b.o. all sts.

FINISHING

Block all pieces.

Sew shoulder seams.

With circular needle, p.u. 71 sts from left front to beg of neck shaping, 58 sts up left front to shoulder, 46 sts across back neck, 58 sts down right front neck to beg of neck shaping, pm, and 71 sts down right front to c.o. edge to give 304 sts.

With RS facing, k 1 row.

Row 2: P to marker; then place buttonholes as follows: *B.o. 2 sts, p9; rep from * until 7 buttonholes have been worked.

Row 3 (RS): K, c.o. 2 sts over b.o. sts on previous row.

Row 4 (WS): K to form fold line.

Work 4 more rows in St st, beg with a k row and working buttonholes on 3rd and 4th rows to correspond to those previously worked.

Fold front band on fold line and slip-stitch into place on WS.

Set in sleeves.

Sew side and sleeve seams.

Sew on buttons.

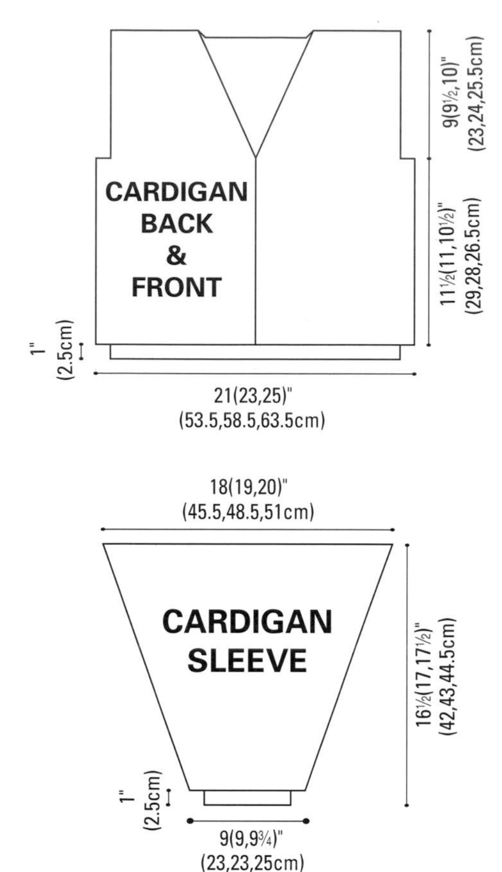

KEY

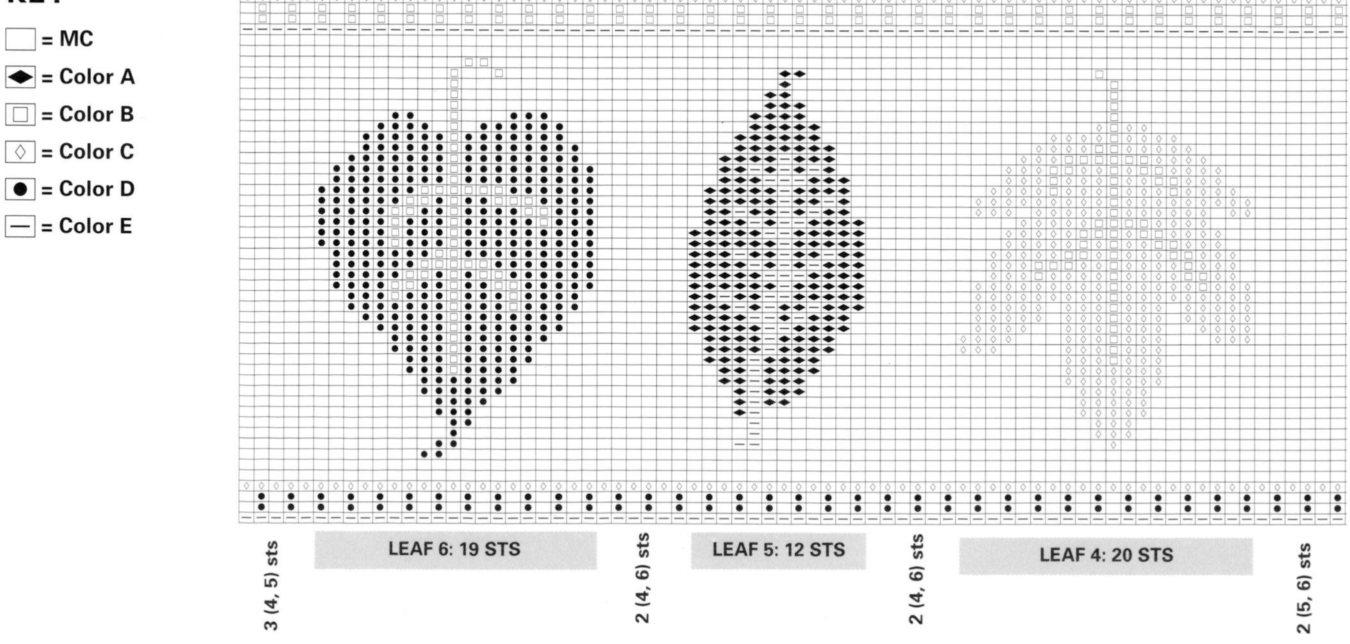

FRONT DIAMOND CABLE CHART

KEY

- | = Knit on RS, p on WS
- — = Purl on RS, k on WS
- 5 = (K1, p1, k1, p1, k1) into 1 st
- 7 = (K1, p1, k1, p1, k1, p1, k1) into 1 st
- ◡ = Knit 5 sts tog
- ● = M1(p.u. horizontal strand & k into the back of it)
- ⇨⇨⇨⇨⇨⇨⇨ = Place 3 sts on cn and hold in back, ssk, k1, k2tog, turn, p3, turn, sl 1 knitwise, k2tog, psso, p3, from cn
- ⇦⇦⇦⇦⇦⇦⇦ = Place 5 sts on cn and hold in front, p3 from cn, ssk, k1, k2tog, turn, p3, turn, k3tog
- ═ = p2tog
- ◢ = Ssk-slip the first and 2nd sts one at a time knitwise; then insert the tip of the left hand needle into the fronts of these 2 sts and knit them tog from this position
- ◣ = K2tog
- △ = Sl 2 sts tog (as if to knit them tog), k1, psso
- = Sl 2 sts to cn and hold in back, k2, k2 from cn
- = Sl 2 sts to cn and hold in front, k2, k2 from cn
- = Sl 1 st on cn and hold in back, k2, p1 from cn
- = Sl 2 sts to cn and hold in front, p1, k2 from cn

LEAF CHART

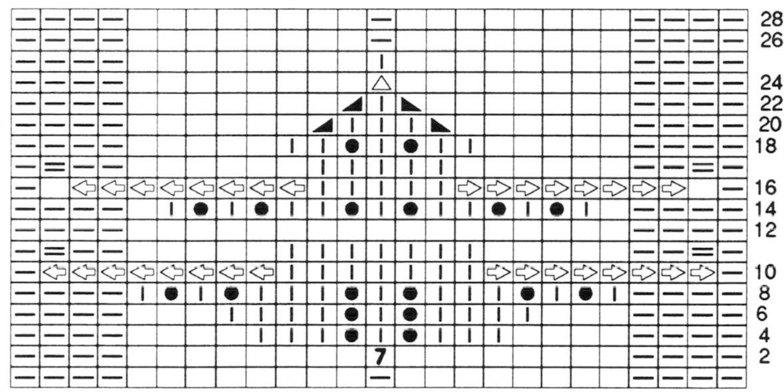

DIAMOND CABLE CHART (for back and sleeves)

4-ST CABLE

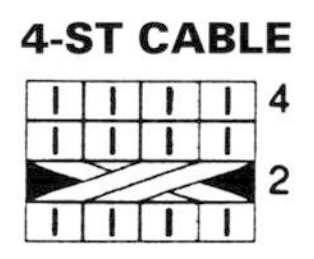

ACORN CHART

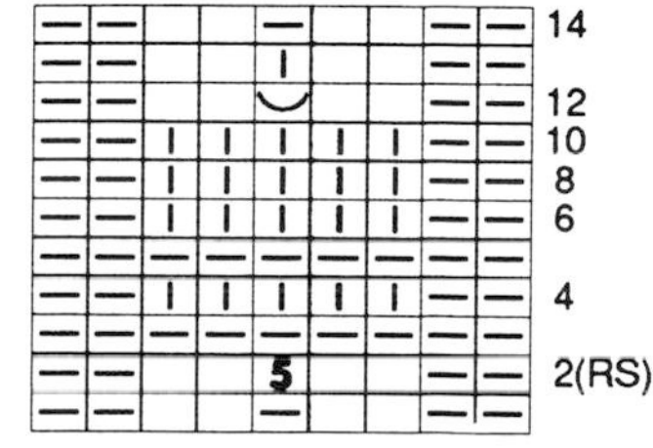

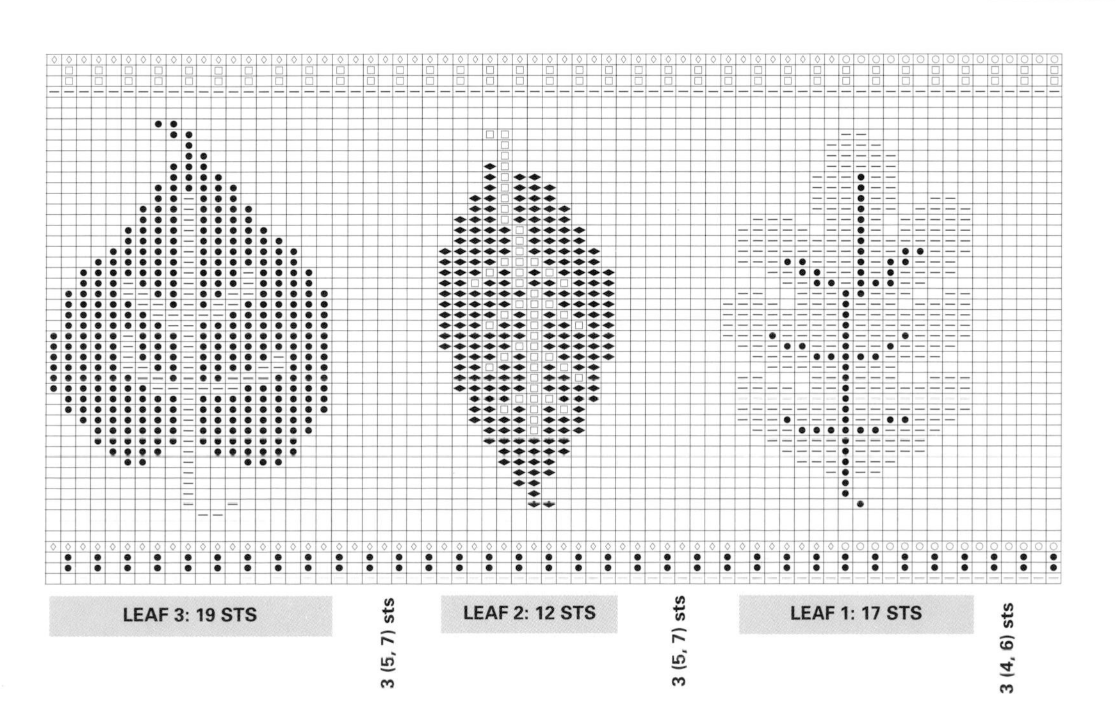

Cabled Raglan Pullover

SIZES

Small (Medium, Large)

Finished measurements: 46½ (50, 54)" (118, 127, 137 cm)

MATERIALS

Tapestry (75% wool, 25% mohair; 50 g = approx. 95 yds/87 m): 24 (25, 26) skeins

Equivalent yarn: 2280 (2375, 2470) yds (2085, 2172, 2259 m) of worsted-weight wool

Knitting needles: sizes 4 and 7 U.S. (3.25 and 4.5 mm), 16" (40.5 cm) circular needle in size 4 U.S. (3.25 mm), cable needle (cn)

Stitch holders

GAUGE

Rev St st with larger needles: 20 sts and 26 rows = 4" (10 cm)

Take time to save time—check your gauge.

PATTERN STITCHES

See charts for cable patterns.

■ Garter Stitch

All rows: Knit all sts.

■ Reverse Stockinette Stitch (RSS)

Row 1 (RS): P all sts.

Row 2: K all sts.

■ 2 x 2 Rib

Row 1 (WS): K2, *p2, k2; rep from *.

Row 2: P2, *k2, p2; rep from *.

■ Decrease Methods

DOUBLE DECREASE (RS row): P3, sl 1, k2tog, psso, work to last 6 sts, k3tog, p3.

SINGLE DECREASE (RS row): P3, sl 1, k1, psso, work to last 5 sts, k2tog, p3.

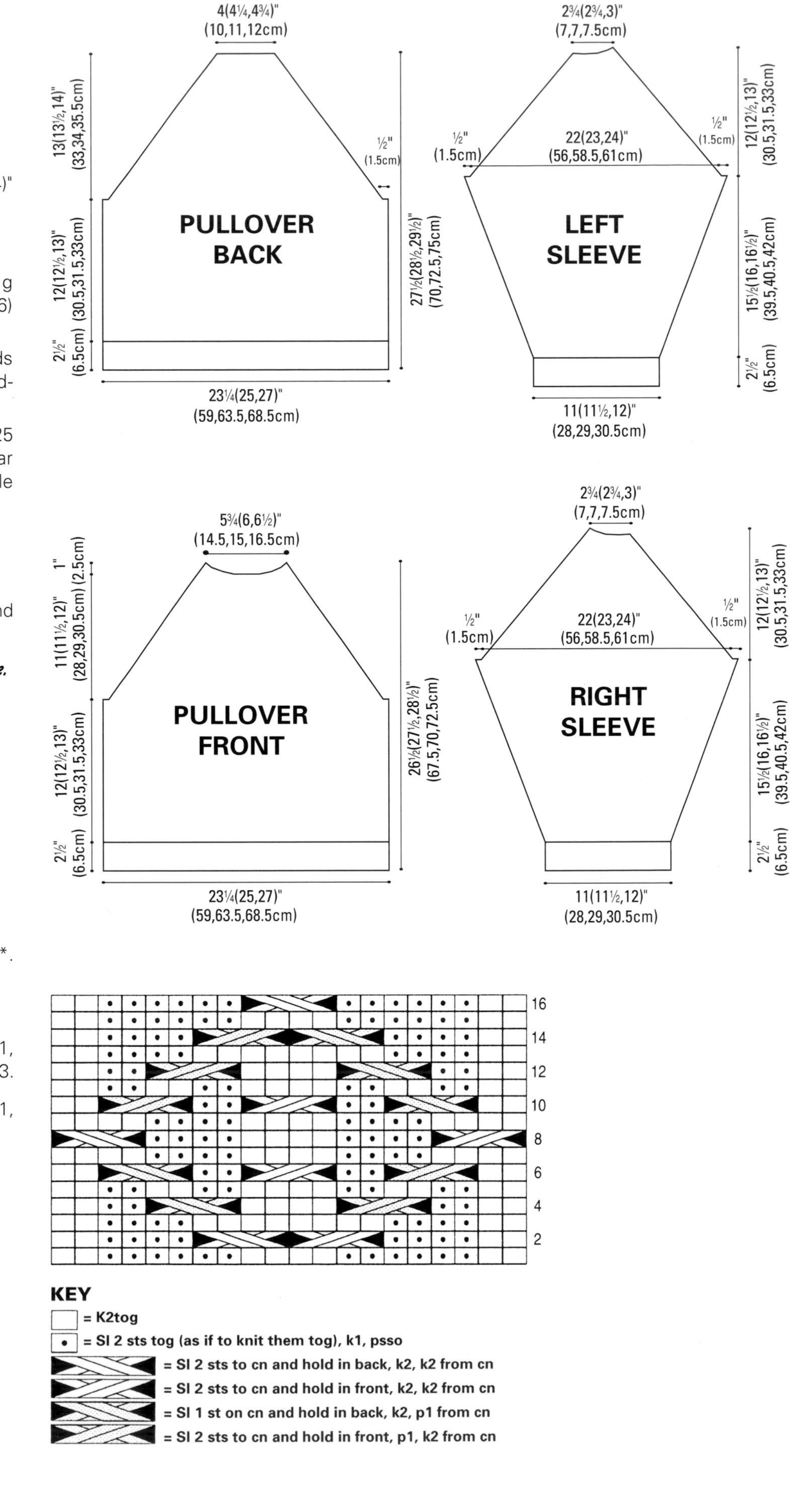

RIGHT SLEEVE

With smaller needles, c.o. 62 (62, 78) sts and work as for back, ending with RS facing.

Change to larger needles and work set-up row as for back to give 72 (76, 80) sts.

Foundation row (WS): *Work 3 (4, 5) sts in RSS, beg row 1 of chart, work next 20 sts in cable patt; rep from * twice, end 3 (4, 5) sts in RSS.

At the same time, keeping in patt, inc 1 st each edge every other row 25 (25, 26) times, then every 4 rows 11 (12, 12) times to give 144 (150, 156) sts.

Cont to work even until piece meas 18 (18½, 19)" (45.5, 47, 48.5 cm), end with a WS row.

RAGLAN SHAPING: B.o. 3 sts at the beg of the next 2 rows to give 138 (144, 150) sts.

Alternate single and double decs with RSS border (as for back) until 79 (83, 85) rows have been completed and 18 (20, 20) sts rem.

SHAPE CAP: B.o. 6 (7, 7) sts at the beg of each RS row twice, then 6 sts once.

LEFT SLEEVE

Work the same as right sleeve until 18 (20, 20) sts rem.

B.o. 6 (7, 7) sts at the beg of each WS row twice, then 6 sts once to reverse angle of cap shaping.

FINISHING

Block all pieces to finished measurements.

Sew raglan seams.

With smaller circular needle, p.u. and k92 (96, 100) sts evenly spaced around neck.

P 1 row, k 1 row, p 1 row.

Work 2 x 2 rib over an even number of sts, beg with *, for 1½" (4 cm).

P 1 row, k 1 row.

B.o. loosely in p.

RAGLAN BANDS (make 4): With smaller needles, c.o. 84 (88, 92) sts.

Work in 2 x 2 rib over an even number of sts, beg with *, for 5 rows.

B.o. all sts loosely.

Sew band neatly over top of RSS raglan border.

Sew side and sleeve seams.

Block seams lightly.

BACK

With smaller needles, c.o. 142 (142, 174) sts.

Work 4 rows in garter st, ending with WS facing.

Work 2 x 2 rib for 13 rows.

Work 4 more rows in garter st (ending with RS facing).

Change to larger needles and work set-up row:

SMALL: *P1, m1, p1, k2, p6, (k1, m1) twice, p6, k2; rep from * to last 2 sts, end p1, m1, p1 to give 164 sts.

MEDIUM: *(P1, m1) twice, k2, p6, (k1, m1) twice, p6, k2; rep from * to last 2 sts, end (m1, p1) twice to give 172 sts.

LARGE: *P1, m1, p2, p2tog, k2, p6, (k1, m1) twice, p6, k2; rep from * to last 6 sts, end p2tog, p2, m1, p1 to give 180 sts.

NOTE: *The cable panel vertical knit sts should line up over the knit sts of the 2 x 2 rib.*

Foundation row (WS): *Work 3 (4, 5) sts in RSS, beg row 1 of chart, work next 20 sts in cable patt; rep from * 6 times, end 3 (4, 5) sts in RSS.

Cont to follow chart as est until piece meas 14½ (15, 15½)" (37, 38, 39.5 cm).

RAGLAN SHAPING: Maintaining cable patt as est, b.o. 3 sts at beg of next 2 rows to give 158 (166, 174) sts.

Alternate single and double decs on all RS rows until 73 (77, 77) rows have been worked, then all double decs until 85 (89, 91) rows have been completed.

At the same time, maintain 3 sts at each side in RSS.

On all WS rows: K3, work in est patt until 3 sts rem, k3.

B.o. rem 26 (28, 32) sts for back neck.

FRONT

Work as for back until 72 (76, 76) rows have been completed to give 50 (52, 60) sts.

NECK SHAPING: B.o. center 14 (16, 20) sts, and work rem sts in est patt.

B.o. 3 sts at each neck edge 3 times to give 3 sts rem on each side.

Place these sts on holders for neck finishing.

Craigside Gardens

Photographed on the grounds of Eglingham Hall Farm, Northumberland, England

designs: **Susan Mills**
knitting rating: **Experienced**
photography: **Philip Newton**

Lace and openwork stitches are especially pretty and delicate in mohair yarn. The woman's pullover has a sampler of lace stitches framed with openwork cables down the center front. The center front of the child's pullover features a lace heart motif. Both designs have easy rolled edges, and the woman's sweater has raglan sleeves and a slightly flared profile for added comfort.

SIZES

ADULT: One size

CHILD: Small (Medium, Large, Extra Large)

Finished measurements: 48" (122 cm) <20 (24, 28, 32)" (51, 61, 71, 81.5 cm)>

MATERIALS

Mini-Mohair (74% mohair, 13% wool, 13% nylon; 1½ oz. = approx. 135 yds/123 m): 9 <3 (4, 4, 5)> skeins

Equivalent yarn: 1215 yds (1111 m) <405 (540, 540, 675) yds (370, 494, 494, 617 m)> of light worsted-weight brushed mohair

Knitting needles: size 6 U.S. (4 mm), 16" (40.5 cm) circular needle in size 6 U.S. (4 mm)

GAUGE

St st: 20 sts and 24 rows = 4" (10 cm)

Take time to save time—check your gauge.

PATTERN STITCHES

See charts for lace stitches.

■ **Reverse Stockinette Stitch** (RSS)

Row 1 (RS): P all sts.

Row 2: K all sts.

■ **Garter Stitch**

K all rows.

Adult's Pullover

NOTE: *Knit front of sweater first; then knit back to same length.*

FRONT

C.o. 115 sts and work in St st for 1¼" (3 cm) for rolled edge, ending with a WSR.

Set-up row: Work 37 sts in RSS, k5 for lace cable, 2 sts in RSS, 27 sts in garter st, 2 sts in RSS, k5 for lace cable, and 37 sts in RSS.

Work 5 more rows as est, working lace cable over 5 k sts.

Beg working lace panel over center 27 sts, working 6 rows in garter st bet lace panels.

SHAPE ARMHOLE: When front meas 14"/35.5 cm (94 rows), b.o. 4 sts at beg of next 2 rows.

Cont in patt and work dec as foll: On RSR, k3, ssk, work across row in patt, and end k2tog, k3.

On WSR, p3, p2tog, work across row in patt, and end p2tog-b, p3.

Dec 2 out of every 3 rows (dec every row once, then every other row once) 7 times; then dec every other row 20 times.

When armhole meas 7" (18 cm), b.o. center 31 sts.

SHAPE NECK: Working each shoulder sep, dec 1 st at each neck edge every other row 4 times to give no sts rem.

BACK

C.o. 115 sts and work rolled edge as for front.

Work in RSS until piece meas 14" (35.5 cm).

Shape armhole as for front.

Work until back meas same length as front, with 39 sts rem.

Place sts on holder for neck finishing.

SLEEVE

C.o. 40 sts and work rolled edge as for back.

Work in RSS, inc 1 st each side every 4 rows 25 times to give 90 sts.

When sleeve meas 16" (40.5 cm), b.o. 4 sts at beg of next 2 rows.

Work dec as foll: Dec 2 out of every 3 rows (dec every row once, then every other row once) 10 times; then dec every other row 16 times.

Place rem 10 sts on holder for neck.

FINISHING

With circular needle, p.u. 94 sts evenly around neck and work in St st for 2½" (6.5 cm) for rolled edge.

Set in sleeves.

Sew side and sleeve seams.

Child's Pullover

BACK

C.o. 50 (60, 70, 80) sts and work in St st for 1½" (4 cm).

Work in RSS until piece meas 13 (15, 17, 19)" (33, 38, 43, 48.5 cm).

B.o. all sts.

FRONT

C.o. 50 (60, 70, 80) sts and work rolled edge as for back.

Work in RSS for 3¼ (4¾, 5¾, 6¾)" (8.5, 12, 14.5, 17 cm) above rolled edge.

Work across 8 (13, 18, 23) sts in RSS, pm, work row 1 of heart panel across 34 sts, pm, work across last 8 (13, 18, 23) sts in RSS.

Work in est patt until chart is complete; then work 2 (1, 2, 3)" (5, 2.5, 5, 7.5 cm) in RSS.

When piece meas 12 (14, 16, 18)" (30.5, 35.5, 40.5, 45.5 cm), shape neck: Work across 9 (14, 17, 22) sts, join another ball of yarn, b.o. center 32 (32, 36, 36) sts, and work across rem 9 (14, 17, 22) sts.

Working each shoulder sep, dec 1 st at each neck edge every other row twice to give 7 (12, 15, 20) sts rem on each shoulder.

Work until front meas same length as back.

B.o. all sts.

SLEEVES

C.o. 25 (30, 35, 35) sts and work in St st for 1½" (4 cm).

Work in RSS, inc 1 st each edge every 2 rows 6 (3, 1, 2) times and every 4 rows 12 (15, 18, 19) times to give 61 (66, 71, 75) sts.

When sleeve meas 10 (11, 12, 13)" (25.5, 28, 30.5, 33 cm), b.o. all sts.

FINISHING

Sew shoulder seams.

P.u. 75 (78, 80, 83) sts and work in St st for rolled neck for 1½ (1½, 2, 2)" (4, 4, 5, 5 cm).

Set in sleeves.

Sew side and sleeve seams.

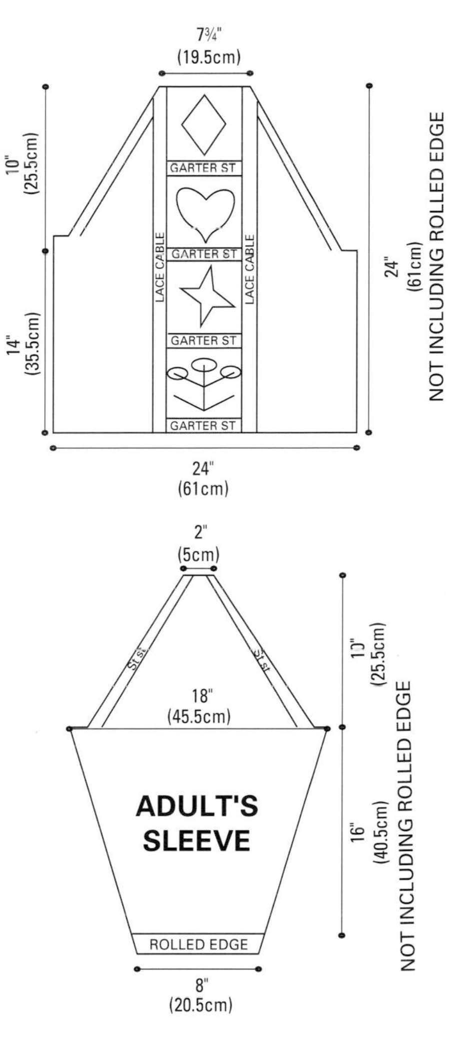

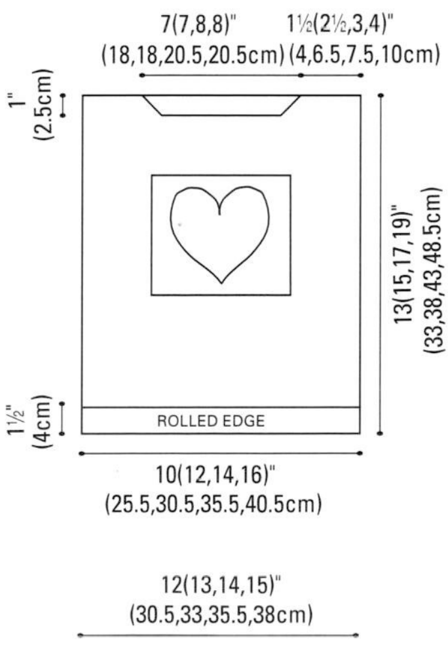

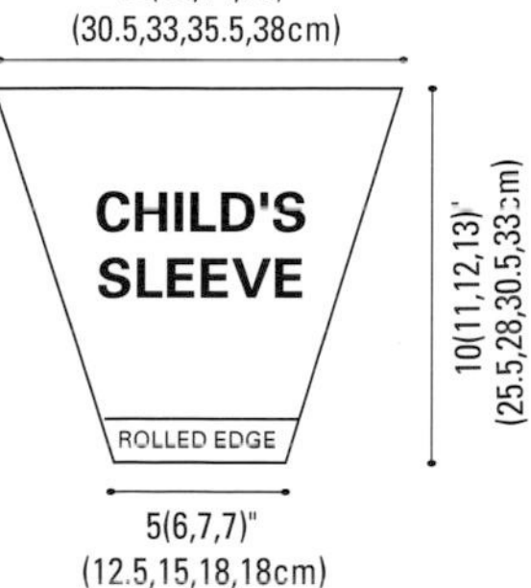

...ULLOVER

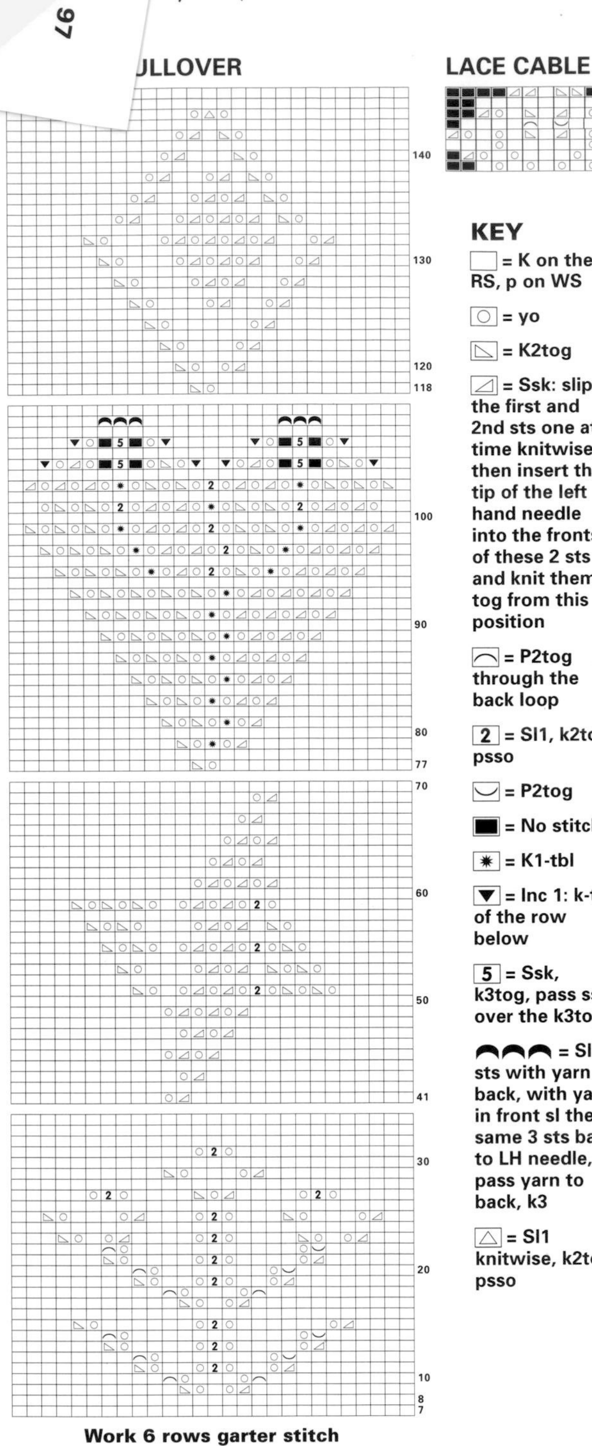

Work 6 rows garter stitch between each lace panel.

LACE CABLE

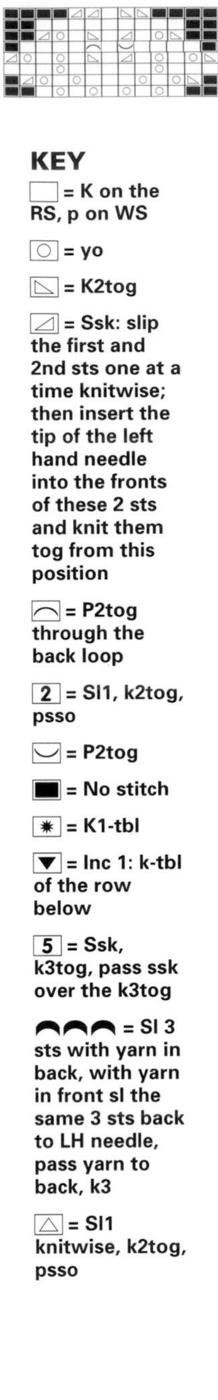

KEY

☐ = K on the RS, p on WS

○ = yo

◺ = K2tog

◿ = Ssk: slip the first and 2nd sts one at a time knitwise; then insert the tip of the left hand needle into the fronts of these 2 sts and knit them tog from this position

⌒ = P2tog through the back loop

2 = Sl1, k2tog, psso

◡ = P2tog

■ = No stitch

✷ = K1-tbl

▼ = Inc 1: k-tbl of the row below

5 = Ssk, k3tog, pass ssk over the k3tog

⌒⌒⌒ = Sl 3 sts with yarn in back, with yarn in front sl the same 3 sts back to LH needle, pass yarn to back, k3

△ = Sl1 knitwise, k2tog, psso

CHILD'S PULLOVER

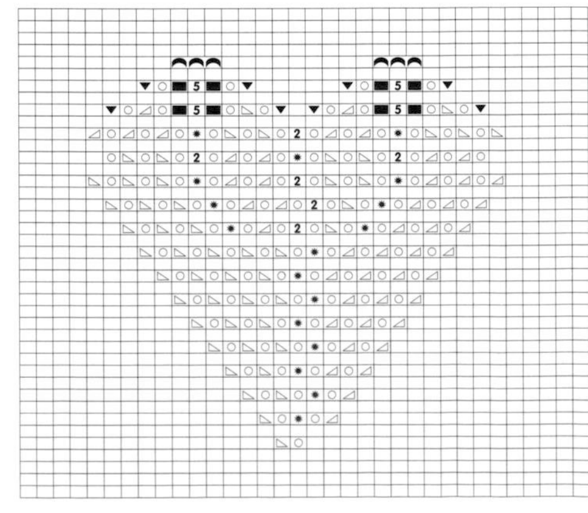

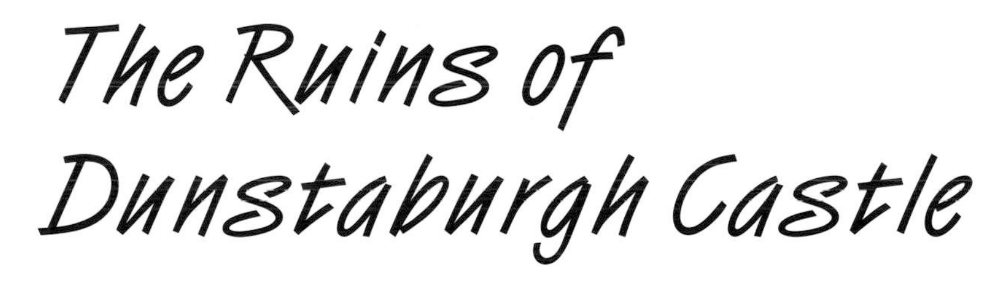

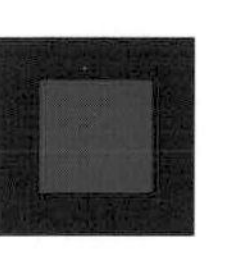

Photographed on the grounds of the remains of Dunstaburgh Castle, Northumberland, England. Dunstaburgh Castle is a property of Great Britain's National Trust and is open to the public.

designs: **Susan Mills** (trinity-stitch vest), **Kristin Nicholas** (Aran pullovers)
knitting ratings: **Intermediate** (vest), **Advanced** (pullovers)
photography: **Philip Newton**

Traditional trinity stitch provides the overall texture for the woman's cropped vest, and simple four-stitch vertical cables are inset at the sides and across the back. With its crew neck and straight edges, this vest creates the effect of a cropped, sleeveless pullover.

The Aran pullovers are edged with trinity stitch and worked in a variety of cable stitches. For added versatility, there are two neckline variations— a ribbed shawl collar and a crew-neck with trinity stitch.

Aran Pullover with Neckline Variations

SIZES

Small (Medium, Large)

Finished measurements: 40 (44, 48)" (101.5, 112, 122 cm)

MATERIALS

MAN'S SHAWL COLLAR: Evergreen Cashmere/Wool (45% cashmere, 45% wool, 10% unidentified fibers; 100 g = approx. 226 yds/207 m): 7 (7, 8) hanks

WOMAN'S CREWNECK: Evergreen Cotton/Wool (45% cotton, 45% wool, 10% unidentified fibers; 100 g = approx. 226 yds/207 m): 7 (7, 8) hanks

Equivalent yarn: 1450 (1580, 1800) yds (1325, 14445, 1646 m) of light worsted-weight wool

Knitting needles: sizes 5 and 7 U.S. (3.75 and 4.5 mm), 16" (40.5 cm) circular needle in size 5 U.S. (3.75 mm), cable needle (cn)

GAUGE

St st and rev St st: 25 sts and 25 rows = 4" (10 cm)

Boxy cable = 2¼" (5.5 cm)

Enclosed cable = 2¼" (5.5 cm)

Open braid cable = 2" (5 cm)

4-St cable = ¾" (2 cm)

Open cable = 1" (2.5 cm)

Ribbed cable = 4¼" (11 cm)

Trinity stitch: 24 sts = 4" (10 cm)

Take time to save time—check your gauge.

PATTERN STITCHES

T3B: Sl next st to cn and hold in back, k2, p1 from cn.

T3F: Sl next 2 sts to cn and hold in front, p1 from left-hand needle, k2 from cn.

T4L: Sl next 3 sts to cn and hold in front, p1, k3 from cn.

T4R: Sl next st to cn and hold in back, k3 sts from left-hand needle, p1 from cn.

T4B: Sl next 2 sts to cn and hold in back, k2, p2 from cn.

T4F: Sl next 2 sts to cn and hold in front, p2 from left-hand needle, k2 from cn.

C4B: Sl next 2 sts to cn and hold in back, k2, k2 from cn.

C4F: Sl next 2 sts to cn and hold in front, k2, k2 from cn.

C6B: Sl next 3 sts to cn and hold in back, k3, k3 from cn.

C6F: Sl next 3 sts to cn and hold in front, k3, k3 from cn.

■ Stockinette Stitch

Row 1 (WS): P all sts.

Row 2: K all sts.

■ **Trinity Stitch** (over multiple of 4 sts)

Row 1 (WS): *(K1, p1, k1) into first st, p next 3 sts tog; rep from *.

Rows 2 and 4 (RS): P all sts.

Row 3: *P3tog, (K1, p1, k1) into next st; rep from *.

■ **Reverse Stockinette Stitch** (RSS)

Row 1 (WS): K all sts.

Row 2: P all sts.

■ **4-Stitch Cable** (over 4 sts)

Rows 1 and 3 (WS): P4.
Row 2: C4F.
Row 4: K4.

■ **Enclosed Cable** (over 12 sts)

Row 1 (WS): K2, p8, k2.
Row 2: P2, C4B twice, p2.
Row 3 and all WSR: Work all sts as they appear.
Row 4: T4B, C4B, T4F.
Row 6: K2, p2, k4, p2, k2.
Row 8: K2, p2, C4B, p2, k2.
Rows 9 to 16: Rep rows 5 to 8 twice.
Row 18: K2, p2, k4, p2, k2.
Row 20: T4F, C4B, T4B.
Rep rows 1 through 20.

■ **Boxy Cable** (over 12 sts)

Row 1 (WS): P4, k4, p4.
Row 2: C4F, p4, C4B.
Row 3 and all WSR: Work all sts as they appear.
Row 4: K2, T3F, p2, T3B, k2.
Row 6: K2, p1, T3F, T3B, p1, k2.
Row 8: K2, p2, C4B, p2, k2.
Row 10: K2, p1, T3B, T3F, p1, k2.
Row 12: K2, T3B, p2, T3F, k2.
Rep rows 1 through 12.

■ **Open Braid Cable** (over 10 sts)

Row 1 (WS): P2, k6, p2.
Rows 2 and 4: K2, p6, k2.
Row 3 and all WSR: Work all sts as they appear.
Row 6: Sl 2 to cn and hold in front, p2, k2, k2 from cn, T4B.
Rows 8, 12, and 16: P2, k2, C4B, p2.
Rows 10 and 14: P2, C4F, k2, p2.
Row 18: Sl 4 to cn and hold in back, k2, p4 from cn, T4F.
Rows 20, 22, and 24: K2, p6, k2.
Rep rows 1 through 24.

■ **Open Cable** (over 5 sts)

Row 1 (WS): P2, k1, p2.
Rows 2, 4, and 6: K2, p1, k2.
Row 3 and all WSR: Work all sts as they appear.
Row 8: Sl 3 sts to cn and hold in back, k2, sl last st on cn to left-hand needle and p it, k2 from cn.

■ **Ribbed Cable** (over 22 sts)

Row 1 (WS): P2, k2, p6, k2, p6, k2, p2.
Row 2: K2, p2, k6, p2, k6, p2, k2.
Row 3 and all WSR except row 19: Work all sts as they appear.
Row 4: K2, p2, C6F, p2, C6B, p2, k2.
Row 6: Rep row 2.
Rows 7 to 18: Rep rows 1 to 6 twice.
Row 19 (transition row): P6, k2, p2, k2, p2, k2, p6.
Rows 20 and 24: K6, p2, k2, p2, k2, p2, k6.
Row 22: C6B, p2, k2, p2, k2, p2, C6F.
Rows 25 to 36: Rep rows 19 to 24 twice.
Rep rows 1 through 36.

BACK

With smaller needles, c.o. 108 (118, 130) sts.

P 1 RSR.

K across next WSR, inc 14 (16, 16) sts evenly to give 122 (134, 146) sts.

Beg trinity st, keeping first and last sts in RSS for 12 rows.

Change to larger needles and beg est cable sequence on WSR: Work 2 sts in RSS, work enclosed cable over 12 sts, work 2 in RSS, work boxy cable over 12 sts, work 2 in RSS, work open braid over 10 sts, work 2 in RSS, work open cable over 5 sts, work 3 in RSS, work ribbed cable over 22 sts, work 3 in RSS, work open cable over 5 sts, work 2 in RSS, work open braid over 10 sts, work 2 in RSS, work boxy cable over 12 sts, work 2 in RSS, work enclosed cable over 12 sts, work 2 in RSS.

SMALL: Work 122 sts as given for cable sequence above.

MEDIUM: Work 2 sts in RSS, work 4-st cable, work cable sequence above over 122 sts, work 4-st cable, work 2 sts in RSS to give 134 sts.

LARGE: [Work 2 sts in RSS, work 4-st cable] twice, work cable sequence above over 122 sts, [work 4-st cable, work 2 sts in RSS] twice to give 146 sts.

When piece meas 26 (27, 28)" (66, 68.5, 71 cm), b.o. all sts.

SHAWL COLLAR FRONT

Work same as back.

When piece meas 18 (19, 20)" (45.5, 48.5, 51 cm), shape neck: Work 49 (55, 61) sts, join 2nd ball of yarn, b.o. center 24 sts, and work to end.

Work each side sep in est patt until piece meas 22 (23, 24)" (56, 58.5, 61 cm).

Dec for neckline: B.o. 1 st at neck edge every other row 3 (4, 8) times, then every 4 rows 4 (4, 2) times to give 42 (47, 51) sts at shoulder.

When piece meas same as back, b.o. all shoulder sts.

CREWNECK FRONT

Work same as back.

When piece meas 24 (25, 26)" (61, 63.5, 66 cm), shape neck: Work 50 (55, 59) sts, join 2nd ball of yarn, b.o. center 22 (24, 28) sts, and work to end.

Working each side sep as est, dec for neckline every other row 4 sts once, 2 sts once, 1 st twice to give 42 (47, 51) sts at shoulder.

When piece meas same as back, b.o. all sts.

SLEEVES

With smaller needles, c.o. 44 (44, 48) sts.

P 1 RSR.

K across next RSR, inc 10 (10, 6) sts evenly across to give 54 sts.

Beg trinity st, keeping first and last sts in RSS for 10 rows.

Change to larger needles and beg est cables on WSR: Work 2 in RSS, work boxy cable over 12 sts, work 2 in RSS, work ribbed cable over 22 sts, work 2 in RSS, work enclosed cable over 12 sts, work 2 in RSS.

Work in est patt, inc out into trinity st but keeping first st in RSS to make seaming easier.

Inc 1 st each end every other row 0 (0, 2) times, then every 4 rows 21 (23, 24) times to give 96 (100, 106) sts.

Work in est patt until piece meas 16½ (17½,18½)" (42, 44.5, 47 cm) or desired length; then b.o. all sts.

FINISHING

Sew shoulder seams.

Meas down 9 (9½, 10)" (23, 24, 25.5 cm) in front and back and mark.

Sew sleeves bet markers.

Sew side and sleeve seams.

SHAWL COLLAR

With RS facing and circular needle, p.u. 154 (154, 158) sts evenly at neckline, leaving center bottom cable sts free.

Row 1 (WS): *P2, k2; rep from *, end p2.

Row 2: *K2, p2; rep from *, end k2.

Work in 2 x 2 rib for 4¼" (11 cm) or until piece fits across opening.

B.o. all sts.

Fasten down at lower center front.

CREWNECK

With RS facing and circular needle, p.u. 90 (94, 100) sts evenly around neck and k in trinity st for 4 rows, then in RSS for 2 rows, dec 6 (8, 10) sts on last row.

B.o. all sts.

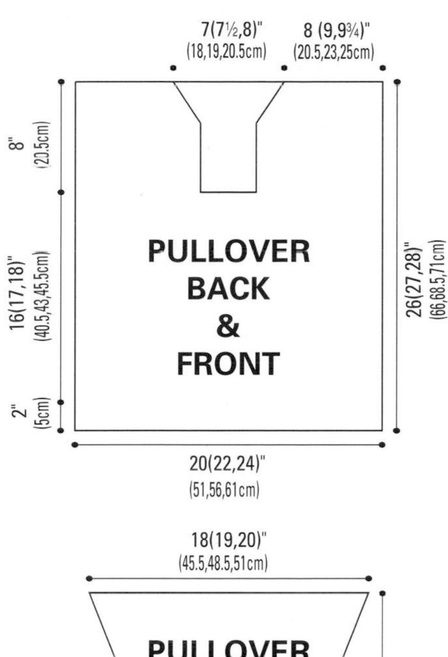

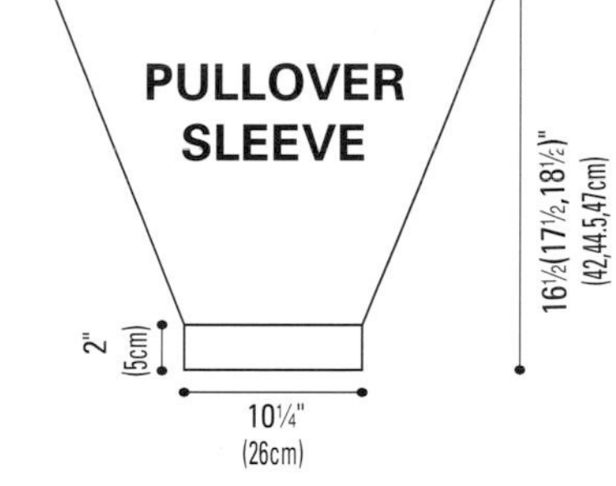

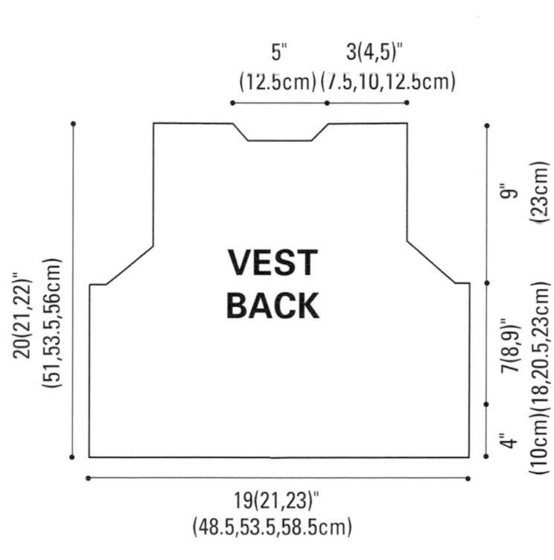

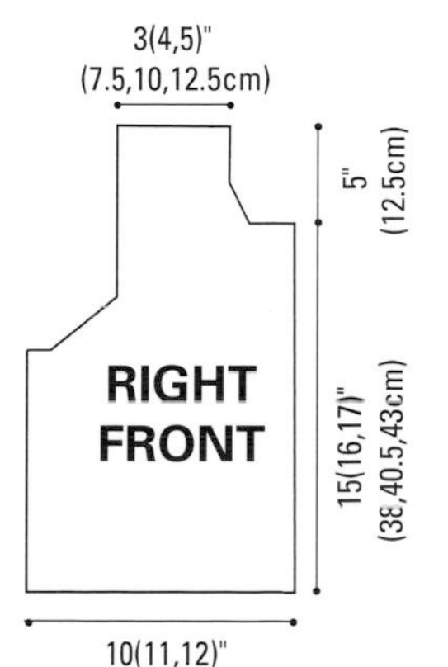

Vest

SIZES

Small (Medium, Large)

Finished measurements: 38 (42, 46)" (96.5, 106.5, 117 cm)

MATERIALS

Evergreen Cashmere/Wool (45% cashmere, 45% wool, 10% unidentified fibers; 100 g = 226 yds/207 m): 3 (4, 4) skeins

Equivalent yarn: 680 (800, 900) yds (622, 732, 823 m) of light worsted-weight wool

Knitting needles: size 6 U.S. (4 mm), cable needle (cn)

Seven ½" (1.5 cm) buttons

GAUGE

Trinity stitch: 24 sts = 4" (10 cm)

Take time to save time—check your gauge.

PATTERN STITCHES

■ **Trinity Stitch** (over multiple of 4 sts)

Row 1 (RS): P all sts.

Row 2: *(K1, p1, k1) into 1 st; p3tog; rep from *.

Row 3: P all sts.

Row 4: *P3tog, (k1, p1, k1) into 1 st; rep from *.

Rep rows 1 through 4.

■ **Cable** (over 4 sts and 8 rows)

Rows 1, 3, and 7 (RS): K all sts.

Rows 2, 4, 6, and 8: P all sts.

Row 5: Sl 2 sts to cn and hold in back, k2, k2 from cn.

BACK

C.o. 114 (126, 138) sts and work in trinity st for 4" (10 cm), working 1 edge st at each side in St st.

Beg working in trinity st with cables as foll: 1 edge st, 4 sts in trinity st, [8 sts in trinity st, 4 sts in cable] 8 (9, 10) times, 12 sts in trinity st, 1 edge st.

When back meas 11 (12, 13)" (28, 30.5, 33 cm), shape armhole: B.o. 11 sts at beg of next 2 rows, 2 sts at beg of next 6 rows, then 1 st each edge every other row 7 times to give 66 (78, 90) sts.

When piece meas 19 (20, 21)" (48.5, 51, 53.5 cm), shape neck: Work across 19 (25, 31) sts, join another ball of yarn, b.o. center 28 sts, and work across rem sts.

B.o. 1 st each neck edge once to give 18 (24, 30) sts.

When back meas 20 (21, 22)" (51, 53.5, 56 cm), b.o. all sts.

RIGHT FRONT

C.o. 60 (64, 72) sts and work in trinity st for 4" (10 cm).

Beg working trinity st with cables as foll: 2 edge sts in St st, 16 (20, 16) sts in trinity st, 4 sts cable, [8 sts trinity st, 4 sts cable] 2 (2, 3) times, 12 sts in trinity st, and 2 edge sts in St st.

Shape armhole as for back.

When piece meas 15 (16, 17)" (38, 40.5, 43 cm), shape neck: B.o. at neck edge 6 sts once, 4 sts once, 2 sts twice, then 1 st 4 times to give 18 (24, 30) sts.

When piece meas same length as back, b.o. all sts.

LEFT FRONT

Work as for right front, reversing all shaping and working trinity st with cables as foll: 2 edge sts in St st, 12 sts in trinity st, 4 sts cable, [8 sts trinity st, 4 sts cable] 2 (2, 3) times, 16 (20, 16) sts in trinity st, and 2 edge sts in St st.

FINISHING

Sew shoulder seams.

P.u. 100 (104, 108) sts around neck, work in 1 x 1 rib for 1" (2.5 cm), and b.o. all sts loosely.

P.u. 88 sts around each armhole, work in 1 x 1 rib for 1" (2.5 cm), and b.o. all sts loosely.

Sew side seams.

P.u. 90 (95, 100) sts along each front edge and work in 1 x 1 rib for 1" (2.5 cm).

Work 7 buttonholes evenly spaced along left front for a man or right front for a woman.

Sew on buttons.

6

Summer Knits

Cotton is the quintessential hot-weather fiber. Available in glossy (mercerized) and matte (natural, untreated) finishes, cotton produces knitwear with a crispness no other fiber can approach. Cables and lace are especially well suited to mercerized cottons because the detailing practically jumps out of the fabric. Cotton sweaters are often quick and easy to knit, allowing them to be completed in time for the hot weather. This fiber is also a great choice for children's sweaters, as most cotton yarns can be washed and dried by machine.

Oceanside Cabana

designs: **Kristin Nicholas**
knitting ratings: **Intermediate** (zigzag eyelet pullover)
Beginner (scoop-neck pullover)
photography: **Philip Newton**

Vertical zigzag strips of lace are interspersed between panels of garter stitch in this quick-to-knit bright summer pullover. The edges are worked in easy garter stitch. This is a great project for knitters who want to try lace for the first time.

The double-stranded stockinette pullover with a scoop-shaped neckline uses a mercerized cotton and a novelty nub cotton. Combining two different yarns produces an overall textured and striated effect.

Zigzag Eyelet Pullover

SIZES

Small (Medium, Large)

Finished measurements: 38½ (45½, 52½)" (98, 115.5, 133.5 cm)

MATERIALS

Newport (100% cotton; 50 g = approx. 70 yds/64 m): 12 (13, 13) balls

Equivalent yarn: 800 (840, 910) yds (732, 768, 832 m) of bulky cotton

Knitting needles: sizes 6 and 8 U.S. (4 and 5 mm)

GAUGE

St st with larger needles: 16 sts and 25 rows = 4" (10 cm)

Take time to save time—check your gauge.

PATTERN STITCHES

SSK (slip, slip, knit): Sl next 2 sts knitwise, one at a time, to right-hand needle; then insert tip of left-hand needle into fronts of these sts and k them tog.

■ Garter Stitch

K every row.

■ Zigzag Eyelet Garter Rib (over multiple of 14 sts plus 7)

Row 1 and all WS rows: K7, *p7, k7*; rep bet *s.

Row 2: *K11, k2tog, yo, k1*; rep bet *s, k7.

Row 4: *K10, k2tog, yo, k2*; rep bet *s, k7.

Row 6: *K9, k2tog, yo, k3*; rep bet *s, k7.

Row 8: *K8, k2tog, yo, k4*; rep bet *s, k7.

Row 10: *K7, ssk, yo, k5*; rep bet *s, k7.

Row 12: *K8, yo, ssk, k4*; rep bet *s, k7.

Row 14: *K9, yo, ssk, k3*; rep bet *s, k7.

Row 16: *K10, yo, ssk, k2*; rep bet *s, k7.

Row 18: *K11, yo, ssk, k1*; rep bet *s, k7.

Row 20: *K12, yo, ssk*; rep bet *s, k7.

BACK

With smaller needles, c.o. 77 (91, 105) sts.

Work in garter st for 8 rows.

Change to larger needles and beg zigzag eyelet garter rib.

When piece meas 23 (24, 25)" (58.5, 61, 63.5 cm), b.o. all sts.

FRONT

Work as for back until piece meas 18 (19, 20)" (45.5, 48.5, 51 cm).

SHAPE NECK: Work 28 (34, 40) sts, join a 2nd ball of yarn, b.o. center 21 (23, 25) sts, and work to end.

Working each side sep, b.o. 1 st at neck edge every other row 8 times to give 20 (26, 32) sts at shoulder.

When piece meas same as back at shoulders, b.o. all sts.

SLEEVES

With smaller needles, c.o. 57 (57, 59) sts.

Work in garter st for 6 rows.

Change to larger needles and est patt as follows: Work 4 (4, 5) sts in garter st, work patt repeat 3 times over center 49 sts, work 4 (4, 5) sts in garter st.

At the same time, inc 1 st each end every 3rd row 8 (9, 10) times in garter st to give 73 (75, 79) sts.

When piece meas 5½ (6, 6½)" (14, 15, 16.5 cm), b.o. all sts.

FINISHING

Sew one shoulder seam.

With small circular needle, p.u. 98 (102, 106) sts evenly around neckline.

Work in garter st for 8 rows.

B.o. loosely.

Sew shoulder and neck seam.

Mark underarm points 9 (9½, 10)" (23, 24, 25.5 cm) down in front and back from shoulder.

Sew sleeve bet points.

Sew underarm and side seams.

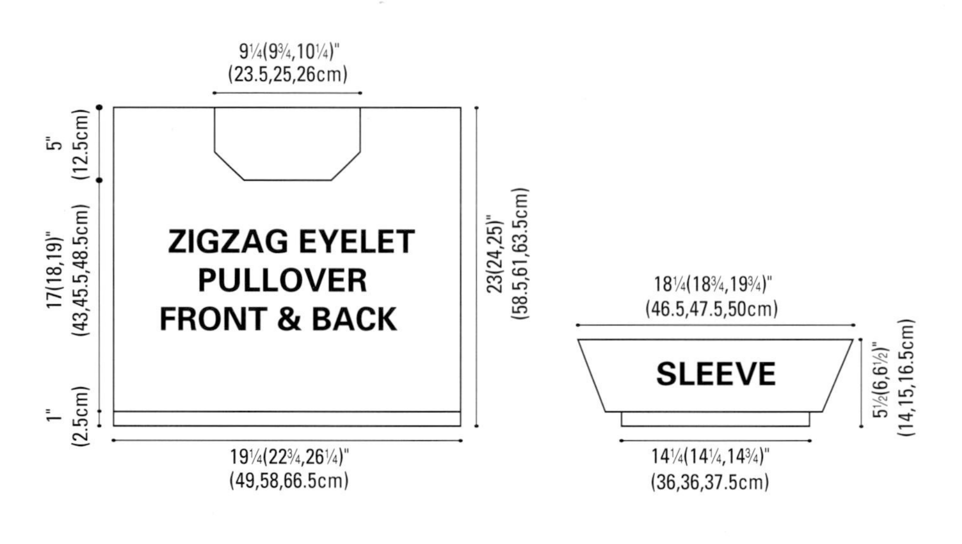

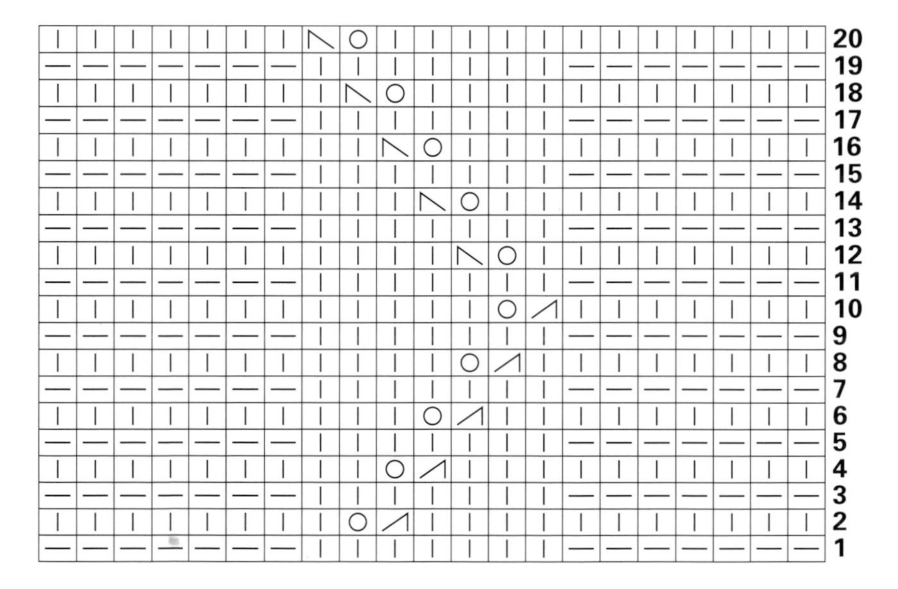

KEY

| = Knit on RS, purl on WS

— = Purl on RS, knit on WS

○ = Yarn over

◺ = Sl1, k1, psso

◿ = K2tog

Scoop-Neck Pullover

SIZES

Small (Medium, Large)

Finished measurements: 42 (44, 46)" (106.5, 112, 117 cm)

MATERIALS

Regatta (100% cotton; 50 g = approx. 123 yds/112 m): 6 (7, 7) hanks and Sea (100% cotton nub; 100 g = approx. 170 yds/155 m): 4 (5, 5) hanks

Equivalent yarn: 700 (740, 860) yds (640, 677, 786 m) each of sport-weight cotton and textured sport-weight nubby cotton

Knitting needles: sizes 7 and 9 U.S. (4.5 and 5.5 mm), 16" (40.5 cm) circular needle in size 7 U.S. (4.5 mm)

GAUGE

St st on larger needles, using 1 strand of each yarn held tog: 15½ sts and 21 rows = 4" (10 cm)

Take time to save time—check your gauge.

PATTERN STITCHES

■ 1 x 1 Ribbing

Row 1 (RS): K1, *p1, k1*; rep bet *s.

Row 2: P1, *k1, p1*; rep bet *s.

■ Stockinette Stitch

Row 1 (RS): K all sts.

Row 2: P all sts.

NOTE: *One strand of each yarn is held together throughout.*

BACK

With smaller needles, c.o. 81 (85, 89) sts.

Work 1 x 1 rib for 3" (7.5 cm).

Change to larger needles and work St st until piece meas 20 (21, 22)" (51, 53.5, 56 cm) from beg.

B.o. all sts.

FRONT

Work as for back until piece meas 17 (18, 19)" (43, 45.5, 48.5 cm).

SHAPE NECK: Work across first 27 (28, 29) sts, join 2nd ball of yarn, b.o. center 27 (29, 31) sts, and work to end.

Working each side sep, b.o. 1 st at each neck edge every other row 7 times to give 20 (21, 22) sts each side.

When piece meas same as back to shoulders, b.o. all sts.

SLEEVES

With smaller needles, c.o. 41 (43, 45) sts.

Work 1 x 1 rib for 1" (2.5 cm).

Change to larger needles and work St st, inc 1 st each end every 2nd row 7 (8, 9) times and every 4th row 5 times to give 65 (69, 73) sts.

When piece meas 7½ (8, 8½)" (19, 20.5, 21.5 cm), b.o. all sts.

FINISHING

Sew shoulder seams.

With circular needle, p.u. 76 (80, 84) sts around neck edge and work 1 x 1 rib for 1" (2.5 cm).

B.o. all sts.

Set in sleeves.

Sew underarm and side seams.

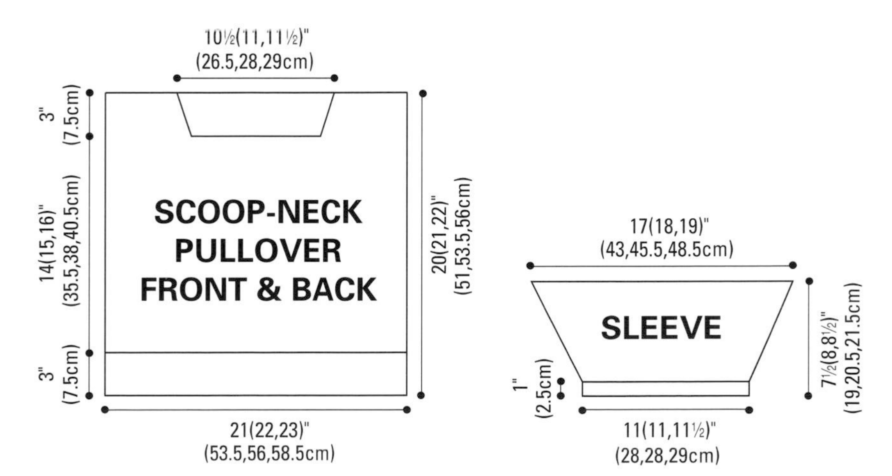

A Day at the Beach

designs: **Kristin Nicholas**
knitting rating: **Beginner**
photography: **Philip Newton**

Stockinette stitch forms the basis for this casual duo. Beginning knitters can master knitting and purling on the fronts, back, and sleeves, then learn cables for the decorative edgings on both the cardigan and pullover. This design could also be easily adapted for knitting by machine and finishing by hand.

V-Neck Pullover

SIZES

Small (Medium, Large)

Finished measurements: 42 (44, 46)" (106.5, 112, 117 cm)

MATERIALS

Boda (68% cotton, 12% linen, 9% acetate, 11% polyester; 100 g = approx. 158 yds/144 m): 7 (8, 8) hanks

Equivalent yarn: 1105 (1175, 1265) yds (1010, 1074, 1157 m) of bulky cotton

Knitting needles: sizes 6 and 8 U.S. (4 and 5 mm), cable needle (cn)

GAUGE

St st on larger needles: 16 sts and 26 rows = 4" (10 cm)

Take time to save time—check your gauge.

PATTERN STITCHES

■ **2 x 2 Ribbing** (over multiple of 4 sts plus 2)

Row 1: *K2, p2*; rep bet *s, end k2.

Row 2: *P2, k2*; rep bet *s, end p2.

■ **Stockinette Stitch**

Row 1 (RS): K all sts.

Row 2: P all sts.

■ **Cable** (over 12 sts)

Rows 1, 3, 5, and 7: K2, p8, k2.

Rows 2, 6, and 8: P2, k8, p2.

Row 4: P2, sl 4 sts to cn and hold in back, k4, k4 from cn, p2.

BACK

With smaller needles and 2 strands, c.o. 78 (82, 86) sts.

Work in 2 x 2 rib for 3½" (9 cm), inc 7 sts evenly spaced across last row to give 85 (89, 93) sts.

Change to larger needles and work in St st until piece meas 23 (24, 25)" (58.5, 61, 63.5 cm) including rib.

SHAPE BACK NECK: Work 31 (32, 34) sts in St st, join a 2nd ball of yarn and b.o. center 23 (25, 25) sts; then work to end.

Working each side sep, b.o. 1 st at neck edge every other row 4 times to give 27 (28, 30) sts at shoulder.

When piece meas 25 (26, 27)" (63.5, 66, 68.5 cm), b.o. all sts.

FRONT

Work same as back until piece meas 15" (38 cm).

SHAPE NECK: Work across first 42 (44, 46) sts, join a 2nd ball of yarn, b.o. center st, and work to end.

Working both sides sep, b.o. 1 st at each neck edge every 4th row 15 (16, 16) times to give 27 (28, 30) sts at each shoulder.

When piece meas same as back, b.o. all sts.

SLEEVES

With smaller needles, c.o. 34 sts.

Work in 2 x 2 rib for 3½" (9 cm).

Change to larger needles and work in St st, inc 1 st each end every 2nd row 0 (3, 2) times, then every 4th row 21 (20, 21) times to give 76 (80, 80) sts.

When piece meas 17 (17½, 18)" (43, 44.5, 45.5 cm), b.o. all sts.

FINISHING

Sew shoulder seams.

With larger needles, c.o. 12 sts.

Work in 12-st cable pattern until piece is equal in length to distance around neck opening.

B.o. all sts.

P.u. 94 (98, 102) sts along cable edge and work in 2 x 2 rib for 3½" (9 cm).

Sew piece to neckline edge, keeping front overlapping section free.

Overlap neckline at front and sew in place.

Sew in sleeves.

Sew underarm and side seams.

Cardigan

MATERIALS

Newport (100% cotton; 50 g = approx. 70 yds/64 m): 16 (17, 17) skeins

Equivalent yarn: 1120 (1150, 1190) yds (1024, 1052, 1088 m) of bulky cotton

Knitting needles: sizes 6 and 8 U.S. (4 and 5 mm), 36" (91.5 cm) circular needle in size 6 U.S. (4 mm), cable needle (cn)

GAUGE

St st on larger needles: 18 sts and 24 rows = 4" (10 cm)

Take time to save time—check your gauge.

PATTERN STITCHES

Same as for pullover

BACK

With smaller needles, c.o. 86 (94, 98) sts.

Work in 2 x 2 rib for 3½" (9 cm), inc 8 (5, 5) sts evenly across last row to give 94 (99, 103) sts.

Change to larger needles and work in St st until piece meas 23 (24, 25)" (58.5, 61, 63.5 cm).

SHAPE BACK NECK: Work 34 (36, 37) sts, join a 2nd ball of yarn and b.o. center 26 (27, 29) sts, work to end.

B.o. 1 st at neck edge every other row 4 times to give 30 (32, 33) sts.

When piece meas 25 (26, 27)" (63.5, 66, 68.5 cm), b.o. all sts.

LEFT FRONT

With smaller needles, c.o. 38 sts.

Work 2 x 2 rib for 3½" (9 cm), inc 3 (5, 7) sts across last row to give 41 (43, 45) sts.

Change to larger needles and work in St st until piece meas 15" (38 cm).

B.o. 1 st at neck edge every 4th row 14 (15, 15) times to give 27 (28, 30) sts at shoulder.

When piece meas same as back, b.o. all sts.

RIGHT FRONT

Work as for left front, but reverse shaping.

SLEEVES

With smaller needles, c.o. 34 sts.

Work in 2 x 2 rib for 3½" (9 cm).

Change to larger needles and work in St st, inc 1 st each end every 2nd row 8 (10, 10) times, then every 4th row 18 times to give 86 (90, 90) sts.

When piece meas 17 (17½, 18)" (43, 44.5, 45.5 cm), b.o. all sts.

FINISHING

Sew shoulder seams.

With smaller needles, c.o. 12 sts.

Work in 2 x 2 rib for 3½" (9 cm).

Change to larger needles and work cable band until it is equal in length to both fronts and back neck when slightly stretched.

Attach to sweater.

With smaller circular needle, p.u. 74 (78, 82) sts from bottom of sweater to shoulder, p.u. 26 (26, 30) sts around back of neck, and p.u. 74 (78, 82) sts to bottom of sweater.

Work in 2 x 2 rib for 3½" (9 cm).

Work 5 buttonholes evenly spaced on right side of band when piece meas 1½" (4 cm).

To do this, b.o. 2 sts and replace them in next row.

Sew in sleeves.

Sew underarm and side seams.

Sew on buttons.

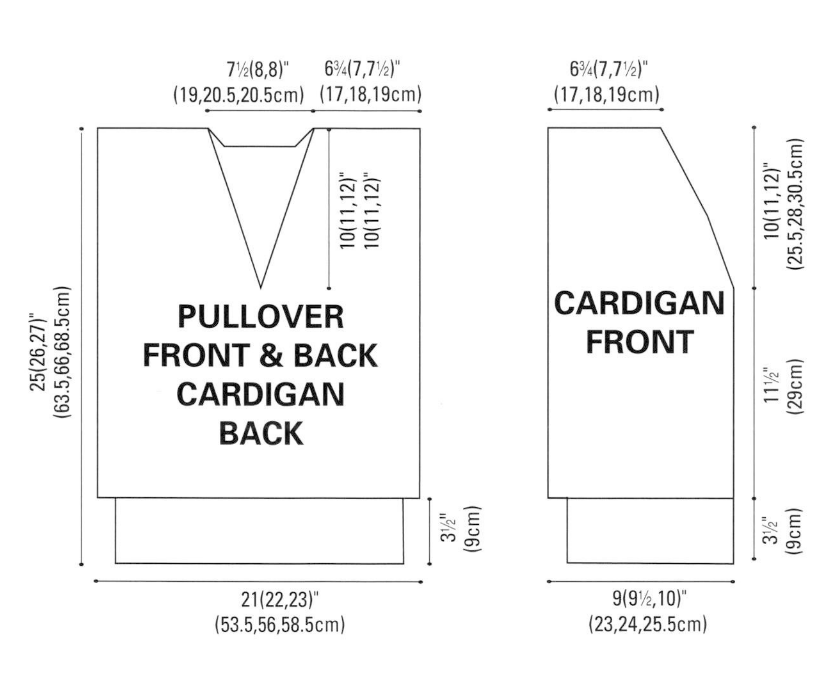

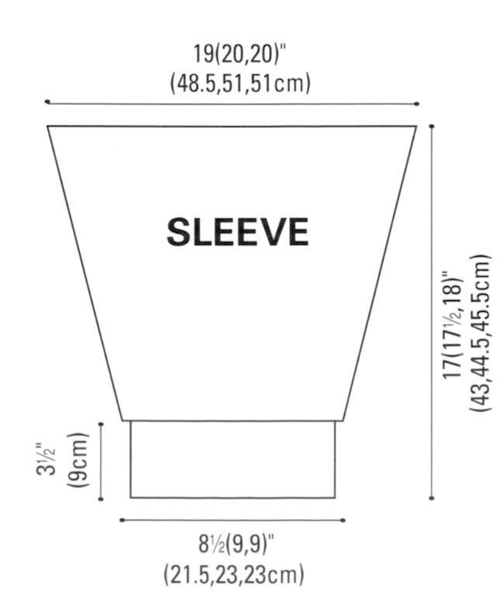

Cotton Gothic

designs: **Susan Mills** (vest)
Cathy Payson (ribbed pullover)
Deborah Newton (textural pullover)

knitting ratings: **Experienced** (vest)
Beginner (ribbed pullover),
Intermediate (textural pullover)

photography: **Philip Newton**

Cotton yarns capture a variety of looks and textures. The openwork vest is worked in a small lace and twist stitch pattern with rounded edges, and it is edged in a picot trim that creates decorative miniature scallops.

The ribbed pullover with a scoop neck is the ultimate in simplicity. The lack of finishing at the hem and cuffs adds an appealing, though subtle, design feature. A single row of crochet provides a delicate finish to the neckline.

Three different textures of yarn are used in the long-sleeve pullover with lace edging and center panel. The center panel, front sides, sleeves, and back all feature different pattern stitches, and the openwork at the bottom border further highlights the differences in texture of the yarns.

Lace Vest

SIZES

Small (Medium, Large)

Finished measurements: 38 (41, 44)" (96.5, 104, 112 cm)

MATERIALS

Willough (35% silk, 65% cotton; 50 g = approx. 136 yds/124 m): 7 (7, 8) hanks

Equivalent yarn: 925 (950, 1090) yds (846, 869, 997 m) of worsted-weight cotton

Knitting needles: size 6 U.S. (4 mm), 24" (61 cm) circular needle in size 5 U.S. (3.75 mm)

Three ½" (1.5 cm) buttons

GAUGE

Hourglass eyelet pattern with larger needles: 20 sts and 25 rows = 4" (10 cm)

Take time to save time—check your gauge.

PATTERN STITCHES

SSK (slip, slip, knit): Sl the first and 2nd sts knitwise, one at a time; then insert the tip of the left-hand needle into the fronts of these two sts from the left, and k them tog from this position.

■ **Hourglass Eyelet** (over multiple of 6 sts plus 1)

Row 1 (RS): K6, *p1, k5*; rep bet *s, end k6.

Row 2: K1, *p5, k1*; rep bet *s.

Row 3: K1, *yo, ssk, p1, k2tog, yo, k1*; rep bet *s.

Row 4: K1, p2, *k1, p5*; rep bet *s, end k1, p2, k1.

Row 5: K3, *p1, k5*; rep bet *s, end p1, k3.

Row 6: K1, p2, *k1, p5*; rep bet *s end k1, p2, k1.

Row 7: K1, *k2tog, yo, k1, yo, ssk, p1*; rep bet *s, end k1 instead of p1.

Row 8: K1, *p5, k1*; rep bet *s.

BACK

With larger needles, c.o. 97 (103, 109) sts.

Work in patt for 10 (11, 12)" (25.5, 28, 30.5 cm).

SHAPE ARMHOLE: Continue in patt and b.o. 6 sts at the beg of the next 2 rows.

Then b.o. 1 st at each end of every row 6 times to give 73 (79, 85) sts.

Continue in patt until piece meas 18 (20, 22)" (45.5, 51, 56 cm), ending with a WSR.

SHAPE NECK: Work across 24 (26, 28) sts in patt, join another ball of yarn, and b.o. 25 (27, 29) sts.

Work across rem 24 (26, 28) sts.

Working each shoulder sep, b.o. 1 st at each neck edge every other row 3 times.

Work even until back meas 19 (21, 23)" (48.5, 53.5, 58.5 cm) to give 21 (23, 25) sts rem for each shoulder.

B.o. all sts.

LEFT FRONT

With larger needles, c.o. 35 (38, 41) sts.

Working in patt, c.o. 3 sts at the end of row 3.

At the end of rows 5, 7, 9, and 11, c.o. 2 sts.

Continue in patt on 46 (49, 52) sts until piece meas 10 (11, 12)" (25.5, 28. 30.5 cm), ending with a WSR.

SHAPE ARMHOLE: B.o. 7 sts at beg of next RSR, then 1 st at the beg of each RSR 5 times.

At the same time, dec 1 st at neck edge at the beg of each WSR 5 times and every other WSR 8 (9, 10) times to give 21 (23, 25) sts rem for each shoulder.

Work even until piece meas same length as back.

B.o. all sts.

RIGHT FRONT

With larger needles, c.o. 35 (38, 41) sts.

Work 2 rows in patt, starting row 1 with k1 (k4, k1) instead of k6.

Continue in patt and inc as follows:

Row 2: C.o. 3 sts at the end of row.

Rows 4, 6, 8, and 10: C.o. 2 sts at the end of the row.

Continue to work in patt on 46 (49, 52) sts until piece meas 10 (11, 12)" (25.5, 28, 30.5 cm), ending with a RSR.

SHAPE ARMHOLE: B.o. 7 sts at the beg of the next row and 1 st at the beg of each WSR 5 times.

At the same time, dec 1 st at neck edge at the beg of each RSR 5 times, and every other RSR 8 (9, 10) times to give 21 (23, 25) sts rem for shoulder.

Work even until piece meas same length as back.

B.o. all sts.

FINISHING

Sew shoulder seams.

P.u. 92 (98, 104) sts along lower back edge and work St st for 8 rows.

Next row: *K2tog, yo*; rep bet *s.

Work St st for 8 more rows; then b.o. all sts.

P.u. 92 (100, 108) sts around each armhole and work as for back edge.

P.u. 298 (314, 330) sts along lower right edge of front, right front edge, back of neck, left front edge, and lower left edge of front and work as for back, making 3 evenly spaced button holes on right front edge (b.o. 2 sts for each buttonhole on row 4 and c.o. 2 sts on row 5).

Work buttonholes on row 4 after picot edge, and c.o. 2 sts over buttonhole on row 5.

Sew side seams and fold each St st band to inside and hem.

Sew on buttons.

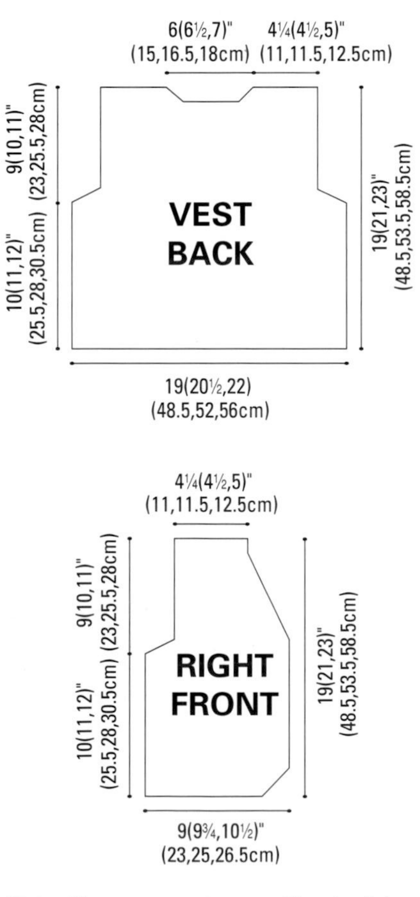

Note: Measurements are without edging.

Ribbed Pullover

SIZES

Small (Medium, Large)

Finished measurements: 42½ (46, 49)" (108, 117, 124.5 cm)

MATERIALS

Sand (100% cotton boucle; 100 g = approx. 154 yds/141 m): 6 (7, 7) hanks

Equivalent yarn: 900 (925, 1075) yds (823, 846, 983 m) of bulky cotton

Knitting needles: sizes 7 and 8 U.S. (4.5 and 5 mm)

Crochet hook in size G

GAUGE

Ribbed patt st on larger needles: 15 sts and 25 rows = 4" (10 cm)

Take time to save time—check your gauge.

BACK

With smaller needles, c.o. 80 (86, 92) sts and begin ribbed patt st:

Row 1: P3 (4, 4), [k6, p6] 5 (6, 7) times, k6, p3 (4, 4).

Row 2: K the k sts and p the p sts.

Rep rows 1 and 2 for 3" (7.5 cm).

Change to larger needles and continue in est patt until piece meas 24 (25, 26)" (61, 63.5, 66 cm).

B.o. all sts.

FRONT

Work as for back until piece meas 20 (21, 22)" (51, 53.5, 56 cm).

SHAPE NECK: Work across first 28 (30, 32) sts, join 2nd ball of yarn, b.o. center 24 (26, 28) sts, and work to end.

Working each side sep, dec 1 st at each neck edge every 5th row to give 23 (25, 27) sts at each shoulder.

When piece meas same as back, b.o. all sts.

SLEEVES

With smaller needles, c.o. 30 sts.

Row 1: [K6, p6] twice, end k6.

Row 2: K the k sts and p the p sts.

Rep rows 1 and 2 for 2" (5 cm).

Change to larger needles and continue as est, inc 1 st each end every 5th row 0 (4, 13) times, every 6th row 15 (15, 8) times, then every 7th row 2 (0, 0) times.

When piece meas 17 (18, 19)" (43, 45.5, 48.5 cm), b.o. all sts.

FINISHING

Sew shoulder seams.

Sew in sleeves.

Sew underarm and side seams.

With crochet hook, work crab stitch (reverse single crochet) around neck edge.

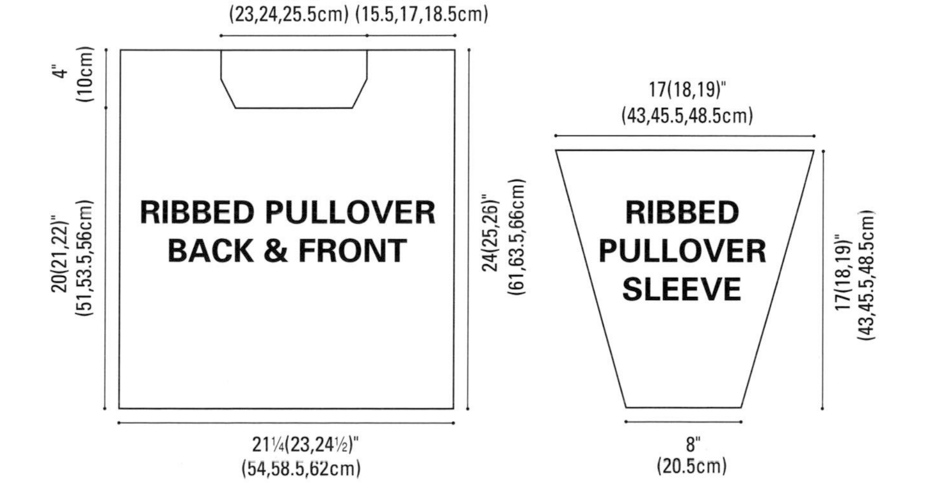

Textural Pullover

SIZES

Small (Medium, Large)

Finished measurements: 42½ (46½, 49)" (108, 117, 124.5 cm)

MATERIALS

Dunes (100% cotton, 100 g = approx. 205 yds/187 m): 7 (8, 9) hanks; Celestial (54% cotton, 43% rayon, 3% polyester; 100 g = approx. 154 yds/141 m): 2 (3, 3) hanks; Waves (97% cotton, 3% polyester; 100 g = approx. 154 yds/141 m): 1 hank

Equivalent yarn: 1435 (1640, 1845) yds (1312, 1500, 1687 m) of thick-and-thin worsted-weight cotton; 300 (450, 450) yds (274, 411, 411 m) of worsted cotton with rayon highlights; 154 yds (141 m) of worsted-weight textured cotton

Knitting needles: sizes 5, 7, and 10½ U.S. (3.75, 4.5, and 7 mm), 16" (40.5 cm) circular needle in size 6 U.S. (4 mm)

GAUGE

Column patt with Dunes yarn and sizes 7 and 10½ needles: 25 sts and 24 rows = 4" (10 cm)

Woven patt with Celestial yarn and size 5 needles: 23 sts and 28 rows = 4" (10 cm)

Take time to save time—check your gauge.

PATTERN STITCHES

■ Scalloped Edging

C.o. 11 sts with Dunes.

Row 1 (RS): Sl 1, k2, yo, p2tog, yo, ssk, (yo, ssk) twice.

Row 2: Yo (to make 1 st), *p1, then (k1, p1) into next st (which is the yo st of previous row); rep from * twice more, p2, yo, p2tog, end k1-b (15 sts).

Row 3: Sl 1, k2, yo, p2tog, k10.

Row 4: Sl 1, p11, yo, p2tog, k1-b.

Row 5: Sl 1, k2, yo, p2tog, k10.

Row 6: B.o. 4 sts purlwise (1 st remains on right-hand needle), p7, yo, p2tog, k1-b (11 sts).

Rep rows 1 through 6.

■ **Column Pattern** (over multiple of 4 sts plus 2 with Dunes)

NOTE: *Use two different needle sizes, 7 and 10½, or those necessary to obtain specified gauge.*

Row 1 (RS): With larger needle, k all sts.

Row 2: With smaller needle, k1, *(skip 3 sts and p the 4th st, drawing it off the needle over the 3 skipped sts), p the 3 skipped sts; rep from *, end k1.

Rep rows 1 and 2.

■ **Woven Stitch** (multiple of 4 sts plus 2 with Celestial)

RT (right twist): K2tog, but do not sl sts off needle; insert right-hand needle between these 2 sts and k the first st again; then sl sts from needle tog.

LT (left twist): Skip 1 st and k 2nd st in back loop, then insert right-hand needle into backs of both sts and k2tog through back loops.

Row 1 (RS): P2, *RT, p2; rep from *.

Row 2: K2, *p2, k2; rep from *.

Row 3: P1, *k2tog, (yo) twice, ssk; rep from *, end p1.

Row 4: P2, *(k1, p1) into the double yo of previous row, p2; rep from *.

Row 5: K2, *p2, LT; rep from *, end p2, k2.

Row 6: P2, *k2, p2; rep from *.

Row 7: P1, yo, *ssk, k2tog, (yo) twice; rep from *, end ssk, k2tog, yo, p1.

Row 8: K2, *p2, (k1, p1) into the double yo of previous row; rep from *, end p2, k2.

Rep rows 1 through 8.

CENTER PANELS (make 2)

With size 5 needles and Celestial, c.o. 32 (36, 36) sts.

P all sts on WSR.

Keeping first 2 sts and last 2 sts in St st (k RS, p WS), work in woven patt over center 28 (32, 32) sts until piece meas 23½ (24, 24½)" (59.5, 61, 62 cm).

B.o. all sts.

SCALLOPED EDGING

With size 7 needles and Dunes, c.o. 11 sts.

Work even in scalloped edging patt until piece meas 42½ (46½, 49)" (108, 118, 124.5 cm) when slightly stretched.

B.o. after full rep is complete.

SIDE SECTIONS (make 2)

With large needles and Dunes, c.o. 102 (110, 118) sts.

Keeping first 2 and last 2 sts in St st (edge sts), work even in column patt over center 98 (106, 114) sts until piece meas 17" (43 cm), ending with a WSR.

ARMHOLE SHAPING: Mark center 2 sts.

Work to center 2 sts, join a 2nd ball of yarn, b.o. 2 sts, and work to end to give 50 (54, 58) sts in each section.

NOTE: *Armhole edges are above 2 b.o. sts at center of piece.*

Next row (WS): In first section, *p2 (edge sts), work in patt over 46 (50, 54) sts, end p2; then with a new ball of yarn in second section, rep from *.

Work both sides at same time until armhole depth meas 7 (7½, 8)" (18, 19, 20.5 cm), ending with a WS.

The piece should meas 24 (24½, 25)" (61, 62, 63.5 cm).

NECK SHAPING: B.o. 2 sts at each outer neck edge 3 times to give 44 (48, 52) sts in each section.

Work even until armhole depth meas 8 (8½, 9)" (20.5, 21.5, 23 cm), ending with a WSR.

SHOULDER SHAPING: B.o. from each inner armhole edge 15 (16, 17) sts twice, then 14 (16, 18) sts once.

SLEEVES

With size 10½ needles and Dunes, c.o. 48 (52, 52) sts.

Keeping first st and last st in St st (edge sts), work in column patt over center 46 (50, 50) sts for 6 rows.

Keep edge sts, inc 1 st each end every 4th row 26 (26, 28) times to give 100 (104, 108) sts.

When piece meas 17 (18, 18)" (43, 45.5, 45.5 cm) or desired length, b.o. all sts.

FINISHING

Steam all Dunes pieces, taking care to steam out any slanting tendencies they may have; then flatten with hands and allow to dry thoroughly.

Steam Celestial panels lightly on WS if necessary.

SLEEVE TRIM: With RS facing, smaller needles, and Waves, p.u. 42 (44, 44) sts evenly along lower sleeve.

K 1 row, p 1 row, b.o. in k.

Sew center panels to side pieces, taking care to match them evenly.

Sew shoulder seams.

NECK TRIM: With circular needle and Waves, p.u. 94 (98, 98) sts evenly around neckline.

P 3 rounds.

B.o. loosely.

Sew sleeves into armholes.

Sew sleeve seams.

Sew ends of scalloped edging tog.

Beg at seam, mark scalloped edging at 4 evenly divided points.

Mark center of sweater at front and back; then mark exact sides of sweater.

Matching markers of edging to markers on sweater and placing seam of edging at side of sweater, sew edging evenly along lower edge, stretching slightly to fit if necessary.

Lay sweater flat, match panels at front and back, and steam again.

Allow to dry thoroughly before wearing.

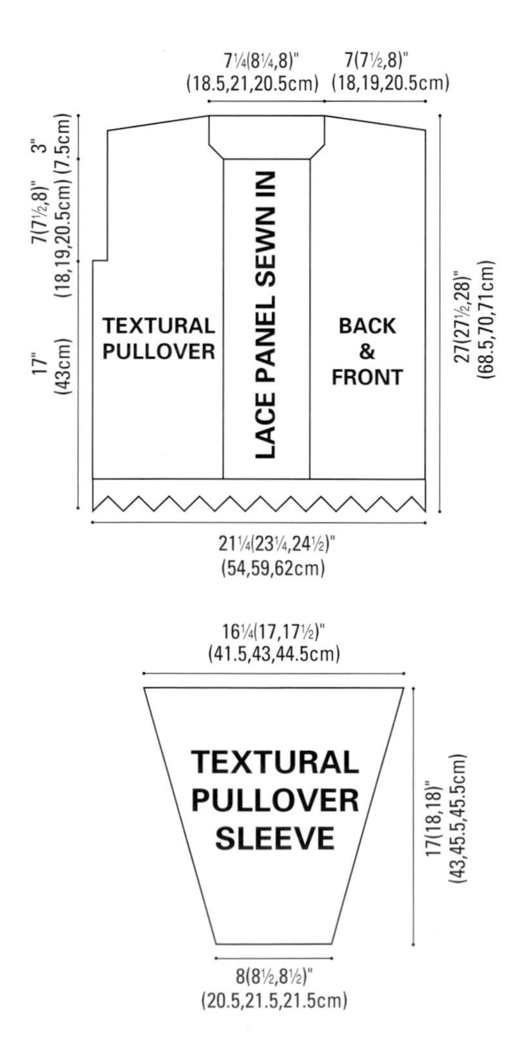

Ruffles & Lace

designs: **Norah Gaughan** (woman's pullover)
Stephanie Gildersleeve (baby's cardigan)

knitting ratings: **Intermediate**

photography: **Philip Newton**

Three-by-three ribbing is separated by columns of lace-edged cables on the woman's short-sleeve, scoop-neck pullover. The eight-row pattern stitch is easily memorized to make a pleasing project for dressy or casual occasions.

The baby's jacket begins with a very large number of stitches, which are quickly decreased to form the bell edging. The body of the cardigan is worked in two different types of ribbing. Choose a very soft cotton for this adorable jacket.

Adult's Cabled T-Shirt

SIZES

Small (Medium, Large)

Finished measurements: 38 (42, 46)" (96.5, 106.5, 117 cm)

MATERIALS

Newport Light (100% cotton; 50 g = approx. 93 yds/85 m): 12 (13, 14) skeins

Equivalent yarn: 1116 (1209, 1302) yds (1020, 1106, 1191 m) of worsted-weight cotton

Knitting needles: size 6 U.S. (4 mm), 24" (61 cm) circular needle in size 4 U.S. (3.25 mm), cable needle (cn)

GAUGE

3 x 3 rib with larger needles: 22 sts and 28 rows = 4" (10 cm)

Take time to save time—check your gauge.

PATTERN STITCHES

See chart.

BACK

C.o. 114 (126, 138) sts.

Work in pattern according to chart until piece meas 20 (21, 22)" (51, 53.5, 56 cm).

SHAPE SHOULDERS AND BACK NECK: Keeping in est patt, b.o. 8 (8, 9) sts, work across 36 (39, 44) sts, join another ball of yarn, b.o. center 26 (32, 32) sts, and work to end of row.

Next row: B.o. 8 (8, 9) sts and work to center b.o. sts.

Working both sides at once, b.o. at neck edge 5 sts 3 times, and at the same time, b.o. at shoulder edge 7 (8, 9) sts 3 (3, 1) times, then 0 (0, 10) sts 0 (0, 2) times.

FRONT

Work as for back until piece meas 17 (18, 19)" (43, 45.5,48.5 cm).

SHAPE FRONT NECK: Work 49 (53, 59) sts, join another ball of yarn, b.o. center 16 (20, 20) sts, and work to end of row.

Working each side sep, b.o. at neck edge 4 sts once, 3 sts twice, 2 sts 3 (4, 4) times, then 1 st 4 (3, 3) times.

When piece meas the same as back to shoulder, shape shoulders as for back.

SLEEVES

C.o. 68 (78, 91) sts.

Work in patt according to chart, and at the same time, inc 1 st each side every 4th row 10 times, keeping all inc sts in 3 x 3 rib.

Work even on 88 (98, 111) sts until piece meas 6" (15 cm) from beg.

B.o. all sts.

FINISHING

Sew shoulder seams.

Neck band: With smaller circular needle, p.u. 132 (144, 144) sts evenly around neck.

Work in 2 x 2 rib (k2, p2 for all rows) for 1½" (4 cm).

B.o. all sts.

Fold rib to inside and sew down.

Sew sleeve and underarm seams.

Baby's Ruffled Cardigan

SIZES

6 months (12 months, 18 months)

Finished measurements: 22½ (24½, 26½)" (57, 62, 67.5 cm)

MATERIALS

Caitlin (100% cotton; 50 g = approx. 154 yds/141 m): 3 (3, 4) balls

Equivalent yarn: 462 (462, 616) yds (422, 422, 563 m) of fingering-weight yarn

Knitting needles: size 2 U.S. (2.75 mm), circular knitting needle in size 3 U.S. (3 mm)

Crochet hook in size B

Five ⅜" (1 cm) buttons

GAUGE

Rib pattern with larger needles: 24 sts and 28 rows = 4" (10 cm)

Twisted rib with smaller needles: 17 sts and 32 rows = 4" (10 cm)

Take time to save time—check your gauge.

PATTERN STITCHES

SL 2, K1, P2SSO: Sl 2 sts as if to knit, k1, pass the 2 slipped sts over.

■ **1 x 3 Rib** (over 4 sts)

All Rows
4 3 2 1

■ **Twisted Ribbing**

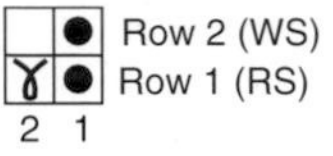

□ = K on the RS, p on the WS

● = P on the RS, k on the WS

Y = K into the back loop

NOTE: *Body is made in one piece, beg at lower edge and divided for fronts and back at armholes. Don't be afraid of the large number of sts to be cast on--they are decreased quickly after row 3. Use a contrasting piece of scrap yarn to mark sts as they are cast on (every 10 or 25 sts) to make counting easier.*

BODY

With circular needle, c.o. 383 (419, 455) sts.

Make ruffled edge:

Row 1 (WS): K3, p1, (k3, p9) 31 (34, 37) times, k3, p1, k3.

Row 2 : P3, k1, p3, (k9, p3) 31 (34, 37) times, k1 p3.

Row 3: Rep row 1.

Row 4: P3, k1, p3, (k3, sl 2, k1, p2sso, k3, p3) 31 (34, 37) times, k1, p3 to give 321 (351, 381) sts.

Row 5: K3, p1, (k3, p7) 31 (34, 37) times, k3, p1, k3.

Row 6: P3, k1, p3, (k3, sl 2, k1, p2sso, k3, p3) 31 (34, 37) times, k1, p3 to give 259 (283, 307) sts.

Row 7: K3, p1, (k3, p5) 31 (34, 37) times, k3, p1, k3.

Row 8: P3, k1, p3, (k1, sl 2, k1, p2sso, k1, p3) 31 (34, 37) times, k1, p3 to give 197 (215, 233) sts.

Row 9: K3, p1, (k3, p3) 31 (34, 37) times, k3, p1, k3.

Row 10: P3, k1, p3, (sl 2, k1, p2sso, p3) 31 (34, 37) times, k1, p3 to give 135 (147, 159) sts.

Row 11: K3, (p1, k3) 33 (36, 39) times.

Row 12: P3, (k1, p3) 33 (36, 39) times.

Rep rows 11 and 12 for 1 x 3 rib until body meas 6 (6, 6½)" (15, 15, 16.5 cm), ending with a WSR.

DIVIDE FOR ARMHOLES: Work 30 (33, 36) sts in 1 x 3 rib, b.o. next 6 sts, work 63 (69, 75) sts in patt, b.o. next 6 sts, and work across rem 30 (33, 36) sts.

LEFT FRONT

Work on first 30 (33, 36) sts in patt for 1" (2.5 cm), ending with a WSR.

Next row (RS): Change to smaller needles (leaving sts for back and right front on circular needle) and beg working in 1 x 1 twisted rib st, centering ribs as est in 1 x 3 rib.

Work until armhole meas 2½ (3, 3½)" (6.5, 7.5, 9 cm).

SHAPE NECK: B.o. 9 (10, 12) sts at neck edge; then dec 1 st at neck edge every other row 3 times.

When piece meas 10" (25.5 cm) from beg, b.o. rem 18 (20, 21) sts.

BACK

With larger needles, beg with a WSR, work 63 (69, 75) sts in patt as est for 1" (2.5 cm), ending with a WSR.

Change to smaller needles and work in 1 x 1 twisted rib until piece meas the same as left front; then b.o. all sts.

RIGHT FRONT

Beg with a WSR, work 30 (33, 36) sts in patt as est for 1" (2.5 cm), ending with a WSR.

Change to smaller needles and work in 1 x 1 twisted rib until armhole meas 2½ (3, 3½)" (6.5, 7.5, 9 cm).

Shape neck as for left front, reversing shaping.

When piece meas 10" (25.5 cm) from beg, b.o. rem 18 (20, 21) sts.

SLEEVES

With larger needles, c.o. 39 (43, 51) sts.

P 1 row (WS).

Next row: P3, work 9 (10, 12) rep of 1 x 3 rib chart.

Cont in 1 x 3 rib and inc 1 st each edge every 6th row 6 (7, 7) times to give 51 (57, 65) sts.

Work even until piece meas 5½ (6, 6½)" (14, 15, 16.5 cm) and b.o. all sts.

FINISHING

Sew shoulder seams.

Sew sleeve seams, leaving ½" (1.5 cm) opening at the upper edge.

Sew in sleeves, stitching each side of upper ½" (1.5 cm) of sleeve to half of the b.o. armhole sts.

EDGING: From RS, (single crochet (sc), chain (ch) 1) along right front, neck, and left front, working sc into every other row and taking care to keep work flat.

Work (sc, ch1, sc) at corners, end sc in lower edge.

Ch 2, turn.

Mark position of 5 buttonholes evenly spaced on right front edge.

Next row: (Sc in ch1 space, ch1) rep along edge, work (sc, ch1, sc) in corner ch 1 sp, dec at curves of neck as necessary, and work (ch 3, skip next ch1 space, sc in ch1 space) at each buttonhole marker, finish row.

Next row: (Sl st into ch1 space, ch1) around and work (sl st, ch1, sl st) in each buttonhole ch 3.

Sew on buttons.

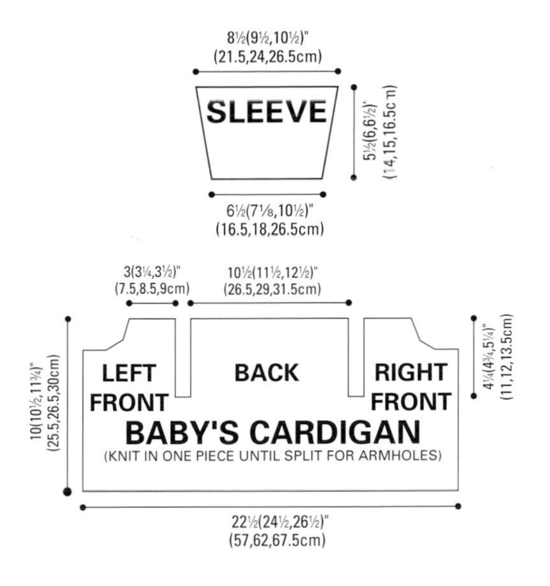

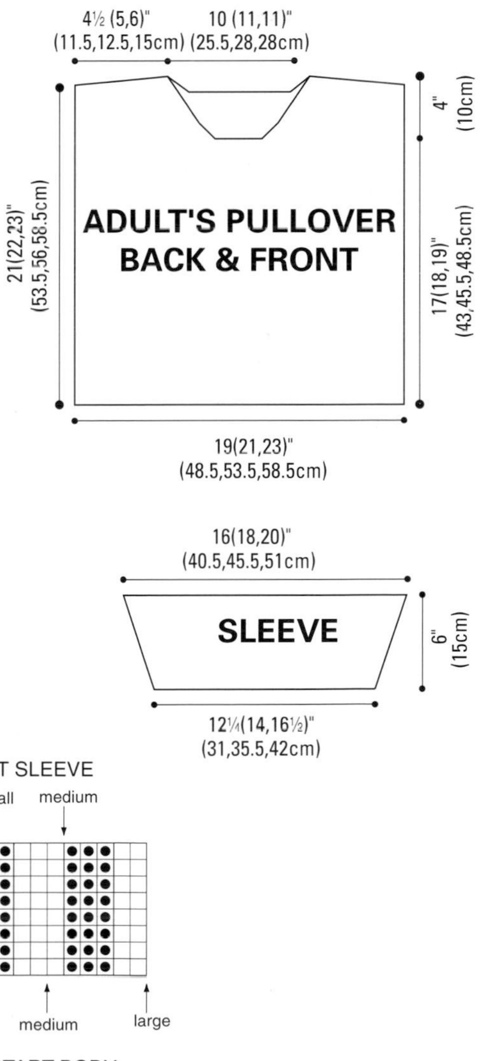

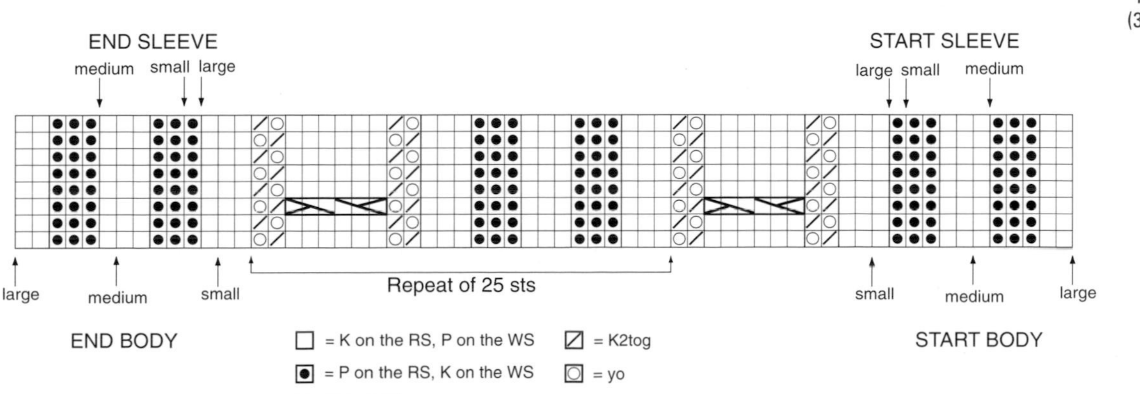

7

International Influences

As the world continues to shrink and the food, music, and artwork of once-foreign cultures become familiar, it becomes more appropriate to envision American knitwear designs in less conventional settings. For this chapter, accessories were combined with sweaters to create a series of ensembles inspired by the cultures of other countries. To further distinguish these designs, we chose a portrait style of photography, using painted back-drops and natural lighting to complement the knitwear. These sweaters range from simple mohair ribs to complex Fair Isle patterns, making them suitable for a variety of lifestyles in whatever country you call home.

Reykjavik, Iceland

designs: **Susan Mills**
knitting rating: **Beginner**
photography: **Philip Newton**

Mohair is a superb yarn for outer wear, and this trio of mohair sweaters, including two pullovers and a cardigan, is very easy to knit. The cardigan is especially well suited for beginners, as it is worked in stockinette stitch with one-by-one ribbing. An overall pattern of ribs with an easy open braid cable inset at each side is featured on the two pullovers in the center–his a tunic and hers a shorter version. The gray V-neck, which is made with two strands of yarn in a four-by-four rib stitch, is very thick and warm.

Cardigan

SIZES

Small (Medium, Large, Extra Large)

Finished measurements: 40 (44, 48, 52)" (101.5, 112, 122, 132 cm)

MATERIALS

La Gran (74% mohair, 13% wool, 13% nylon; 1½ oz = approx. 90 yds/82 m): 11 (11, 12, 13) balls for cropped version or 14 (15, 15, 16) balls for tunic

Equivalent yarn: 990 (990, 1080, 1170) yds (905, 905, 988, 1070 m) of brushed bulky mohair for cropped version or 1260 (1350, 1350, 1440) yds (1152, 1234, 1234, 1317 m) for tunic

Knitting needles: sizes 7 and 9 U.S. (4.5 and 5.5 mm)

Five 1" (2.5 cm) buttons

GAUGE

St st on larger needles: 16 sts = 4" (10 cm)

Take time to save time—check your gauge.

PATTERN STITCHES

■ Stockinette Stitch

Row 1 (WS): P all sts.

Row 2: K all sts.

■ 1 x 1 Rib (over an even number of sts)

All rows: *K1, p1; rep from *.

BACK

With smaller needles, c.o. 80 (88, 96, 104) sts.

Work 1 x 1 rib for 1" (2.5 cm).

Change to larger needles and work in St st until back meas 20 (20½, 21, 22)" (51, 52, 53.5, 56 cm) for cropped version or 26 (26½, 27, 27½)" (66, 67.5, 68.5, 70 cm) for tunic.

B.o. all sts.

RIGHT FRONT

With smaller needles, c.o. 38 (42, 46, 48) sts and work 1 x 1 rib for 1" (2.5 cm).

Work in St st until piece meas 17 (17½, 18, 19)" (43, 44.5, 45.5, 48.5 cm) for cropped version or 23 (23½, 24, 24½)" (58.5, 59.5, 61, 62 cm) for tunic, ending with a WSR.

SHAPE NECK: At neck edge, b.o. 4 sts 0 (0, 0, 1) time, 3 sts 1 (2, 2, 1) times, 2 sts 4 (3, 3, 3) times, and 1 st 2 (2, 2, 3) times.

B.o. all sts.

LEFT FRONT

Work as for right front, reversing all shaping.

SLEEVES

With smaller needles, c.o. 32 (34, 36, 38) sts.

Work 1 x 1 rib for 1" (2.5 cm).

Change to larger needles and beg working in St st.

At the same time, inc 1 st every other row 8 times, every 4th row 10 times, and every 6th row 2 (2, 2, 3) times.

When sleeve meas 15½ (16, 16½, 17)" (39.5, 40.5, 42, 43 cm) or desired length, b.o. all sts.

FINISHING

Sew shoulder, side, and sleeve seams.

With smaller circular needle, p.u. 52 (56, 60, 64) sts around neck, work 1 x 1 rib for 1" (2.5 cm), and b.o. all sts loosely.

P.u. 74 (76, 78, 82) sts for cropped version or 98 (100, 102, 104) sts for tunic evenly along left front and work 1 x 1 rib for 6 rows.

RIGHT FRONT: Work rib as for left front; then work 5 buttonholes for cropped version or 7 buttonholes for tunic, spacing them evenly.

To make buttonholes: B.o. 2 sts for each buttonhole on the 3rd row; on row 4, c.o. 2 sts where you b.o. 2 sts on 3rd row.

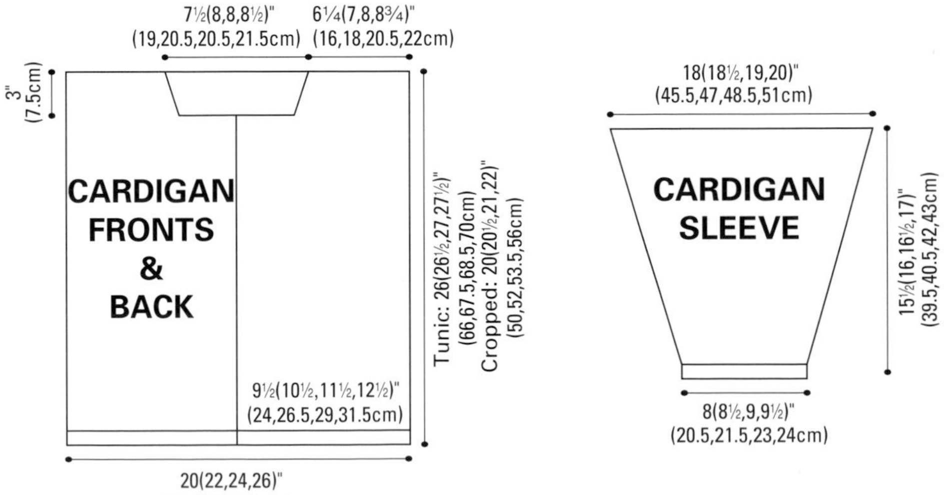

Big Cable Pullover

SIZES

Small (Medium, Large, Extra Large)

Finished measurements: 41½ (46½, 49, 54)" (105.5, 118, 124.5, 137 cm)

MATERIALS

La Gran (74% mohair, 13% wool,13% nylon; 1½ oz = approx. 90 yds/82 m): 9 (10, 10, 11) balls for cropped version or 12 (13, 13, 14) balls for tunic

Equivalent yarn: 810 (850, 900, 990) yds (741, 777, 823, 905 m) of bulky brushed mohair for cropped version or 1080 (1140, 1170, 1260) yds (988, 1042, 1070, 1152 m) for tunic

Knitting needles: sizes 6 and 9 U.S. (4 and 5.5 mm), 16" (40.5 cm) circular needle in size 6 U.S. (4 mm), cable needle (cn)

GAUGE

2 x 2 rib with larger needles: 13 sts and 20 rows = 4" (10 cm) when blocked or slightly stretched

Open braid cable: 13 sts = 2¾" (7 cm)

Take time to save time—check your gauge.

PATTERN STITCHES

■ **2 x 2 Rib** (over multiple of 4 sts plus 2)

Row 1 (WS): *P2, k2; rep from *, end p2.

Row 2: *K2, p2; rep from *, end k2.

Rep rows 1 and 2.

Open Braid Cable (over 13 sts)

FC (front cross): Sl 2 sts to cn and hold in front, p1, k2 from cn.

BC (back cross): Sl 1 st to cn and hold in back, k2, p1 from cn.

4CB: Sl 2 sts to cn and hold in back, k2, k2 from cn.

4FC: Sl 2 sts to cn and hold in front, k2, k2 from cn.

Row 1 (WS): K3, p4, k2, p2, k2.

Row 2: P2, FC, BC, FC, p2.

Row 3 and all WSR: Work sts as they appear.

Row 4: P3, 4CB, p2, k2, p2.

Row 6: P2, BC, FC, BC, p2.

Row 8: P2, k2, p2, 4FC, p3.

BACK

With smaller needles, c.o. 76 (84, 88, 96) sts.

Work 14 (18, 18, 22) sts in 2 x 2 rib, 13 sts in open braid cable, 22 (22, 26, 26) sts in 2 x 2 rib, 13 sts in open braid cable, and 14 (18, 18, 22) sts in 2 x 2 rib.

Cont working in est patt, changing to larger needles after 3" (7.5 cm).

When piece meas 20 (21, 22, 23)" (51, 53.5, 56, 58.5 cm) for cropped version or 26 (27, 28, 29)" (66, 68.5, 71, 73.5 cm) for tunic, b.o. all sts.

FRONT

Work as for back until 2" (5 cm) less than desired length.

SHAPE NECK: Work across 30 (34, 34, 38) sts, place center 16 (16, 20, 20) sts on holder, join another ball of yarn, and work across rem 30 (34, 34, 38) sts.

Working each side separately, b.o. 1 st each neck edge every other row 3 times to give 27 (31, 31, 35) sts rem on each shoulder.

When piece meas the same length as back, b.o. all sts.

SLEEVES

With smaller needles, c.o. 22 (22, 26, 26) sts.

Work in 2 x 2 rib for 3" (7.5 cm).

Change to larger needles and cont working in 2 x 2 rib; at the same time, inc 1 st each edge every other row 5 times, then every 4th row 13 (15, 15, 15) times to give 58 (62, 66, 66) sts.

Work even until sleeve meas 16 (16½, 17, 17½)" (40.5, 42, 43, 44.5 cm).

B.o. all sts.

FINISHING

Sew shoulder, side, and sleeve seams.

With circular needle, p.u. 56 (56, 64, 64) sts around neck, including sts on holder at neck front.

Work 2 x 2 rib for 1" (2.5 cm), matching rib patt with ribs at the center front of sweater.

B.o. all sts loosely.

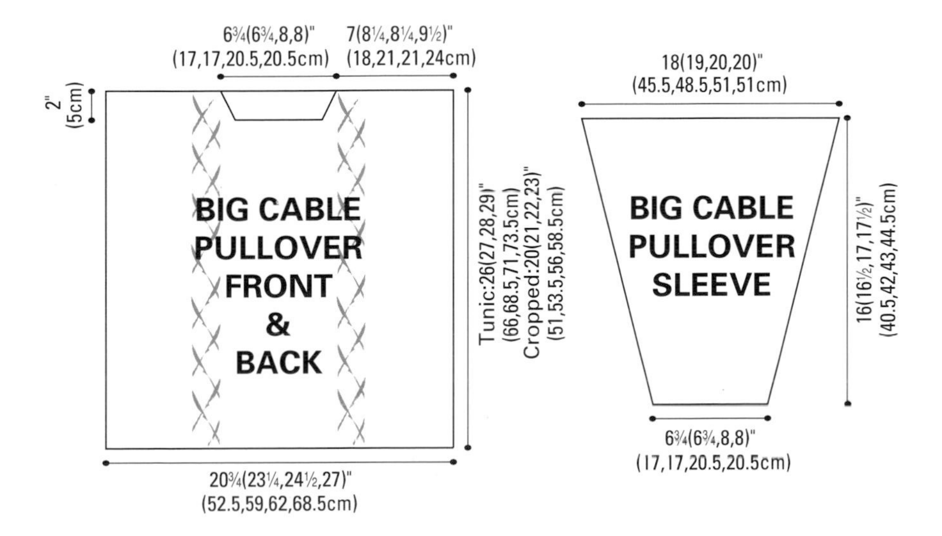

V-Neck Pullover

SIZES

Small (Medium, Large)

Finished measurements: 41½ (48, 54½)" (105.5, 122, 138.5 cm)

MATERIALS

La Gran (74% mohair, 13% wool, 13% nylon; 1½ oz = approx. 90 yds/82 m): 13 (14, 15) balls

Equivalent yarn: 1170 (1260, 1350) yds (1070, 1152, 1234 m) of bulky brushed mohair

Knitting needles: size 10-1/2 U.S. (7 mm)

OPTION: *Use one strand of La Gran and one strand of Sharon or Montera for a different texture.*

GAUGE

4 x 4 rib with 2 strands of yarn: 10 sts and 14 rows = 4" (10 cm) when slightly stretched

Take time to save time—check your gauge.

PATTERN STITCHES

SSK: Sl the first and 2nd sts knitwise, one at a time; then insert the tip of the left-hand needle into the front of these 2 sts from the left, and k them tog from this position.

TBL: through the back loop.

■ **4 x 4 Rib** (over multiple of 8 sts plus 4)

Row 1 (RS): *K4, p4; rep from *, end k4.

Row 2: *P4, k4; rep from *, end p4.

■ **Left Front Decrease**

RSR: Work in patt to last 4 sts, k2tog, k2.

WSR: P2, p2tog, work in patt to end of row.

■ **Right Front Decrease**

RSR: K2, ssk, work in patt to end of row.

WSR: Work in patt to last 4 sts, p2tog-tbl, p2.

BACK

With 2 strands of yarn, c.o. 52 (60, 68) sts and work 4 x 4 rib until piece meas 24 (26, 28)" (61, 66, 71 cm) or desired length.

B.o. all sts.

FRONT

Work as for back until piece meas 16 (17, 18)" (40.5, 43, 45.5 cm) or 8 (9, 10)" (20.5, 23, 25.5 cm) less than back.

DIVIDE FOR NECK: Work across 26 (30, 34) sts, join another ball of yarn, and work across rem 26 (30, 34) sts.

Work dec at neck edges every 3rd row until 18 (20, 23) sts rem for each shoulder.

Work even until same length as back.

B.o. all sts.

SLEEVES

With 2 strands of yarn, c.o. 20 sts.

Beg working in 4 x 4 rib, and at the same time, while keeping in patt, inc 1 st each edge every other row 5 times, then every 4th row 9 (11, 12) times to give 48 (52, 54) sts.

When sleeve meas 16 (17, 18)" (40.5, 43, 45.5 cm), b.o. all sts.

FINISHING

Sew shoulder, sleeve, and side seams.

Block to required size.

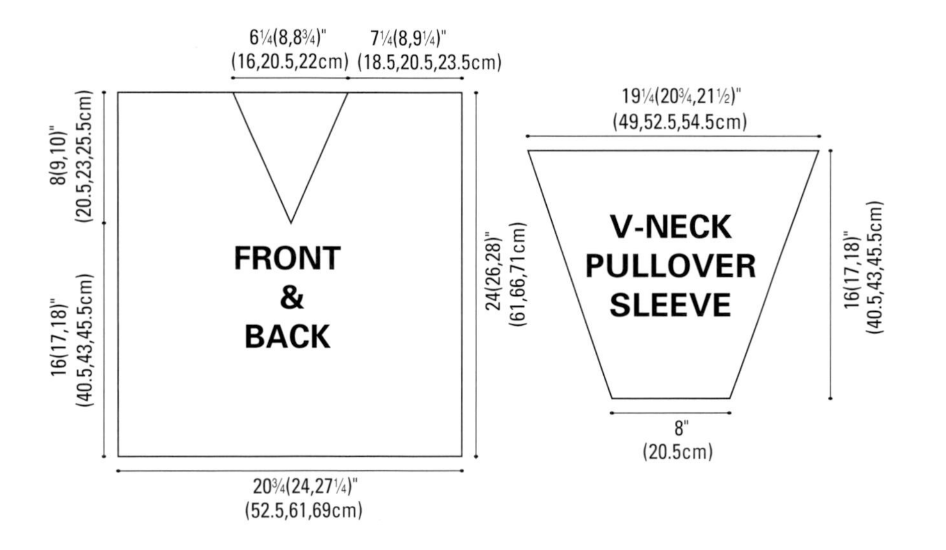

Santiago, Chile

designs: **Kristin Nicholas**
knitting rating: **Experienced**
photography: **Philip Newton**

In the style of men's formal wear, the front of this pocketed vest has a multicolored Fair Isle pattern, and the back is worked in a single color in an overall textured stitch. The edges are trimmed with one-by-one ribbing.

The woman's cropped pullover is worked in double seed stitch that is inset with traveling miniature cables. A modified diamond cable with a central braid fills the central panel, and the neckline is finished in miniature cables.

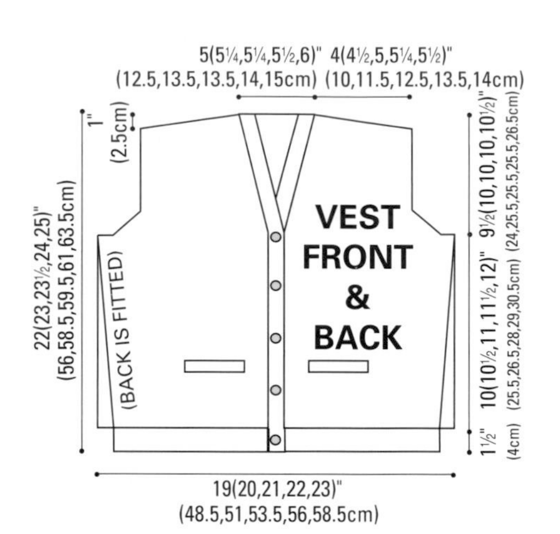

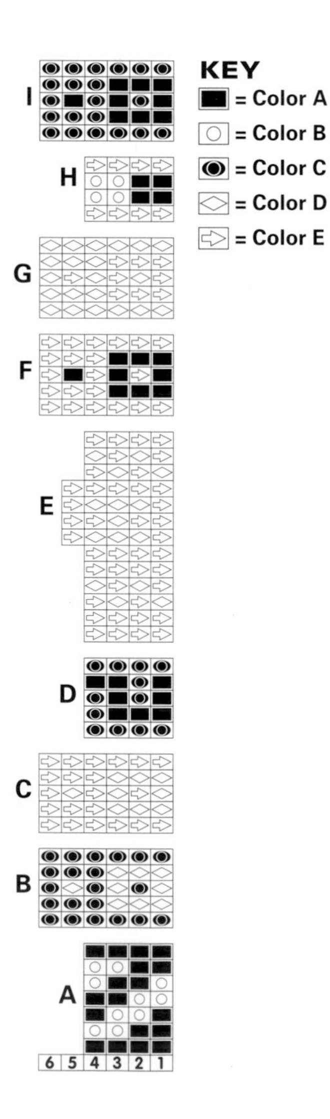

Fair Isle Vest

SIZES

Extra Small (Small, Medium, Large, Extra Large)

Finished measurements: 38 (40, 42, 44, 46)" (96.5, 101.5, 106.5, 112, 117 cm)

MATERIALS

Inca alpaca (100% alpaca; 50 g = approx. 115 yds/105 m): 1 hank each of colors A, C, and D; 5 hanks of B; 2 hanks of E

Equivalent yarn: 115 yds (105 m) of sport-weight alpaca in each of colors A, C, and D; 500 (510, 525, 550, 575) yds (457, 466, 480, 503, 526 m) of B; 230 yds (210 m) of E

Knitting needles: sizes 5 and 7 U.S. (3.75 and 4.5 mm)

Two stitch holders

Seven ¾" (2 cm) buttons

GAUGE

St st on larger needles: 24 sts and 24 rows = 4" (10 cm)

Textured stitch on larger needles: 20 sts and 28 rows = 4" (10 cm)

Take time to save time—check your gauge.

PATTERN STITCHES

■ Stockinette Stitch

Row 1 (RS): K all sts.

Row 2 (WS): P all sts.

In the rnd: K all sts.

■ Fair Isle Stitch

Work in St st as shown on chart, carrying yarn loosely behind work.

■ Twisted 1 x 1 Rib (over an odd number of sts)

Row 1: *P1, k1 into back of st (k1-b); rep from *, end p1.

Row 2: K1, *p1, k1; rep from *.

■ Textured Stitch (over 4 sts)

Row 1: K all sts.

Row 2 and all WSR: P all sts.

Row 3: K2, p2.

Row 5: K all sts.

Row 7: P2, k2.

Rep rows 1 through 8.

BACK

With smaller needles and color B, c.o. 77 (81, 85, 91, 95) sts.

Work in 1 x 1 twisted rib for 1½" (4 cm).

In last row of rib, inc 7 (11, 11, 9, 9) sts evenly across to give 84 (92, 96, 100, 104) sts.

Change to larger needles and work in textured st.

At the same time, inc 1 st each end every 10 rows 5 (4, 5, 5, 6) times to give 94 (100, 106, 110, 116) sts.

When piece meas 11½ (12, 12½, 13, 13½)" (29, 30.5, 31.5, 33, 34 cm), shape armholes: B.o. 5 sts at beg of next 2 rows, then 1 st each end every 2nd row 10 times to give 64 (70, 76, 80, 86) sts.

When piece meas 21 (22, 22½, 23, 24)" (53.5, 56, 57, 58.5, 61 cm), shape shoulders: B.o. 6 (7, 8, 8, 9) sts at beg of next 2 rows, b.o. 7 (7, 8, 9, 9) sts at beg of next 2 rows, and b.o. 7 (8, 9, 9, 10) sts at beg of next 2 rows.

B.o. rem back neck sts.

POCKETS (make 2)

Using color E, c.o. 24 sts on larger needles.

Work in St st until piece meas 4" (10 cm).

Slip sts to holder.

RIGHT FRONT

With smaller needles and color B, c.o. 51 (53, 57, 59, 61) sts.

Work in 1 x 1 twisted rib for 1½" (4 cm).

In last rows of rib, inc 6 (7, 6, 9, 10) sts to give 57 (60, 63, 68, 71) sts.

Change to larger needles and beg Fair Isle pattern on RS on first st.

Work charts as est in following sequence: A, B, C, D, E, A, B, F, G, D, E, A, B, H, G, I, E, A, B, H.

When piece meas 5½" (14 cm) and you are beg WS, insert pocket back.

Work 15 sts, sl next 24 sts to holder, work 24 sts from pocket, work to end.

Cont in patt as est until piece meas 11½ (12, 12½, 13, 13½)" (29, 30.5, 31.5, 33, 34 cm).

SHAPE ARMHOLES: B.o. 6 sts at armhole edge.

Then b.o. 1 st at armhole edge every other row 12 times to dec armhole edge by 18 sts total.

At the same time, b.o. 1 st at neck edge now and every 4th row 15 (16, 15, 17, 18) times total to give 24 (26, 30, 31, 33) sts rem at shoulder.

When piece meas 21 (22, 22½, 23, 24)" (53.5, 56, 57, 58.5, 61 cm), shape shoulder: At armhole edge, b.o. 8 (7, 10, 10, 11) sts twice, then 8 (8, 10, 11, 11) rem sts.

LEFT FRONT

Work same as right front, reversing shaping and pocket placement.

To beg Fair Isle patt and make center front match exactly, beg on first st on the WSR.

FINISHING

BUTTON BAND: With smaller needles and color B, c.o. 11 sts.

Row 1 (RS): K1, *k1-b, p1; rep from *.

Row 2: *K1, p1; rep from *, end k1.

Rep until piece meas same as from bottom of front vest to center back of neck while stretching slightly.

Sew purl st edge of band to vest.

Place markers for buttons 1" (2.5 cm) from bottom of vest and at first center front neck dec.

Evenly space rem 5 markers for other buttons.

BUTTONHOLE BAND: Work as button band, working buttonholes opposite markers.

Row 1 (RS): *P1, k1-b; rep from *, end k1.

Row 2: *K1, p1; rep from *, end k1.

Work buttonhole by b.o. center st and c.o. over b.o. st in next row.

Sew purl st edge of band to vest.

ARMHOLE BAND: Using smaller circular needle, p.u. 85 (89, 89, 89, 93) sts evenly around armholes.

Work in 1 x 1 twisted rib for 1" (2.5 cm).

B.o. all sts.

Sew side seams.

POCKETS

Using smaller needles, p.u. sts on holder.

Work in 1 x 1 twisted rib for 1" (2.5 cm), dec 1 st in first row to give odd number of sts.

B.o. all sts.

Tack at edges.

Sew pockets to inside.

Sew on buttons.

Cropped Aran

SIZES

Small (Medium, Large)

Finished measurements: 44 (48, 52)" (112, 122, 132 cm)

MATERIALS

Camden (100% cotton; 100 g = approx. 192 yds/176 m): 6 (7, 7) hanks

Equivalent yarn: 1150 (1300, 1350) yds (1052, 1189, 1234 m) of worsted-weight cotton

Knitting needles: sizes 5 and 7 U.S. (3.75 and 4.5 mm), 16" (40.5 cm) circular needle in size 5 U.S. (3.75 mm), cable needle (cn)

GAUGE

Double moss st with larger needles: 18 sts and 23 rows = 4" (10 cm)

Cable pattern: 20 sts = 4" (10 cm)

Take time to save time—check your gauge.

PATTERN STITCHES

■ **Double Moss Stitch** (over an odd number of sts)

Row 1: *P1, k1; rep from *, end p1.

Row 2: *K1, p1; rep from *, end k1.

Row 3: *K1, p1; rep from *, end k1.

Row 4: *P1, k1; rep from *, end p1.

■ **Center Cable Pattern** (over 70 sts)

See chart.

BACK

With smaller needles, c.o. 108 (120, 130) sts.

Work 19 (25, 30) sts in double moss st, work center cable patt over 70 sts, end with 15 (25, 30) sts in double moss st.

When 2" (5 cm) are complete, change to larger needles, and cont as est.

When piece meas 19 (20, 21)" (48.5, 51, 53.5 cm) or desired length, b.o. all sts.

FRONT

Work same as back.

When piece meas 17 (18, 19)" (43, 45.5, 48.5 cm), shape neck: Work 41 (46, 50) sts, join 2nd ball of yarn, and b.o. center 26 (28, 30) sts.

Work to end.

At neck edge, b.o. 1 st every other row 5 times to give 36 (41, 45) sts at shoulder.

When piece meas same as back, b.o. all sts.

SLEEVES

With smaller needles, c.o. 35 (35, 39) sts.

Work for 2" (5 cm).

Change to larger needles and inc 1 st each end every 2nd row 0 (2, 0) times, then every 4th row 23 (23, 25) times to give 81 (85, 89) sts.

When piece meas 16 (17, 17½)" (40.5, 43, 44.5 cm) or desired length, b.o all sts.

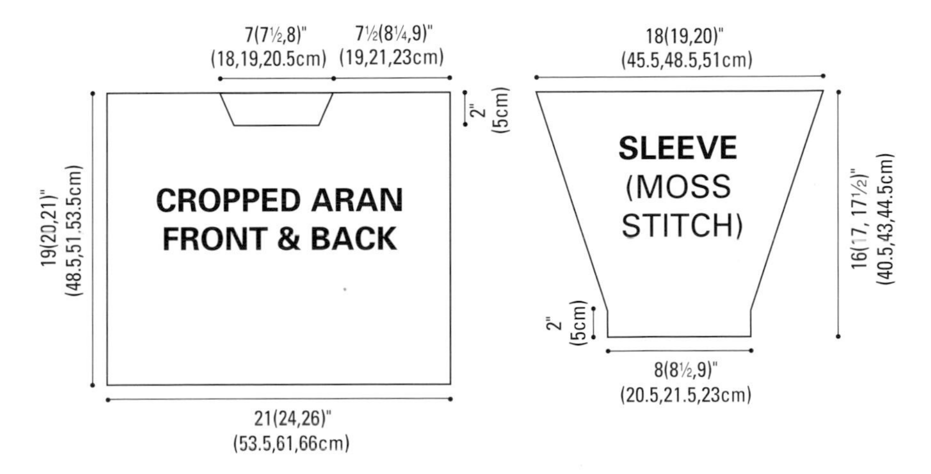

FINISHING

Sew shoulder seams.

With circular needle, p.u. 90 (90, 99) sts evenly around neckline.

Work in rnd for cabled rib:

Rnds 1 and 3: P5, k4.

Rnd 2: P5, sl 1 st to cn and hold in front, k1, k1 from cn, sl 1 st to cn and hold in back, k1, k1 from cn.

Rnd 4: P5, sl 1 st to cn and hold in back, k1, k1 from cn, sl 1 st to cn and hold in front, k1, k1 from cn.

Work in rib for 3" (7.5 cm).

If neckline seems too loose, p2tog at p5 section of pattern.

When piece meas 3½" (9 cm), b.o. all sts.

Meas down 9 (9½, 10)" (23, 24, 25.5 cm) from shoulder in front and back.

Sew sleeve bet these points.

Sew underarm and side seams.

= P on RS, k on WS

= Sl 2 sts to cn and hold in back, k2, k2 from cn

= Sl 2 sts to cn and hold in front, k2, k2 from cn

= Sl 1 st to cn and hold in back, t2r, t2l, p1 from cn

= Sl 1 st to cn and hold in back, t2l, t2r, p1 from cn

= Sl 4 sts to cn and hold in front, p1, t2r, t2l from cn

= Sl 4 sts to cn and hold in front, p1, t2l, t2r from cn

= Sl 1 st to cn and hold in back, t2r, t2l, k1 from cn

= Sl 1 st to cn and hold in back, t2l, t2r, k1 from cn

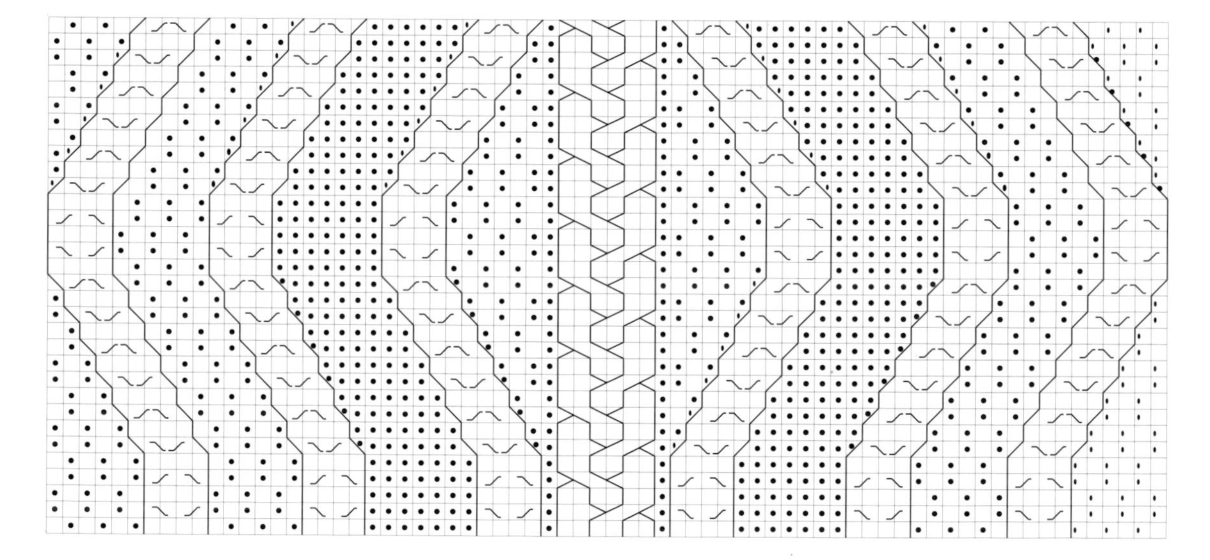

Jaffna, Sri Lanka

designs: **Susan Mills**
knitting rating: **Beginner**
photography: **Philip Newton**

The oversized tunic with a rolled edge is worked in stockinette stitch with absolutely no edge finishing. Knit with three strands of worsted-weight cotton, this is a great project for knitters who dislike working ribs.

The subtly striped pullover is knit in garter stitch and drop stitch, using multiple strands of yarn. The sleeves are picked up at the armholes and knit down, and the only finishing required is to sew the side and underarm seams. Because of the simplicity of these designs, the choice of interesting yarns—both in color and texture—becomes paramount.

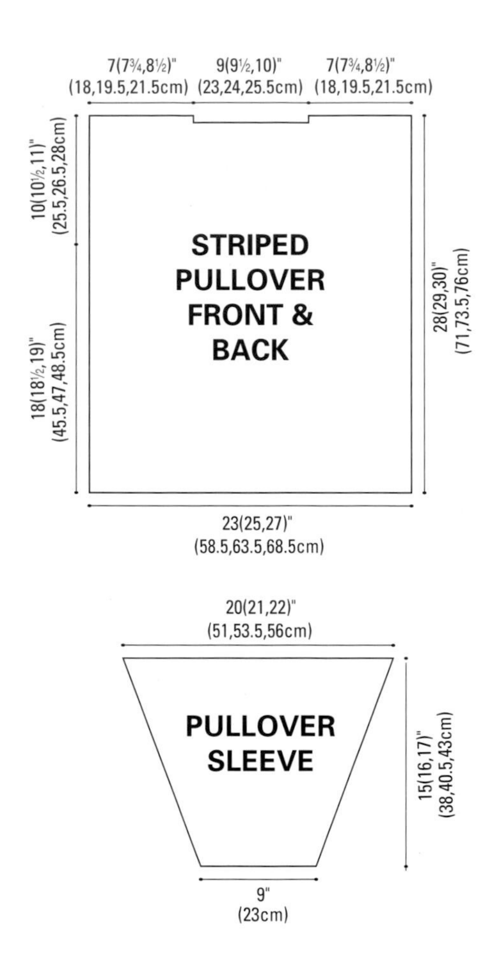

Striped Pullover

SIZES

Small (Medium, Large).

Finished measurements: 46 (50, 54)" (117, 127, 137 cm)

MATERIALS

Sea (100% cotton; 100 g = approx. 170 yds/155 m): 2 (2, 3) hanks; Velure (100% cotton chenille; 100 g = approx. 319 yds/292 m): 2 hanks; Stone (50% linen, 50% cotton; 100 g = approx. 186 yds/170 m): 2 (2, 3) hanks; Rain (44% rayon, 31% cotton, 20% linen, 5% silk; 100 g = approx. 181 yds/166 m): 2 (2, 3) hanks

Equivalent yarn: 340 (450, 520) yds (311, 411, 475 m) each of two cotton worsted-weight novelty yarns and 375 (490, 550) yds (343, 448, 503 m) each of two different cotton worsted-weight novelty yarns

Knitting needles: size 10 U.S. (6 mm), cable needle (cn)

GAUGE

Pattern stitch: 12 sts = 4" (10 cm)

Take time to save time—check your gauge.

PATTERN STITCHES

■ Body Pattern

With 1 strand each of Sea and Velure,

Rows 1 to 4: K all sts.

With 1 strand each of Stone and Rain,

Row 5: K, wrapping yarn around needle twice.

Row 6: K, dropping the extra loop.

Rep rows 1 through 6.

■ Sleeve Pattern

With 1 strand each of Sea and Velure,

Rows 1 to 3: K all sts.

With 1 strand each of Stone and Rain,

Row 4: K all sts.

Row 5: K, wrapping yarn around needle twice.

With 1 strand each of Sea and Velure,

Row 6: K, dropping the extra loop.

Rep rows 1 through 6.

BACK AND FRONT

C.o. 69 (75, 81) sts.

Work in patt st for front and back until piece meas 18 (18½, 19)" (45.5, 47, 48.5 cm) and pm on edges for sleeve placement.

Continue until piece meas 27½ (28½, 29½)" (70, 72.5, 75 cm), ending with row 6.

Next row: Keeping in pattern, k across 21 (23, 25) sts, b.o. center 27 (29, 31) sts, and work across rem 21 (23, 25) sts.

Work 1 more row and place sts on holders.

When both back and front are completed, k sts tog at shoulders.

SLEEVES

P.u. 60 (63, 66) sts bet sleeve markers.

With 1 strand each of Sea and Velure, k 1 row.

Work sleeve patt for 6 (6, 12) rows.

Cont in patt, and at the same time, dec 1 st each edge on rows 1 and 3 of patt until 28 (27, 28) sts rem.

When sleeve meas 15 (16, 17)" (38, 40.5, 43 cm) or desired length, ending with row 3, b.o. all sts.

FINISHING

Sew side and sleeve seams.

Chunky Tunic

SIZES

Small (Medium, Large)

Finished measurements: 48 (52, 56)" (122, 132, 142 cm)

MATERIALS

Camden (100% mercerized Egyptian cotton; 125 g = approx. 192 yds/175 m): 5 hanks; Telluride (100% cotton chenille; 50 g = approx. 99 yds/90 m): 8 (8, 9) hanks; Stone (50% linen, 50% cotton; 100 g = approx. 186 yds/170 m): 5 (5, 6) hanks

Equivalent yarn: 800 (850, 900) yds (731, 777, 823 m) each of three different cotton worsted-weight novelty yarns

Knitting needles: size 15 U.S. (11 mm), 16" and 32" (40.5 and 81.5 cm) circular needles in size 15 U.S. (11 mm)

GAUGE

St st with 3 strands: 8 sts and 10 rows = 4" (10 cm)

Take time to save time—check your gauge.

PATTERN STITCHES

■ Stockinette Stitch

In the rnd: K every rnd.

Back and forth:

Row 1 (RS): K all sts.

Row 2: P all sts.

BODY

With large circular needle, c.o. 96 (104, 112) sts.

Join and work in St st until piece meas 16 (18, 20)" (40.5, 45.5, 51 cm).

Divide body into front and back.

BACK: Work St st back and forth over 48 (52, 56) sts until back meas 27 (29, 31)" (68.5, 73.5, 78.5 cm) from beg.

B.o. all sts.

FRONT: Work as for back until front meas 25 (27, 29)" (63.5, 68.5, 73.5 cm), or 2" (5 cm) less than back length.

SHAPE NECK: Work across 19 (20, 21) sts, join a 2nd ball of yarn, b.o. center 10 (12, 14) sts, and work across rem 19 (20, 21) sts.

Working each side separately, b.o. 1 st at each neck edge every other row 3 times to give 16 (17, 18) sts rem for each shoulder.

When piece meas the same length as back, b.o. all sts.

SLEEVES

With straight needles, c.o. 18 sts.

Work in St st, and at the same time, inc 1 st each edge every other row 5 (8, 11) times, then every 4th row 6 (5, 4) times.

When sleeve meas 15 (16, 17)" (38, 40.5, 43 cm), b.o. all sts.

FINISHING

Sew shoulder, side, and sleeve seams.

For optional roll neck (not shown): With smaller circular needle, p.u. 38 (42, 46) sts around neck.

Work in St st for 3" (7.5 cm) and b.o. all sts loosely.

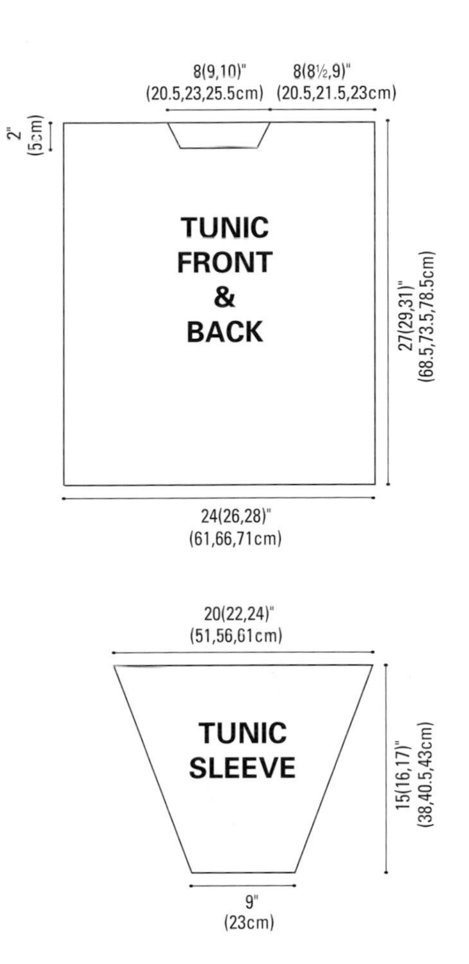

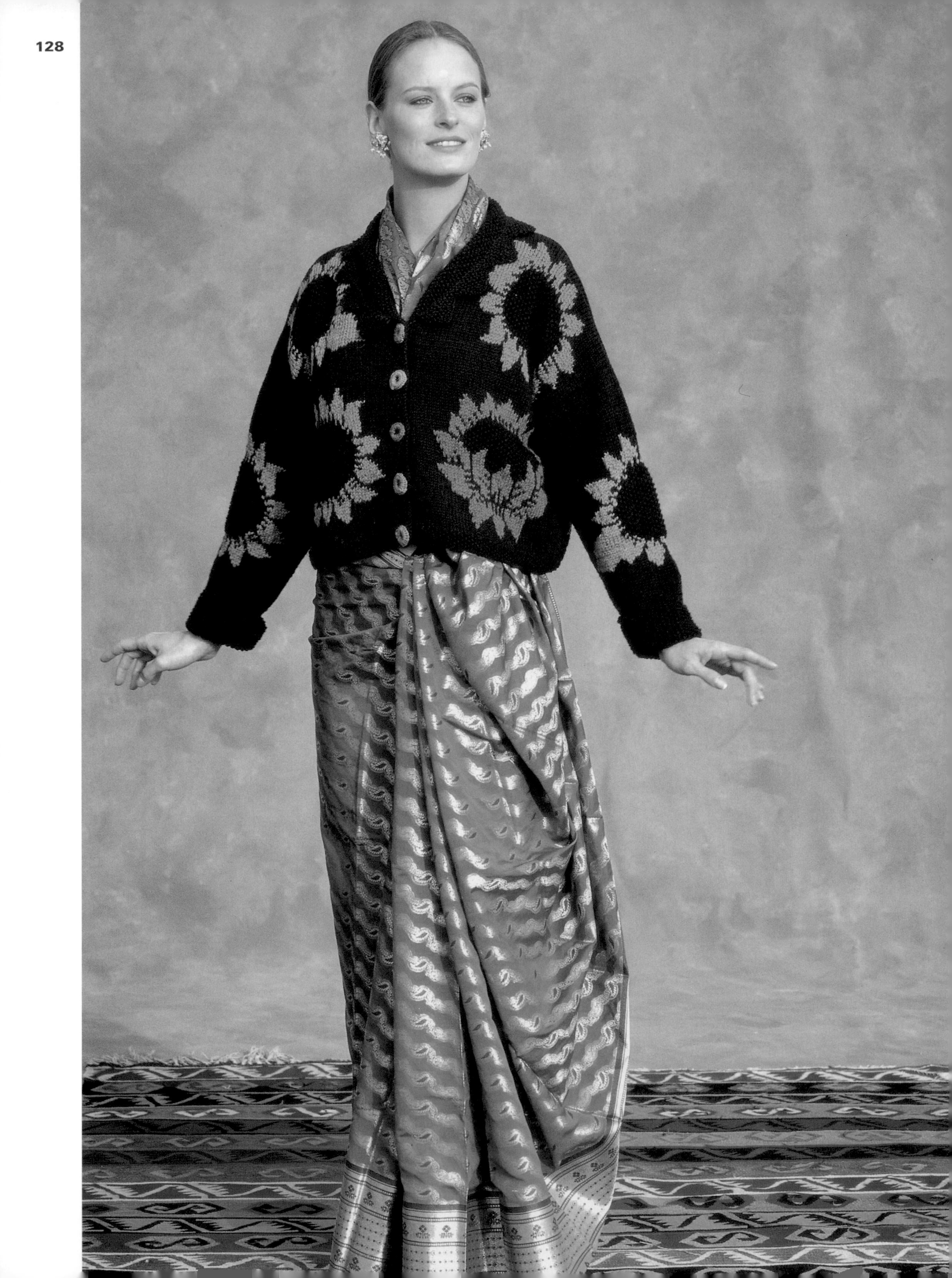

Bombay, India

design: **Julie Hoff**

knitting rating: **Experienced**

photography: **Philip Newton**

This cropped cardigan features a cheerful sunflower motif trimmed with seed stitch and an extremely flattering shawl collar. Both the collar and sleeves are cleverly finished with petal-shaped seed stitch edging. The handmade buttons are constructed by crocheting several colors of yarn around drapery rings.

SIZES

Small (Medium, Large)

Finished measurements: 46 (48, 50)" (117, 122, 127 cm)

MATERIALS

Tapestry (75% wool, 25% mohair; 50 g = approx. 95 yds/87 m): 11 (12, 12) skeins of main color (MC), 2 skeins of color A, 1 skein each of colors B, C, and D

Equivalent yarn: 1045 (1080, 1140) yds (956, 988, 1042 m) of worsted-weight wool in main color; 190 yds (174 m) of color A; 95 yds (87 m) each of colors B, C, and D

Knitting needles: sizes 7 and 8 U.S. (4.5 and 5 mm)

Two stitch markers

Five ¾" (2 cm) drapery rings

Crochet hook in size F

Tapestry needle

GAUGE

St st with larger needles: 20 sts and 26 rows = 4" (10 cm)

Take time to save time—check your gauge.

PATTERN STITCHES

■ **Seed Stitch**

Row 1 (RS): *K1, p1; rep from *.

All other rows: P the k sts, k the p sts.

■ **Seed Stitch Points**

C.o. 2 sts.

Row 1: K1, p1.

Row 2: (K1, k1-b) into first st, k1.

Rows 3 and 4: (K1, k1-b) into first st, (p1, k1) across row.

Rows 5 and 6: (K1, k1-b) into first st, (k1 p1) across row.

Rep rows 3 to 6 until you have 12 sts.

Cut yarn and push these 12 sts to end of needle.

With other needle, c.o. 2 sts, and rep sequence until desired number of points have been worked.

BACK

With smaller needles and MC, c.o. 114 (120, 126) sts and work 8 rows in seed st.

Change to larger needles and work 0 (3, 6) rows St st.

Work chart for back.

After completing chart, work a further 0 (3, 6) rows in St st.

SHAPE SHOULDERS: B.o. 12 (12, 14) sts at beg next two rows, 13 (14, 15) sts at beg next two rows, and 13 (15, 15) sts at beg next two rows.

B.o. rem 38 sts.

RIGHT FRONT

With smaller needles and MC, c.o. 57 (60, 63) sts and work 8 rows seed st.

Change to larger needles and work St st for 0 (3, 6) rows.

Begin working chart for right front.

When piece meas 11½ (12½, 13½)" (29, 31.5, 34 cm), shape neck: At neck edge, dec 1 st every other row 19 times to give 38 (41, 44) sts rem for shoulder.

At the same time, after completing chart, work 0 (3, 6) rows St st; then shape shoulder as for back.

LEFT FRONT

Work as for right front, using chart for left front and reversing all shaping.

RIGHT SLEEVE

With smaller needles and MC, work 4 seed st points.

Keeping in patt, work seed st across all 4 points, joining them to give 48 sts for cuff.

Cont in seed st, and at the same time, dec 1 st each edge every 4th row 3 times.

Cont in seed st until cuff measures 3 (3, 3½)" (7.5, 7.5, 9 cm) from base of points (the first joining row).

Change to larger needles and beg working in St st.

Inc 1 st each edge every other row 6 times, every 4th row 14 times, and every 6th row 3 times to give 88 sts.

At the same time, when you have 58 sts, work chart for sleeve with color A for sunflower and color D for leaf.

Position chart as follows: On RSR, k6, pm, work chart (51 sts), pm, k1.

After completing chart, cont in St st until piece meas 14½ (15, 15½)" (37, 38, 39.5 cm) from top of cuff.

B.o. all sts.

LEFT SLEEVE

Work as for right sleeve, but work chart with color B for sunflower and color D for leaf.

FINISHING

Block all pieces.

Sew shoulder seams.

CROCHET BUTTONS: With desired color, work in single crochet around drapery ring to completely fill ring.

Pull yarn through the last loop, leaving a 12" (30.5 cm) tail.

Thread through tapestry needle.

Take needle through back of every other stitch and pull yarn tightly to fill in center of ring; use MC to pull sts tog in center of ring, if desired.

Sew on buttons.

COLLAR

With smaller needles and MC, c.o. 236 (244, 252) sts and work 3 rows seed st.

Row 4: Work 5 buttonholes as follows: Seed 2 sts, b.o. 2 sts, *seed 12 (13, 14) sts, b.o. 2 sts; rep from * 3 times total, seed 11 (12, 13) sts, b.o. 2 sts, work in seed st to end of row.

Row 5: Work in seed st to first b.o. sts.

C.o. 2 sts over b.o. sts in row 4.

Cont in seed st for a total of 8 rows.

B.o. 59 (63, 67) sts at beg next row, work 118 sts seed st, and b.o. rem 59 (63, 67) sts.

Cont in seed st on the 118 sts.

B.o. 1 st at beg of next 2 rows, 2 sts at beg next 10 rows, 9 sts at beg next 4 rows, 10 sts beg next 2 rows; then b.o. rem 40 sts.

Sew collar to jacket, placing buttonholes along right front and attaching last 40 sts b.o. on collar to back neckline.

POINTED BORDER: With smaller needles, work 12 seed st points.

Work across all 12 points and cont in seed st.

Work two more rows and b.o. all sts.

Sew border to collar from start of shawl collar shaping around the edge to the corresponding point on second side.

Gently block pointed border and shawl collar.

Mark 9¼" (23.5 cm) from shoulder seam on right front and back.

Sew sleeves bet markers, matching center of sleeve to shoulder seam.

Sew side and sleeve seams.

Gently block seams.

Sew on buttons.

SLEEVE

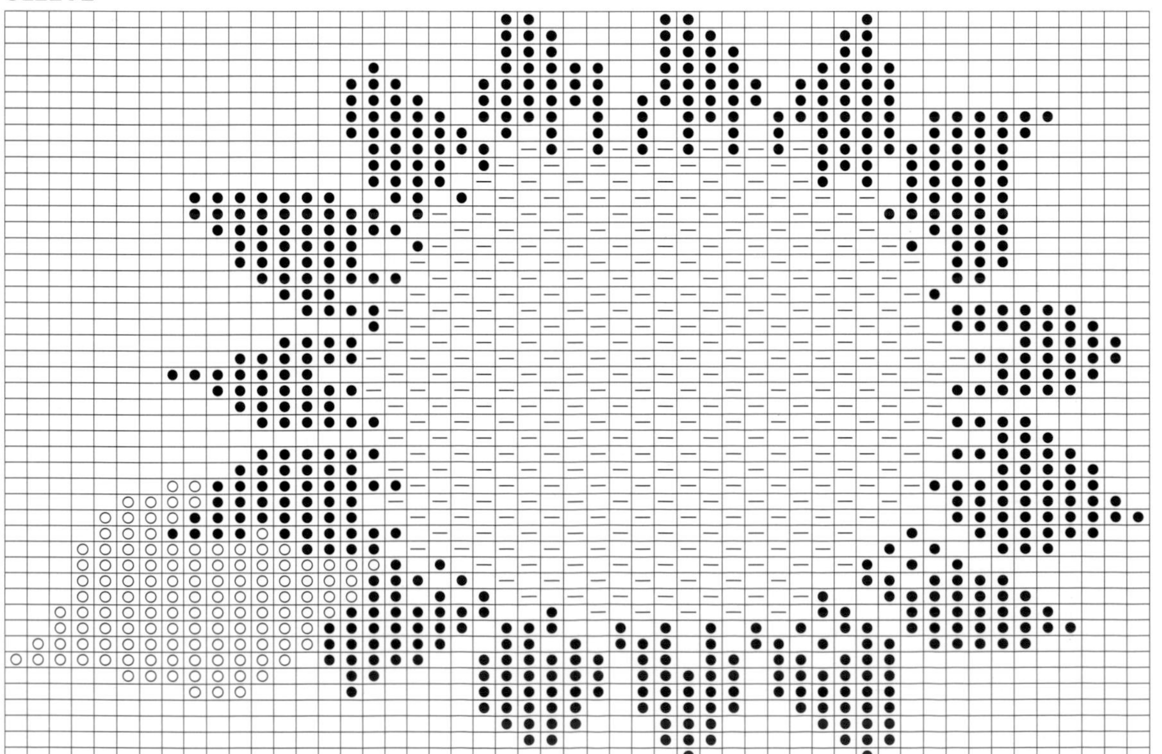

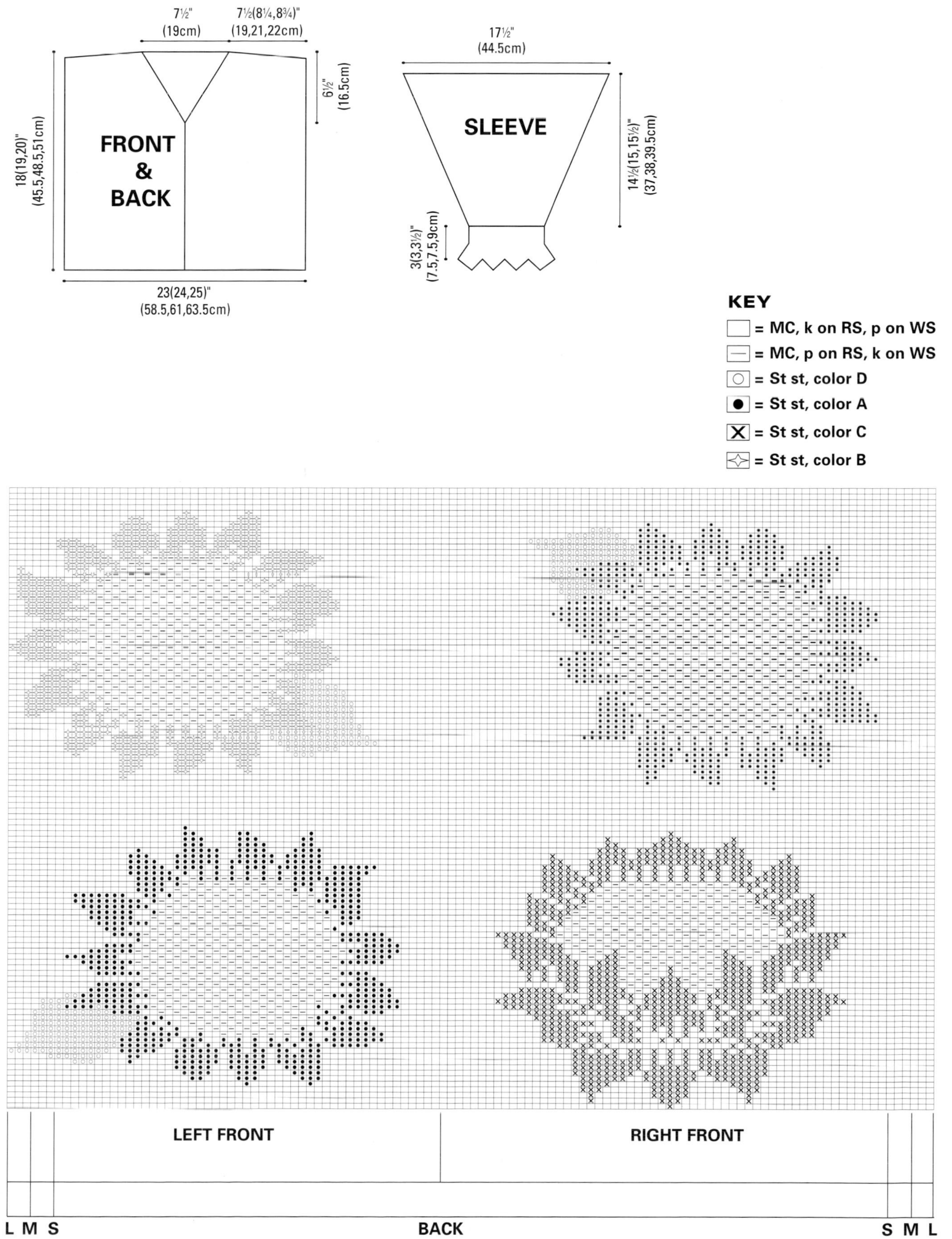
7½"
(19cm)
7½(8¼,8¾)"
(19,21,22cm)
6½"
(16.5cm)
18(19,20)"
(45.5,48.5,51cm)
FRONT
&
BACK
23(24,25)"
(58.5,61,63.5cm)
17½"
(44.5cm)
SLEEVE
14½(15,15½)"
(37,38,39.5cm)
3(3,3½)"
(7.5,7.5,9cm)
KEY
= MC, k on RS, p on WS
= MC, p on RS, k on WS
= St st, color D
= St st, color A
= St st, color C
= St st, color B
LEFT FRONT
RIGHT FRONT
L M S
BACK
S M L

Knitting Basics

The projects in this book range in difficulty from very easy to quite challenging, making them appropriate for beginners and skilled knitters alike. Many of these sweaters are worked in more than one color, and others include textural stitches, such as cables, bobbles, and knitted lace. In case you're not feeling totally confident of your skills in these and other areas of knitting, this chapter provides a brief refresher course.

Before You Begin

Selecting Your Yarn

In the materials section of the instructions for each pattern, the featured yarn is described and the required amount listed. For those who wish to substitute another yarn, the generic yarn requirements (i.e., the number of yards/meters needed to complete the project and the type of yarn you should use) are also given. This yardage and yarn type should be used only as a guide, however. Because each type of yarn has unique characteristics, it will knit differently from any other. The thickness, loft, twist, and texture of the yarn all affect the gauge you will obtain when knitting. Be sure to test your yarn before beginning a project (see "Testing the Gauge," opposite).

All of the patterns in this book were designed for particular yarns produced by Classic Elite. As time passes, new yarns are developed and some of the earlier products must be discontinued. At right is a chart that indicates the appropriate current product to use for the sweater you choose to knit.

FEATURED YARN	DESCRIPTION	CURRENT PRODUCT TO USE
Applause	Bulky	Available
Boston	Worsted	Tapestry
Cambridge	Worsted	Tapestry
Evergreen Cotton/Wool	Worsted	Available
Evergreen Cashmere/Wool	Worsted	Available
Inca Alpaca	Light Worsted	Available
Kelso Wool Tweed	Bulky/Worsted	Available
Kilimanjaro	Bulky Novelty Thick-and-Thin	Available
Lace Brushed Mohair	Light Worsted	Available
La Gran Brushed Mohair	Bulky	Available
Montera	Bulky	Available
Mackenzie	Bulky	Available
Mini Mohair	Worsted	Available
Newport Light Mercerized Cotton	Worsted	Provence
Newport Mercerized Cotton	Bulky/Worsted	Camden
Paisley Light	Light Worsted	Tapestry 2-Ply
Paisley Wool/Rayon	Bulky/Worsted	Tapestry
Regatta	Light Worsted	Provence
Sea	Light Worsted	Fame
Sharon	Bulky	Available
Tapestry	Light Worsted	Available
Willough	Light Worsted	Provence

If you're working with yarn that you've already purchased, the following chart will help you determine its weight. Refer to the ball band for the stitch gauge in stockinette stitch and find the corresponding yarn type below. Then choose a pattern that is appropriate for the type of yarn you have. (The type of yarn used for each sweater shown is given in the generic yarn information.)

YARN TYPE	APPROXIMATE STS/INCH (2.5 CM)
Bulky	3¼ to 3¾
Bulky/Worsted	4 to 4½
Worsted	4¾ to 5
Light Worsted	5 to 5½
Sport Weight	5½ to 6

How Much Yarn Will You Need?

To figure out how much yarn to purchase, determine the number of yards/meters in each skein by referring to the ball band. Take that number and divide it into the total number of yards or meters needed for the sweater. If your answer includes a fraction, round up to the nearest whole number. This figure is the total number of skeins required for the project.

You may feel more comfortable having some extra yarn on hand, especially if you think you may not complete your project within a month. Inventory levels can change very rapidly, and you may find there is no more yarn available in a particular dye lot when you need it. Dye lots do vary from batch to batch, and if you want to prevent having abrupt color variations in your sweater, purchase enough yarn to complete the project.

If you make an error and run out of yarn while you're knitting the body of the sweater, work a row from each ball—one from the new dye lot and one from the old—for a transition period of 2 inches (5 cm) before completely switching to the new dye lot. Often you can work the ribs and collar in a different dye lot without showing an obvious difference because of the change in texture of the stitch.

Testing the Gauge

No matter how many times the directions specify that a sample gauge should be knitted, even the best knitters often eliminate this short, very worthwhile step. The importance of testing your chosen yarn using the needles and stitches specified cannot be overemphasized. You can't rely on achieving the same gauge specified on the ball band because the gauge of an individual yarn varies with the stitch knitted. For instance, in stockinette stitch the gauge on a worsted-weight yarn may be 5 stitches per inch; in moss stitch it may be 4¾ stitches per inch; in a fancy cable it may be 6 stitches per inch. All of these gauges are correct, and most will differ from the specified gauge on the ball band. This is okay!

A ball band is designed by the manufacturer to be used as a guide for a knitter, not as gospel. Beginning knitters may think they must use the needle size indicated on the ball band, but each knitter should check the gauge in the pattern stitches to determine the correct size needles to use.

To be accurate, a gauge swatch must be at least 4 inches (10 cm) wide and 4 inches (10 cm) long, not including selvage stitches. Work a roughly square piece in the stitch specified in the gauge portion of the pattern; then count the number of stitches and rows within the 4-by-4-inch (10 x 10 cm) square. If you have more stitches than the number specified in the pattern, increase the needle size you are using; if you have fewer, decrease the needle size. Continue working swatches until you get the correct gauge to make sure your sweater will fit properly.

In many Aran-style patterns, the gauge section specifies the width for each type of cable you will work. Because an Aran design is composed of many patterns, the total width of the sweater is figured by adding all the cables plus a textured stitch at each side. It's recommended that you knit each cable pattern and measure it before beginning the sweater. If your measurement is off, you can adjust the total width by varying the textured stitches at the side seams.

A second consideration with Aran stitches is that as the piece is combined and gets heavier, the stitches tend to stretch slightly. Therefore, if the gauge on your swatches is just a little small, the sweater will most likely grow sufficiently after blocking.

A gauge swatch is also valuable for testing whether the finished garment will be washable. Washing distorts some knitwear, and depending on the stitch and gauge used for the finished sweater, your garment may shrink or stretch. Loose, lacey stitches tend to stretch much more than firmly knit stockinette stitches. If you want to determine how a sweater will react, wash and dry the swatch as you plan to treat the garment. Measure the swatch before and after laundering and compare the measurements. If the swatch was 4 inches (10 cm) before laundering and is 4½ inches (11.5 cm) afterward, it has stretched 12.5 percent. Likewise, the garment you make will become 12.5 percent larger after washing. If you're unhappy with this outcome, knit another swatch and try a different method of laundering it.

When making a multicolored garment, it's also important to test how all the colors will launder when combined. Work a swatch in all the colors that will be used in the garment; then wash and dry it in the normal manner. If one color is going to bleed into another, the swatch will tell you! You then have the option to change the color or the laundering method.

Techniques and Tips

Determining What Size To Knit

It's amazing how many knitters don't know how to select the proper size. They look at the finished measurements shown in the schematic diagram with each pattern and guess! The fit of a sweater has everything to do with how much the sweater will be enjoyed by its owner. No matter how beautiful or well knit, if the garment doesn't fit properly, it won't be worn often.

The first aspect to consider is the weight and loft of the yarn you intend to use. A bulky yarn requires a generous amount of ease in order for the garment to hang properly. If you're using a very lightweight yarn, the amount of ease can be much less.

The design of the sweater is next in importance. Sweaters with heavy cable patterns look better if they fit loosely. Textured stitches add thickness and bulk to a garment, and if the sweater is too tight, the patterns will distort and become very unflattering. An identical garment that is worked in a plain stockinette stitch can be made smaller.

A third consideration is how you plan to use the sweater: Casual sweaters tend to look better and be more comfortable if they're loose and baggy. For dressy occasions, a tighter fit may be desired.

A very basic rule of thumb for determining size is to measure a comparable sweater that fits comfortably. To be comparable, the sweater you measure should be made of yarn that is close in thickness to the yarn you plan to use, and it should have a similar amount of stitch design. Measure the chest or bust of the sweater and work the instructions for your new sweater that are closest in size.

Don't make the mistake of knitting a sweater to fit your chest or bust size; if you do, you will have a very small sweater that hugs your figure and is probably unwearable.

For convenience, several sizes are given for each design shown. The smallest size is given first, and larger sizes follow within parentheses; e.g., small (medium, large, extra large). Once you have decided on the correct size, note its position within the sequence. For example, if you're a size medium and the instructions include small, medium, and large, always work the first set of numbers just inside the parentheses.

Working from Charts

Many of the designs in this book include charts, either for colorwork or for textured stitchery, such as knit-and-purl combinations or cables. Charts for knitting may look intimidating to the novice, but once you understand how they work, they will become second nature. In recent years the number of knitters who prefer using charts has grown. If you've shied away from using charts, take the time to try knitting from those shown on pages 139 and 140. The effort you invest now will be well worth it in years to come!

Charts show the right side of the fabric only. When you're knitting back and forth on straight needles (as done in almost all the sweaters in this book), both right and wrong sides of the fabric need to be worked. When working on the right side of the fabric, follow the chart from right to left. When working on the wrong side, read it from left to right.

At the bottom of each chart is a key that gives the knitting motion you are to perform for each symbol. On the right side, work the stitches as they appear on the chart. On the wrong side, work the opposite of how the stitch appears on the chart. For instance, if the chart shows a knit stitch on the right side, purl the stitch on the wrong side. You can usually see how a stitch should be worked on the wrong side by how it appears on the knitted piece. If it looks like a purl stitch, it should be purled; if it looks like a knit stitch, it should be knit. If a difficult, manipulative stitch is done on the wrong side, specific instructions will be stated in the symbol key.

Starting and ending points are noted for each size at the bottom and sides of most charts. Sometimes the rows are numbered, and the instructions may denote the stitch or row with which you should begin. When beginning and ending according to a chart, it's imperative that you start and end at the same stitch on each row for the same side of the fabric. When shaping for armholes and necklines, these points will change as the decreases progress. To make it easier to keep track of where you are on the pattern, you can draw the chart on graph paper and mark the shaping details. After you become familiar with a pattern, you will automatically sense how to continue it while doing the shaping.

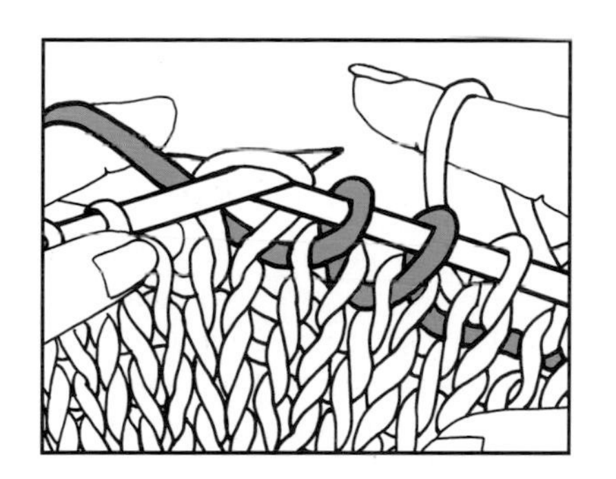

Knitting with right hand, stranding with left

Purling with right hand, stranding with left

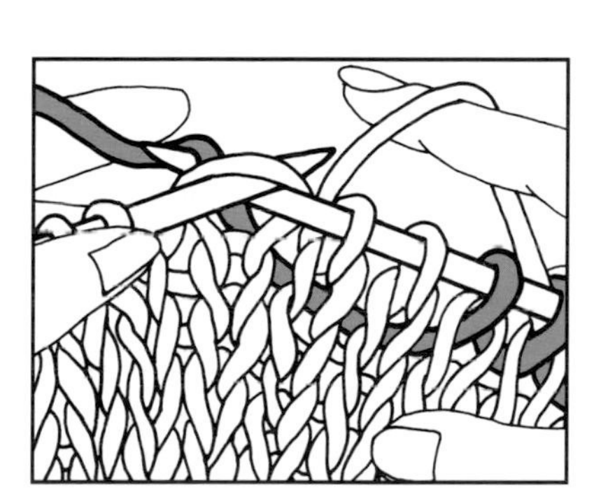

Knitting with left hand, stranding with right

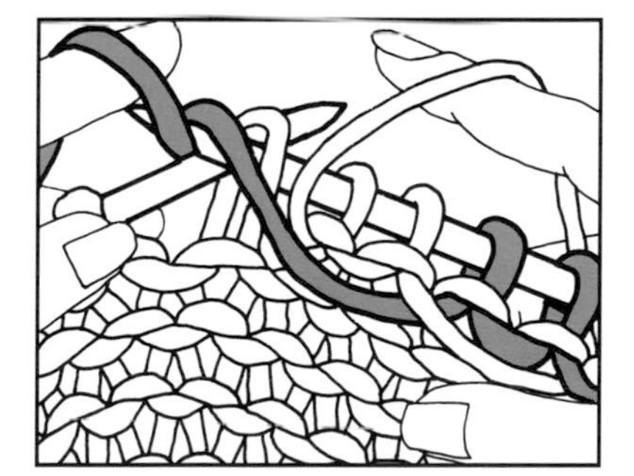

Purling with left hand, stranding with right

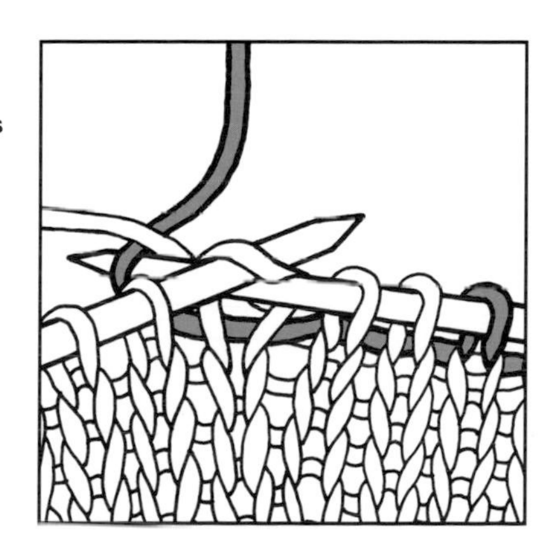

Weaving yarns when changing colors on knit rows

Colorwork Techniques

FAIR ISLE KNITTING

Many of the designs for multicolored garments in this book are knit using the Fair Isle technique, a traditional form of knitting that uses two different colors of yarn in each row to produce a patterned fabric. The color not being used is stranded behind the work and picked up later. This method produces a warm fabric that is thicker than regular knitting because the carried yarn adds extra bulk. Common Fair Isle motifs include geometric shapes, florals, small pattern repeats, and animals. Fair Isle knitting is reminiscent of Scandinavia, the Scottish Shetland Isles, and Iceland, although most cultures with a knitting history practice Fair Isle knitting.

The illustrations at left show how to work Fair Isle in either right- or left-handed knitting. If you plan to do a lot of Fair Isle knitting, it's highly recommended that you learn both left- and right-handed knitting. Then you can combine both methods, using each hand for a different color.

To work in Fair Isle successfully, it's necessary not only to work the colors into the row, but you must also obtain the proper tension with the floating yarn. A puckered, uneven fabric usually results from carrying the unused yarn too tightly behind the work. To produce the correct tension, stretch out the stitches on the right-hand needle after they are knit. Then stretch out the next color of yarn behind the knitting so that it will lie flat when the piece is off the needles.

If a pattern skips more than five stitches, the floating color should be caught into the work to avoid long, messy floats. To do this, pull the unused yarn close to the fabric and knit the next stitch around the unused color to hold it flat. Make sure to maintain proper tension.

Some knitters like the back of the fabric to look even and neat, and they weave the floating yarn into the back side of the work. This is done by laying the unused color between the active yarn and the back side of the fabric. This catches the yarn and prevents any floats. The resulting fabric is neat on the wrong side but won't drape very well; it's suitable for jackets where a stiff fabric is desired.

Wool yarns are the most forgiving of fibers and are highly recommended for knitters who are attempting Fair Isle for the first time. When Fair Isle work comes off the needles, it often looks lumpy, even when completed by the most experienced of knitters. You can flatten the fabric either by washing and laying it flat to dry or by steaming it. Steaming will not, however, flatten out stitches that don't have the proper amount of float on the wrong side. Many experienced knitters have a sweater or two, made when they were just beginning Fair Isle, that won't fit anyone! The mark of a real expert knitter is a Fair Isle sweater knit in a fine gauge cotton; cotton cannot be steamed to correct unevenness!

INTARSIA KNITTING

Intarsia knitting is sometimes called picture knitting. This is because large blocks of color are worked in one color over a large space to result in an overall motif or shape. Unlike Fair Isle knitting, the yarn not being used is not carried across the back of the fabric. Instead, different colors of yarn are held in bobbins behind the work and picked up when specified on a chart. Intarsia knitting highly resembles the tapestry method of weaving. The most difficult part of intarsia knitting is the joining of the two colors. This makes a fabric that is not bulky or extraordinarily heavy. It also uses less yarn than Fair Isle knitting.

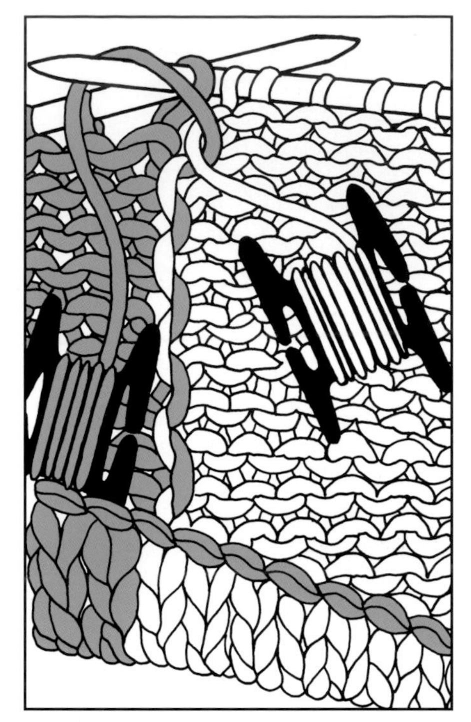

Using bobbins for intarsia knitting

To work intarsia knitting, follow the chart given, and where indicated, change the color. Work the specified number of stitches in the first color; then join the second color by twisting the new color around the stitch just knit and continue with the second color. Continue the piece, twisting the yarns around each other every row to form a join. When the piece is completed, it may be necessary to even out the joins by picking the stitches loose with a tapestry needle. Sometimes holes result where the yarns were not wrapped around each other neatly. To correct them, pull the loose stitch to the wrong side and take a stitch with an extra piece of yarn of the same color.

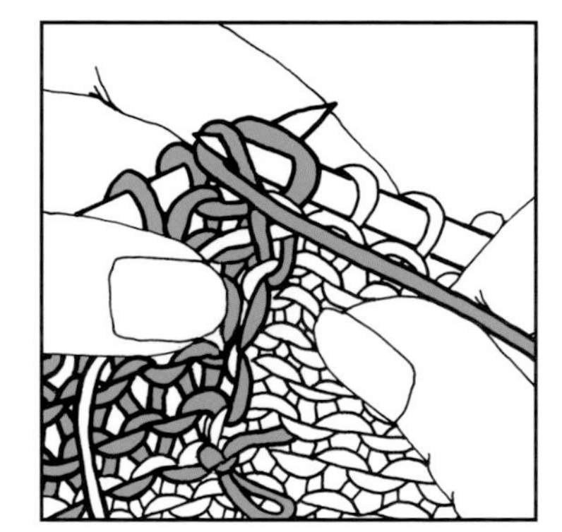

Intarsia knitting with long strands

Bobbins are commonly used by many knitters to hold the various colors to be worked in intarsia. A money-saving technique borrowed from tapestry weavers can quickly and easily be employed to produce butterflies for intarsia knitting. Leaving a 5- to 6-inch (12.5 to 15 cm) tail of yarn between your ring and middle fingers, wrap the yarn in a figure eight around your thumb and little finger until you have the needed amount. Remove the butterfly from your fingers and wrap the end still connected to the ball of yarn five or six times tightly around the middle of the butterfly. Cut the yarn and end it off by tucking the loose yarn under the tightly wrapped yarn. Begin knitting from the end that was held between your fingers.

In the 1980s Kaffe Fassett, an American artist who lives in London, began working in knitwear. Kaffe made popular the intarsia method of knitting by designing knitwear with many small sections of different colors. His preferred method for holding the yarn behind his knitting is to work with short strands of yarn that are not wound. Colors can be added more freely to result in a painterly fabric, and the yarn can be untangled with relative ease because the strands are short.

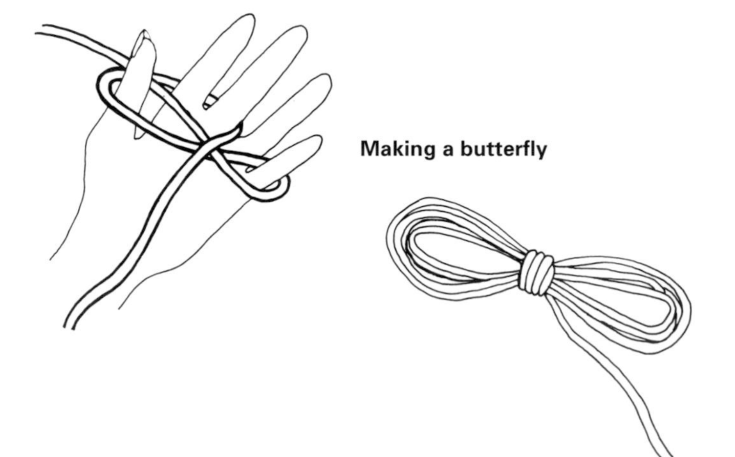

Making a butterfly

As with any technique, each knitter should choose the method that is easiest. Combinations of techniques can be used to develop efficient work methods.

DUPLICATE STITCH

Duplicate stitch, sometimes called Swiss darning, is an embellishing technique that is applied to garment pieces after knitting has been completed. It's similar to embroidery and is primarily used to add colors that aren't easily included while knitting. When applied to plain pieces of stockinette stitch knitting, duplicate stitch resembles intarsia knitting.

This is a technique that requires a little practice, but when skill is obtained, its uses are endless. Small flowers, animals, and many other motifs can be done in duplicate stitch, and Fair Isle patterning, which uses only two colors in each row, can also be enhanced with duplicate stitch. Similarly, large blocks of intarsia knitting can be made more complex by adding colors in duplicate stitch.

When working duplicate stitch, you're actually tracing an existing knit stitch, and it's important to cover the entire original stitch with the new color to give a neat presentation. It's best to work with a large, blunt needle because sharp needles tend to split the stitch and are more difficult to handle. You can avoid tangles and knots by using a relatively short piece of yarn—about 1 yard (91.5 m)—while you work.

Before and after adding duplicate stitch

To begin, take one or two small stitches on the wrong side of the fabric, leaving a tail of about 1 inch (2.5 cm). Bring the needle up through the center of the base of the stitch; then, following the stitch, put the needle under the two strands at the top of the stitch and pull the yarn through. Complete the stitch by inserting the needle next to the starting point at the base of the stitch. If only one stitch is to be covered, pull the needle to the wrong side; when covering a large block of stitches, push the needle through the base of the next stitch and pull it to the right side. After making each stitch, it's advisable to smooth it with your fingers to relax the tension and make the added yarn entirely cover the original stitch.

Duplicate stitch works best when applied horizontally or diagonally. If you work it vertically up the center of a series of stitches, it has a tendency to sink into the fabric and disappear.

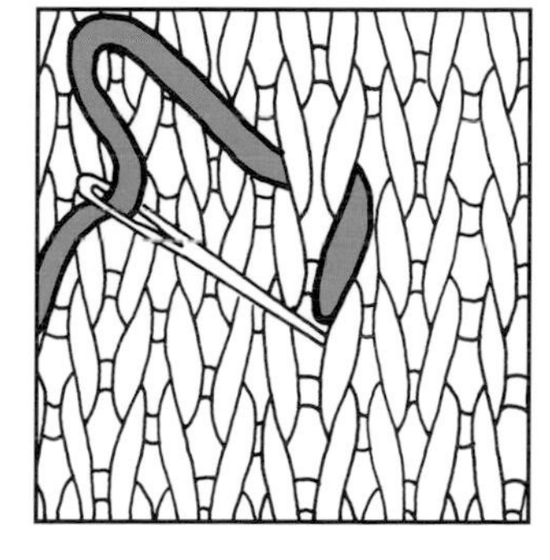

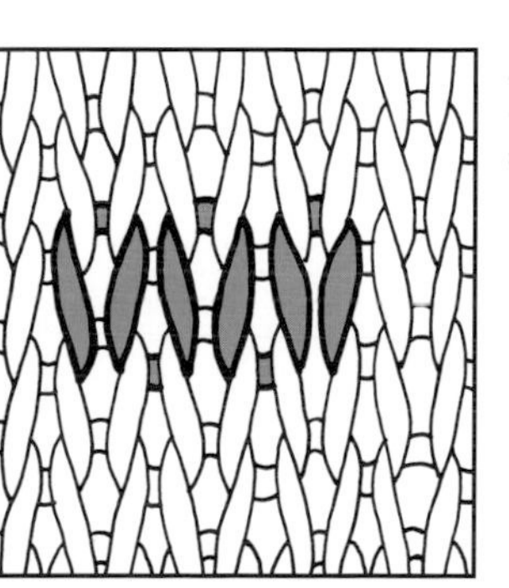

Adding duplicate stitch

EMBROIDERY STITCHES

Many embroidery stitches that are traditionally worked on woven fabrics can also be used on knits. Embroidery adds a decorative, free-flowing element to knitted fabric, which is usually quite geometric in appearance. Stitches such as chain stitch, outline stitch, and satin stitch are especially useful for introducing different shapes and textures to knitted motifs. The key to embroidering on knitwear is to develop a loose, creative approach to your embellishments. The diagrams shown here provide a selection of embroidery stitches you may enjoy using.

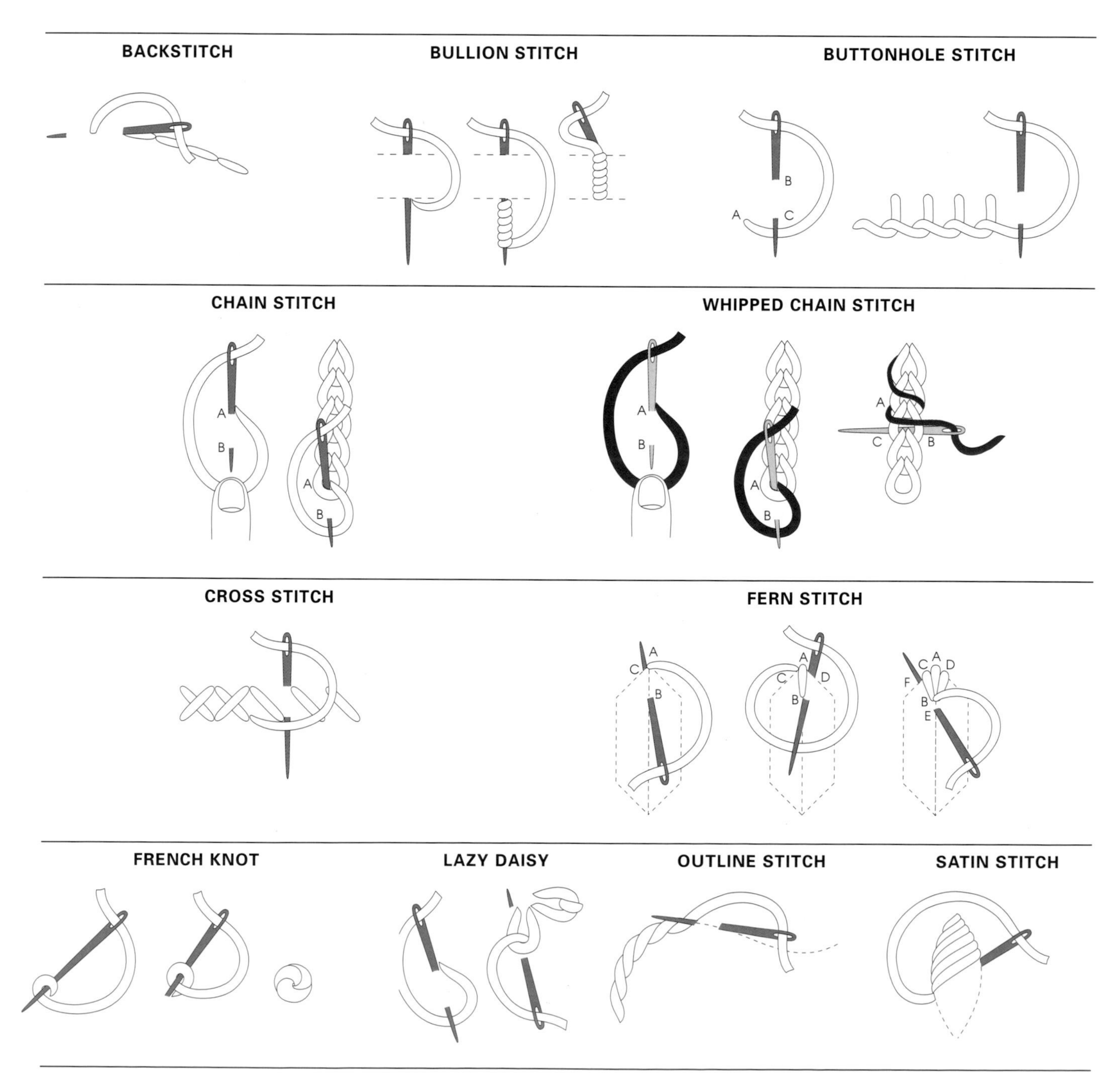

Textural Knitting

MAKING CABLES

Cables have become an inherent part of the American knitwear scene. Although they look rather complicated, they're actually quite simple, and once the concept of a cable is learned, the variations are endless. A cable is made by crossing a group of specified stitches, using an extra needle called a cable needle. A cable needle is U-shaped and pointed at both ends. Alternatively, a short double-pointed needle or a tapestry needle can be used for working cables.

Cables are formed by crossing a group of stitches either to the right or to the left.

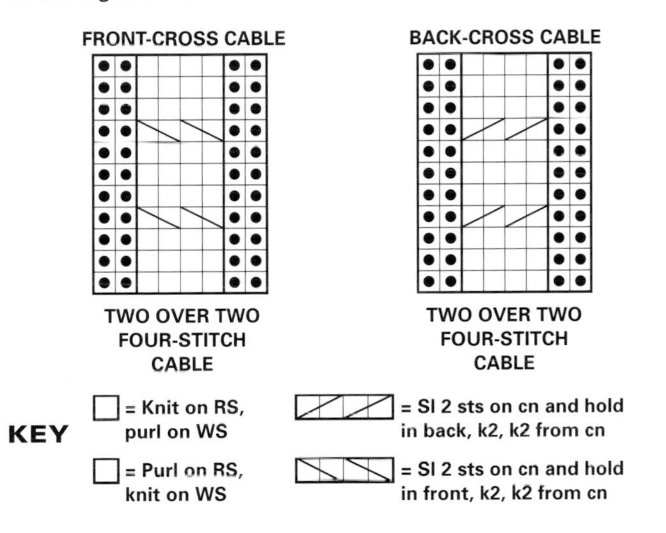

To work a four-stitch cable that crosses to the left, slip two stitches to a cable needle and hold them in front of the work, pull the yarn tightly, and knit the next two stitches on the left-hand needle; then knit the two stitches that are on the cable needle. This is called a front-crossing cable because the stitches are held in front of the work.

To work a four-stitch cable that crosses to the right, slip two stitches to a cable needle and hold them in back of the work, pull the yarn tightly, and knit the next two stitches on the left-hand needle; then knit the two stitches that are on the cable needle. This is called a back-crossing cable.

Cables can be worked to form diamonds, ribs, chevrons, diagonal lines and more. Their size can be varied just by using different numbers of stitches. In general, the more stitches that are crossed, the more the fabric will compress, producing a denser piece of knitwear. Although many cables are worked on a ground of reverse stockinette stitch (the purl side of the fabric faces outward), textured stitches, such as seed or garter stitch, can be inserted between them to create more interest.

Most of the instructions for the cabled designs shown in this book are given in chart form. This is a very easy way to describe cables because the charts themselves resemble the cable produced, and each pattern follows a repetition. The charts at left show a front- and a back-crossing cable. Keep in mind that the charts show only the right side of the fabric. Follow the chart from right to left for the right side of the fabric and from left to right for the wrong side.

BOBBLES

Adding bobbles is a great way to give texture to your knits. They're easy to make and can be done in many sizes for different effects. In general, bobbles are made by increasing a series of stitches into a designated stitch, working this as a separate piece, then decreasing again.

To make a five-stitch bobble:

- Make five stitches in one stitch: knit into the front loop of the stitch, then into the back loop, without slipping any stitches off the needle; repeat this sequence once more; then knit into the front loop one more time. Now slip all five stitches from the left needle. The increases can also be made by working a yarn over instead of knitting into the front and back of the stitch. This increase would be worked as [k1, yo, k1, yo, k1] into one stitch.
- Turn the work and purl these five stitches; turn the work and knit these five stitches; then repeat this sequence once more.
- Using the left needle, slip the second, third, fourth, and fifth stitches—one at a time—over the first stitch and off the right needle. This completes the bobble.

The bobble can be made larger by using more stitches to increase the designated one. Because small increases can have noticeable effects, experiment first by increasing the number by two or three stitches instead of four. Similarly, you can increase the number of rows that are worked on the bobble. The more rows that are worked, the larger the bobble will be.

The number of combinations is endless, and bobbles will add interest to any knitter's repertoire. Bobbles can be worked in reverse stockinette stitch or inserted into a cable pattern to add extra texture. A textured pattern itself can be made by placing bobbles in a geometric pattern. Bobbles that are worked in contrasting colors are very intriguing.

HANDKNIT LACE

Knitted lace fabric looks technically amazing, but it is actually a very simple technique once the concept is understood. Consisting of a series of increases and decreases in a given pattern, the resulting fabric has an open, delicate appearance.

Handknit lace is a perfect choice for summer-weight knits, as it is lightweight and cool to wear. Lace knit in wool or mohair is equally beautiful and is suitable for dressier occasions. It too is very lightweight and thus takes a smaller quantity of yarn than cabled or colorwork projects. Projects can be as complex or simple as you desire, and knitting lace is an addictive pastime for many knitters.

Lace is made by combining specified numbers of increases and decreases to create geometric openwork designs. The increase technique used in lace is a simple yarn over. Placed next to the yarn over is either a right- or left-leaning decrease. Although there are several different ways to work both kinds of decreases, the preferred methods are as follows.

RIGHT-LEANING DECREASE (on the right side): Knit two stitches together. This is abbreviated as k2tog.

LEFT-LEANING DECREASE (on the right side): Slip the next two stitches knitwise; then insert the tip of the left-hand needle into the fronts of these two stitches and knit them together. This is abbreviated in this book as ssk.

Lace patterns can be written out or charted. Knitting lace from charts is much easier than it looks, and this is the technique most lace knitters prefer once they develop their skills and comfort level with lace.

SIMPLE LACE PATTERN

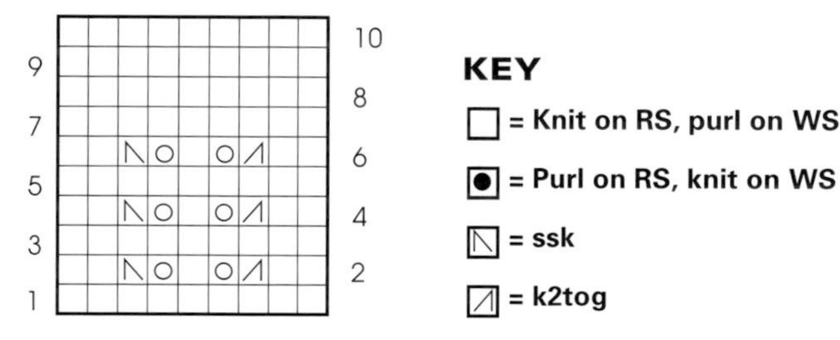

Finishing & Caring for Knits

BLOCKING & STEAMING

Blocking is one of the most important techniques you can use to finish a garment professionally. It is the final step that properly completes any garment, and a knitted garment that isn't blocked can be compared to an unironed cotton shirt!

An added bonus of blocking is that if the proper gauge was not obtained during knitting, the fabric can be stretched to correspond to the needed measurement. It is almost impossible to shrink the fabric.

Begin with a padded surface, such as a bed or a rug with a pad underneath it. To protect the surface in case the yarn bleeds or runs, cover it with a sheet or towel. Then attach the pieces to the surface using large T-pins, stretching each piece until its measurements match the schematic drawing given for the design. For natural fibers, use a steam iron full of water on a high steam setting. Slowly steam the entire piece, holding the iron 2 to 3 inches (5 to 7.5 cm) away from the garment. Don't press on the knit fabric, or you'll flatten the stitchwork, and the fabric may scorch. Let the pieces dry completely with the pins remaining in the fabric. If it takes too long for the fabric to dry, as when steaming cotton on a humid day, you may need to remove the pieces before they are completely dry so that they won't mildew.

An alternative method for blocking is to completely seam and finish the garment. Quickly dip the garment in cold water. Squeeze as much of the water out of the garment as possible without wringing. If you own a washing machine with a reliable delicate spin cycle, spin the water out quickly (1 to 2 minutes), using the last portion of the setting on the machine. Pin the garment to the surface as described above to stretch it to the desired width and length.

LAUNDERING YOUR KNITWEAR

Yarn manufacturers test their yarns in order to instruct knitters on the proper laundering method. You should always follow the instructions on the ball band.

Certain dyes have a tendency to bleed when washed. Although bleeding often won't affect the finished garment, a large degree of dye residue can stain multicolored garments, especially those made with large contrasting color areas, such as black against white. Certain colors are less stable than others; those that tend to bleed are bright teal, red, bright green, and black.

The gauge swatch you worked before you started your project makes a perfect sample for testing the washability of the yarns you used. If your swatch bleeds when washed according to the recommended method, you can be sure the garment will too. Bleeding causes colors to run into each other, which results in fuzzy lines appearing or whole areas turning a dull shade of the color that bled. This is not a reversible process.

If a solid-colored garment bleeds, you can simply wash the garment separately the first few times and lay it flat to dry on several old towels. Most yarns having excess dye will stop bleeding after a few washes. The exceptions to this are the many denim yarns now available for hand-knitting. These yarns will continue to fade throughout the life of the garment, and they should always be washed and dried separately, just like a pair of new denim jeans.

KNITTING ABBREVIATIONS

-b	through back of stitch
beg	beginning
bet	between
b.o.	bind (bound) off
c.o.	cast on
cont	continue
dec	decrease (decreasing)
dpn	double-pointed needle(s)
est	established
foll	follows
inc	increase (increasing)
k	knit
m	make
MC	main color
meas	measures
p	purl
patt	pattern
pm	place marker
psso	pass slipped stitch over
p.u.	pick up
rem	remaining
rep	repeat
rev	reverse
rnd	round
RS(R)	right side (row)
RSS	reverse stockinette stitch
sep	separate(ly)
sl	slip
ssk	slip, slip, knit
st(s)	stitch(es)
St st	stockinette stitch
tog	together
WS(R)	wrong side(row)
yo	yarn over

Technical References

This book is a collection of designs for knitters of all skill levels. Should you need further instructional guidance on techniques, consult any of the following basic knitting books for excellent diagrams and techniques.

1800 Patterns. Paris: Mon Tricot, 1989.

Don, Sarah. *The Art of Shetland Lace*. London: Bell and Hyman, 1986.

Fassett, Kaffe. *Glorious Knits*. New York: Clarson Potter, 1985.

Gibson-Roberts, Priscilla A. *Ethnic Socks and Stockings*. Sioux Falls, South Dakota: Knitter's Magazine, 1995.

Goldberg, Rhoda Ochser. *The New Knitting Dictionary, 1000 Stitches and Patterns*. New York: Crown, 1984.

The Harmony Guide to Knitting Stitches, vols 1, 2, and 3. London: Lyric, 1990.

The Harmony Guide to Aran Knitting. London: Lyric, 1991.

The Harmony Guide to Knitting Techniques. London: Lyric Books, Ltd., 1990.

Mountford, Debra. *The Harmony Guide to Knitting, Techniques and Stitches*. New York: Harmony, 1992.

Newton, Deborah. *Designing Knitwear*. Newtown, CT: Taunton, 1992.

Norbury, James. *Traditional Knitting Patterns*. New York: Dover, 1979.

Stanley, Montse, *The Reader's Digest Guide to Knitting*. Pleasantville, New York: Reader's Digest, 1993

Starmore, Alice. *Alice Starmore's Book of Fair Isle Knitting*. Newtown, CT: Taunton, 1988.

Thomas, Mary. *Mary Thomas's Book of Knitting Patterns*. New York: Dover, 1972.

______. *Mary Thomas's Book of Knitting*. New York: Dover, 1973.

Thompson, Gladys, *Patterns for Guernseys, Jerseys, and Arans*. New York: Dover, 1979.

Van der Klift-Tellegen, Henriette, *Knitting from the Netherlands*. Asheville, NC: Lark, 1983.

Vogue Knitting editors. *Vogue Knitting Book*. New York: Pantheon, 1989.

Walker, Barbara G. *Charted Knitting Designs: A Third Treasury of Knitting Patterns*. New York: Charles Scribner's Sons, 1972.

______. *A Second Treasury of Knitting Patterns*. New York: Charles Scribner's Sons, 1970.

______. *A Treasury of Knitting Patterns*. New York: Charles Scribner's Sons, 1968.

Zimmermann, Elizabeth. *Knitting Without Tears*. New York: Charles Scribner's Sons, 1971.

History of Classic Elite Yarns

Yesterday: Massive turbines, driven by the waters of the Merrimack River, powered the spinning mills in Lowell, Massachusetts, during the 1920s.

(PHOTO BY PHILIP CHAPUT, COURTESY OF LOWELL NATIONAL HISTORICAL PARK)

CLASSIC ELITE YARNS had its origin in the late 1940s, when Ernest Chew, the company's founder, became a partner in Warley Worsted Mills, an old-line textile mill in Lowell, Massachusetts.

The city of Lowell has been a major center for textile production since the beginning of the American Industrial Revolution. In the late 1800s, Frances Cabot Lowell and several business associates developed a canal system fed with water from the Merrimack River, paving the way for several mill complexes to be built throughout the city. In the basements of the mills, massive turbines fed power through leather pulley systems to the looms and spinning frames on the top floors.

Mr. Chew's direction transformed Warley into a specialty mill, the only one of its day to produce fine brushed and looped mohair yarn. Mohair, a product of Angora goats, is a long, slick fiber that is difficult to process. To handle the fibers, Mr. Chew modified nineteenth-century equipment and designed custom machinery.

Today, as in previous decades, Mr. Chew's machinery transforms the mohair fibers from a thick, ropelike mass into looped novelty yarn. Some of the looped yarn is packaged and sold under the trade name Sharon, but the majority receives additional processing, where it is brushed to produce a fuzzy, elegant, quick-knitting yarn known as La Gran.

In 1979, Classic Elite Yarns was created as a marketing division of Warley to cater mainly to hand weavers and designers. As handknitting became popular in the early 1980s, Classic Elite expanded its product line beyond mohairs to include additional natural fibers produced under its direction by other mills worldwide. Prepackaged kits, new specialty yarns, and an annual collection of knitting designs were added. Soon Classic Elite became the parent company of the mill, and its new products and designs began to make the pages of international fashion magazines.

Today Classic Elite Yarns is owned by Patricia Chew and managed primarily by women. Maintaining its traditions, it's still located in the historic mill on the banks of the Merrimack, although the spinning frames are no longer powered by the water below. Its annual design collections have become increasingly popular among handknitters everywhere, and its product line has grown to include yarns made of cotton, silk, llama, alpaca, wool, rayon, cashmere, and mohair fibers, all stocked in a large variety of classic and fashion-forward colors.

And today: Classic Elite's trademark mohair yarns are still spun in the original mill building, although precision equipment has taken the place of the earlier spinning frames, and the machines are is no longer powered by the river below.

(PHOTO BY JOHN GOODMAN)

Contributing Designers

JODI BERKEBILE

Jodi was taught to knit by her mother as part of a Girl Scout troop project. She never knit much again until she became a stay-at-home mom after years of being a professional accountant. To keep her sanity, she began knitting. Not one to follow the rules exactly, Jodi began experimenting with altering patterns. She entered a design contest sponsored by The Knitting Guild of America, and she won! Ever since, she has sold her knitwear designs professionally to *Vogue Knitting*, *Knitters*, *McCall's Needlework* and Classic Elite Yarns.

NORAH GAUGHAN

Best known for her innovative stitch designs, Norah Gaughan has been named one of *Vogue Knitting's* Master Knitters of the '90s. Her design talents surfaced early; she learned to knit when she was 14 years old and had her first knitwear design published just four years later. Currently Norah creates designs for several hand-knitting companies and the New York garment industry.

STEPHANIE GILDERSLEEVE

Stephanie Gildersleeve began her career as a textile artist by crocheting cotton bikini tops during the mid-1970s. Later she taught herself to knit and sharpened her design skills while working as a pattern editor for *McCall's Needlework and Crafts*. Now she works out of her home in California, where she creates designs for several yarn companies and knitwear magazines.

JULIE HOFF

While studying in Austria, Julie Hoff learned to design and knit simultaneously. Instead of using a pattern, she learned to knit a gauge swatch, determine the finished width of the garment, cast on, and go! For several years she designed a line of machine-knit sweaters that were sold in exclusive boutiques and larger stores. Currently she enjoys designing for yarn companies from her home in Wheeling, West Virginia.

SALLY LEE

Sally Lee grew up among talented needleworkers who taught her how to knit and encouraged her natural abilities. Although she's had no formal design training, she is one of the most talented colorists working in the United States today. At present she is the co-owner of the Flatiron Workshop in New York City, where she produces exceptional garments for better boutiques and large stores.

SUSAN MILLS

A self-taught knitter, Susan Mills took up weaving while working toward her mathematics degree in college. The influences of her weaving are evident in the textures and color combinations in her sweater designs. In addition to her work as the customer service director and senior pattern editor at Classic Elite, Susan also manages her own small weaving business and shows her work at craft fairs.

DEBORAH NEWTON

The author of *Designing Knitwear* (Taunton, Newtown, CT, 1992), Deborah Newton has designed sweaters for many publications, written pattern instructions, and designed knitted fabrics for the garment industry. She is one of *Vogue Knitting's* Master Knitters of the '90s, and today she conducts design workshops across the country and co-owns an educational map business.

CATHY PAYSON

Cathy Payson began knitting while in college and later started designing for herself and for friends' children. In 1989, she joined Classic Elite Yarns, where she quickly developed her signature style of casual, comfortable, easy-to-make knitwear. Cathy is now an assistant knitwear designer at Susan Bristol, a sportswear company in Charlestown, Massachusetts.

LINDA PRATT

Linda enjoys playing with her knitting needles—making the yarns wrap around, under, and over to create motifs that are sometimes difficult to explain in words or charts. She fervently hopes that every knitter will start doing the same and transform their projects into one-of-a-kind improvisational knitting studies. She is also the sales manager at Classic Elite Yarns

KATHY ZIMMERMAN

Kathy Zimmerman has been a knitter from the time she was a teenager. She especially enjoys developing unique ribbing patterns and stitch work, and her designs have been published in *Knitters*, *McCall's Needlework and Crafts*, and *Cast On* magazines. She is a founder of the Laurel Highlands Knitting Guild and the owner of Kathy's Kreations, a yarn store in Ligonier, Pennsylvania.

Acknowledgments

This collection of handknits originates in the minds and hands of our many talented knitwear designers. I'm proud to work among our in-house designers--Susan Mills, Cathy Payson, Linda Pratt--who miraculously fit their design duties in between many other assorted responsibilities at a small company. Our freelance designers, Jodi Berkebile, Norah Gaughan, Stephanie Gildersleeve, Julie Hoff, Sally Lee, Deborah Newton, and Kathy Zimmerman generously create beautifully styled and developed knitwear for our collections.

The photographs in this book result from the efforts of a group of talented people. Special thanks go to our photographers, especially Philip Newton; to our fashion stylist, Karen Harrison, who coordinates the costumes; to the hair and make-up artists (especially Michael Tammaro); and to the people who house, feed, and drive our entourage. Without their cooperation and exquisite taste, these photos would not be as beautiful or inspired.

Space limitations preclude listing all the sample knitters who have helped us through the years. Our thanks go to one and all! Our pattern proofreaders, Dee Neer, Carla Patrick Scott, Dorothy Ratigan, and Sheila Richardson, have used their knowledge of knitting and mathematics to perfect the instructions before you. David Xenakis of Golden Fleece Publications assists us with computer technology, and he developed the indispensable knitter's font, which is used in many of the charts in this book. If it were not for the encouragement and interest of B. J. Berti, neither this book nor *Knitting the New Classics* (Sterling/Lark, 1995) would have been possible. Patricia Chew, owner of Classic Elite Yarns, has given me the freedom to create what I see fit for American knitters.

Special thanks go to Pete and April, proprietors of Eglingham Hall Farm in Northumberland, England, who made us feel especially welcome at their country estate. In Watch Hill, Rhode Island, and Stonington, Connecticut, many thanks go to Mickey Pugh of Heartwood Farm, Jane Barber, Mrs. H. Laughlin Blair, Carole Campbell, Liz Crawford, Jo Flanagan, Nancy Frye, Jane Kellogg, Marguerite Moore, Grace Panciera, Bob Sneider at Dodson's Boat Yard, and Terry and Louis Weeks. Special thanks go to the following child models and their parents for donating their time and personalities to our photos: John James Ahearn; Leslie, Julie, and Andrew Barber; Alec and Caitlin Gorski; Hillary and Rachel Greene; Nicholas Martinez; Jeffrey and Matthew Phillips; and Trevor Utley.

Most of all, I would like to acknowledge all of the devoted employees of Classic Elite Yarns; they keep the yarn spinning, the shipments on schedule, and the spirit alive. Without them, today's handknitters would not have such beautiful yarns at their fingertips.

Index